THE ON-LINE INVESTOR

THE ON-LINE INVESTOR

How to Find the Best Stocks
Using Your Computer

Revised and Updated Edition

Ted Allrich

REGISTERED INVESTMENT ADVISOR, MBA

St. Martin's Griffin ❦ New York

Material on page 7 from *Stocks, Bonds, Bills, and Inflation
1995 Yearbook*™, Ibbotson Associates, Chicago (annually updates
work by Roger G. Ibbotson and Rex E. Sinquefield). Used with
permission. All rights reserved.

Material on page 130 reprinted by permission of *Investor's
Business Daily*, July 16, 1992. Copyright © INVESTOR'S BUSINESS
DAILY INC., 1992 (800-831-2525).

Material on pages 188–190 is reprinted with permission from
Morningstar Closed-End Funds, Morningstar, Inc.,
225 West Wacker Drive, Chicago, IL 60606 (312-696-6000).

Design by SONGHEE KIM

Library of Congress Cataloging-in-Publication Data

Allrich, Ted.
    The on-line investor : how to find the best stocks using your
computer / by Ted Allrich. — Rev. ed.
        p.   cm.
    ISBN 0-312-15183-7
    1. Investments—United States—Databases.   2. Stocks—United
States—Databases.   3. Small capitalization stocks—United States
—Databases.   4. Investments—Computer network resources.
5. American Online (Online service)   I. Title
HG4515.95.A44   1997
332.63'22'0285467—dc20   96-43900
                                                               CIP

First St. Martin's Griffin Edition: January 1997
10   9   8   7   6   5   4

THIS BOOK IS DEDICATED TO the three loves of my life: my son, Scott, my daughter, Alison and especially Robyn, whose constant support made me feel as if I were being held in the hands of an angel.

CONTENTS

PREFACE: Play a New Game   ix

ACKNOWLEDGMENTS   xi

INTRODUCTION by William O'Neil   xiii

1. Think Small: Why and How   1

2. The Right Wares: Hard and Soft   21

3. Small-Cap Information: Discovering
   Stocks with Your Computer   41

4. Investment News: Here's the Scoop   63

5. Stock Evaluation: Analyzing Your Treasures   89

6. Buying and Selling Stocks: Season to Your
   Own Taste   124

7. Developing Your Portfolio: Small Pieces
   of a Big Pie   150

8. Small-Cap Mutual Funds, Big Rewards   169

9. A Session on America Online   201

10. Now Go Do It!   219

APPENDIX A: Small-Cap Newsletters   226

APPENDIX B: Evaluation Sheet Math   228

APPENDIX C: Portfolio Software   235

APPENDIX D: Mutual Fund Information   238

BIBLIOGRAPHY   241

PLAY A NEW GAME ◄----

Do you sometimes feel, as an individual investor in the stock market, as if you're trying to play Major League baseball, but at a terrific disadvantage? You're always facing superstars; it's always your turn at the plate, and you're swinging a matchstick!

If so, maybe it's because you're playing in the wrong park, against the wrong players and with the wrong equipment. The truth is, with the information in this book, you can hit game-winning home runs in another league and leave the unfair competition of the big leagues to the pros, giant institutional investors such as mutual funds, insurance companies and investment advisors.

You should be playing in a league made for individual investors: small-capitalization stocks, stocks of exciting small growth companies. As a group, "small-cap" stocks have been the best-performing stock or bond investment for the last 70 years. How do you find these super stocks?

In the 1990s, a new era of investing is dawning, an era in which individuals have access to information at a reasonable price. With a personal computer and a modem, you can obtain timely information from databases previously reserved only for the largest investment firms.

With $2,000 or less in computer equipment and any amount to invest, along with your brains and a little effort, you can become a big-time winner.

In simple terms, this book explains how to use computers and data-bases to make you an informed investor. You will learn an investment strategy that identifies stocks with strong potential for profits, but without intense competition to buy or sell them. These are the "small-cap" stocks, the stocks of small companies. Because of their small market capitalization—the number of shares a company has out-standing times the price of the stock—large institutional investors don't buy them; in many cases, they can't buy them. However, you *can* and *should*.

This decade will be an exciting and rewarding time for the pre-pared investor. You can be one if you combine new technology with a proven investment strategy. If you're willing to play a new game and invest in yourself, you can become the newest success story: the desktop tycoon.

ACKNOWLEDGMENTS

My journey on the path of computing began with the patient help of Tom Latinovich, Sunny Tong and Steve Leonard. Without their initial guidance, I would not have been able to write this book. When the idea for this book was first conceived, I presented it to Mike Larsen, now my agent, who demanded my best work before it would be submitted. I thank him for his tenacity on the project and for his demanding nature.

As the book evolved, I needed help in certain areas. Both Tom Latinovich and Ed Beddow were without peer. Of course, the book had to be read and reread, and Robyn Roberts never tired in that effort, always offering support and constructive comments.

Special thanks to Blanche Brann, Elizabeth Pomada, Bill O'Neil, David Baird, J. B. Harrington and Jim Kirk.

And finally, my thanks to George Witte, who made the process seem almost easy.

The day of the individual investor has arrived. Armed with a computer, sound buying and selling rules and an investment strategy, individuals can find data, calculate ratios and buy stocks by simply clicking a few buttons. But most of them don't.

Here's the problem: The technology is available and the databases are there from on-line services or the Internet, but there is no resource to explain how to use either or both together—until now.

The On-Line Investor takes readers, whether seasoned or novice computer users or investors, and clearly and easily guides them through the necessary steps to become a more successful stock investor. It covers the hardware and software needed as well as the many databases—now available to individuals—that only a few years ago would have been too expensive for most people to buy. Now thanks to Prodigy, America Online and similar services on the Internet, the cost has become affordable to everyone.

When I built our database on companies and began supplying graphs combining fundamental and technical data to institutional investors, there were literally no competitors. And it was and still is very expensive to gather, store, analyze and then create computer-based research services.

With computers continually increasing in efficiency, however, you can buy a great deal of information everyday in the newspaper I founded, *Investor's Business Daily*. The newspaper was started over ten years ago, and its fundamental premise was to give business leaders, institutional and individual investors, timely and useful information not available anywhere else, even at a great price. Now some of that data can be seen on a computer screen, thanks to on-line services, making it easier and cheaper for everyone to receive the information they need.

But too often investors look at the screen and they are intimidated. If they can find the databases, they know what they're looking at is probably important, but there seems to be too much information. They are stunned into paralysis that usually ends with clicking off the computer and a feeling of frustration.

Turn your computer back on. If you don't have one, buy one. Help is on the way. This book explains which of the numbers matter, how to find them, and then how to use them. And it's done in a way anyone can understand. It will turn the average investor into a more educated stock picker. Every investor and computer owner should read this book.

—William O'Neil,
Founder and Chairman,
Investor's Business Daily,
June 1995

CHAPTER ONE

THINK SMALL: ◄┈┈┘
WHY AND HOW

There has never been a better time to be an individual investor. With a personal computer and a modem, you can use information from databases at an affordable cost, store and process that data with the right software and develop your own formula for investing. This is a major step toward becoming successful in the stock market, and you don't have to be gifted or brilliant to take it. Best of all, when you focus on "small-cap" stocks instead of "large-cap" stocks, a distinction that will be explained shortly, you increase your odds for success.

THE BAD OLD DAYS

Of course, it was always possible to be a successful investor, but it took much more time, effort and, in many cases, money. Several years ago, you needed a full-service broker to buy and sell a stock even if you did all or most of the research.

Full-service brokers provided, and still do, scores from the ball games, jokes, research reports and investment ideas. However, when you did all the work on stocks, you still paid for their research staff and other overhead with your commissions. You were levied a relatively large amount just for having a stockbroker answer your phone call, execute a buy or sell order and take you to a free lunch.

For information on stocks, you had to subscribe to various publications, with each one having only part of what you needed, or you had to trek to one or more libraries in hopes of finding the books or newspapers you wanted. If you lived in a major city, you had a competitive advantage because your library had a bigger budget and more publications. Your disadvantage was that more people permanently checked out the best books.

THE GOOD NEW DAYS

Fortunately for you, information access and brokers have changed. Now, there are many discount brokers who will take your call, execute your order and charge you a minimum fee. They have no research staff or other departments to support. Their only function is to buy and sell securities for you at the least expensive cost. Also, major discount brokers such as Schwab, Fidelity and Quick and Reilly have software that allows you to place your orders directly from a home computer and receive an additional discount on your commissions. You, however, get no free lunches.

The majority of the information you need to make good investment decisions is now on affordable database services that can be viewed on your home computer via a modem and then stored on your computer. In addition, the publications listed in this book will provide you with specific data you need to implement a successful investment strategy. Once you learn how to use all these tools, you might feel you can compete with the large institutional investors. Suppress the urge.

You can't and here's why: You can't get information as quickly as the large institutional investors. Their stockbrokers are constantly on the phones talking with the brokerage firms' research staff or watching the various news service wires and then relaying that information to their clients. Those timely, to-the-minute messages advising whether to sell or buy, based on news from research or the ticker tape, make a big difference in profit and loss.

INSTITUTIONAL NEWS IS NEWS; YOUR NEWS IS HISTORY

By the time you hear news on a stock, whether it's an hour or day later, the stock has already adjusted for it. If the news is really bad, the adjustment can be excruciatingly painful.

As an individual investor, you can't possibly get news that stampedes the large investors until it's too late. Institutions always get the first call because on Wall Street, money doesn't talk; it screams. And the more money an institution manages, the more information, and especially timely information, it receives, in a loud and clear voice. Think of information as a TV program. You're a TV with no antenna, and the institutions are TVs with cable.

Institutional investors such as bank trust departments, insurance companies, mutual funds and pension funds, represent large commissions, big dollar income to stock brokerage firms and, therefore, get the kind of service those dollars demand: instant and often.

One of the rarest commodities a brokerage firm has is good, timely information. It's part of being in the big leagues, and one of the main reasons the individual investor can't compete in this arena.

As an individual investor, you may still receive good service from your stockbroker, even wonderful service, but your broker isn't part of the timely news pipeline. Retail brokers get crucial news after the institutional brokers, as determined by the pecking order in the brokerage world, which is established by money. The formula is simple: The more dollars you control, the sooner you hear.

BIGGER IS BETTER; YOU'RE NOT BIGGER

Once the large institutions receive significant news, they move in or out of stocks quickly. They can afford it. First of all, their transaction fees are small; some pay less than three cents per share to buy or sell stocks. Compare that to what you, the small shareholder, pay per share to buy or sell a hundred shares of stock.

Unless you're using a deep discount broker like eBroker, which charges $12 per trade for listed securities regardless of the number of shares traded, you can't approach the per share trade costs of the big investors. (eBroker requires a minimum account of $10,000.) For large institutions, even if a stock is up only an eighth of a point (a point equals one dollar), 12.5 cents per share, they still can make money by selling it. By contrast, individual investors usually need a move of one point—one dollar per share—or more to break even after commission costs.

Second, institutions hold diversified portfolios. Most single stock positions represent less than 3% of their holdings. If a stock must be sold at a loss, it doesn't wipe out the portfolio. It's a small portion, and even if the whole investment is lost, no one stock can do devastating damage. As an individual investor, you probably don't have that much diversification, and you're paying higher commissions than institutions. Therefore, the same stocks cost you more, and their movements are more significant, good or bad, to your portfolio.

BACK TO THE NEWS

Remember, by the time you hear bad news about your stock or stocks, the price has already adjusted for it. And if you read about your stock in the newspaper, it isn't news.

Every business news item, whether released by a company or discovered by a reporter, first appears on a news service ticker tape, such as Reuters or Dow Jones News Service. Every brokerage firm subscribes to one or more of these news services, and they are monitored constantly. In fact, every stock or bond trading floor of a brokerage firm has a large electronic version, like a Broadway marquee, running on the front wall of the trading room, and traders immediately react to any news, especially bad news. They sell or buy within seconds.

So where does that leave you when you read or hear bad news? Usually you grab the nearest paper to check your stock's price, your eyes race down the quote page to find your beloved investment and see how much damage has been done. You find your stock, and there comes a uniquely disturbing pain. Your countenance transforms from one of hope to anguish. Your stock is down, dramatically. You age internally. Open wounds rubbed with salt feel better than this. You vow to do better next time. You certainly don't tell your spouse.

THE BIG BOYS

Most institutional investors must invest in stocks with large capitalizations, known as large-cap stocks. Capitalization refers to the amount of shares a company has outstanding times the price of the company's stock. For example, if a company has 20 million shares outstanding and the stock is $50, it is said to have a capitalization of $1 billion. For defining a large-cap stock, there are different demarcations, but it is generally agreed that the Fortune 500 companies represent the majority of this group.

Most professionals use $1 billion of capitalization as the dividing point between small-cap stocks and large-cap stocks. The actual size is not important. It's the concept of knowing which stocks the institutions are buying or selling, signifying that these are the stocks in which individual investors are at a distinct informational disadvantage.

Institutions have little choice when investing in the stock market. The Securities and Exchange Commission, the SEC, prevents mutual funds from holding more than 10% of a company's shares and limits holdings of one stock to 5% of a given fund's assets. If the fund is managing $1 billion, it obviously needs to invest in large-cap stocks, under the above restrictions.

If you are a fund manager, you stay employed by making money for your shareholders. If you don't, the shareholders withdraw their money along with your job. Therefore, you, as the manager, must choose stocks that will appreciate in value, and your position in them must be large enough to impact performance in a positive way.

PRETEND YOU MANAGE A $1 BILLION MUTUAL FUND

You need to invest $30 million, 3% of your assets. You find a great small-cap company with a capitalization of $100 million. But you can't invest all $30 million because that would exceed the 10% ownership restriction. Of course, you could invest $10 million in the company, but then you would probably be the single largest shareholder and selling your shares could be difficult because most other institutions (faced with the same restrictions) will not buy small-cap issues. And if you did go ahead and buy it, you've only invested 1% of your assets. Even if the stock moved up dramatically, it would hardly be noticed in your overall portfolio.

You need to find bigger companies, large-cap companies such as IBM or General Motors, with capitalizations in the tens of billions of dollars. These are the kinds of stocks that have liquidity, which is the ease of buying and selling shares, and the size required for institutional portfolios.

BACK TO REALITY: YOUR PORTFOLIO

Isn't it great you aren't burdened with all that money and those restrictions? You have the whole investment world for your consideration. There are more than 30,000 publicly traded companies—60 times as many as the Standard & Poor's 500, an index of the largest 500 stocks. That leaves you with more than 29,500 stocks that most institutions rarely buy.

Of all stocks, about 7,800 are listed on the major exchanges: the New York Stock Exchange, the American Stock Exchange, the NASDAQ and the Over the Counter Market. For purposes of liquidity, an investor would do well to buy from this group. The New York Stock Exchange only trades about 2,400 of these.

Brokerage firms mostly write about and recommend the large-cap stocks. After all, their biggest customers prefer to invest in them. So invest in the S&P 500 sparingly, please, and focus your attention on companies in which access to information is equal for all investors. Then, if you do your homework, you will know as much or more than anyone else investing in a particular stock, because most small-cap stocks don't have major brokerage firms following them.

SMALL-CAP PERFORMANCE

Let's get down to the real reason you invest: to maximize your wealth beyond your ability to count. The question then becomes: How do these small-cap stocks perform when compared with large-cap stocks, Treasury bills, Treasury bonds, and the rate of inflation? Look at the graph on the opposite page.

The returns for small-cap stocks are much better than any investment shown. This is exciting, isn't it? However, please don't place your order to buy stocks yet. You've only seen the best-looking horses; you haven't checked their teeth.

Notice the length of time required to achieve the returns and the importance of timing.

Obviously, the last 70 years have been rewarding to the investor who bought the right small-cap stocks and held them. You'll look a long time to find one person who did that. Still, the graph underscores the importance of holding on to stocks with solid earnings through good times and bad and being patient. You should also remember that all large-cap stocks were once small-cap stocks.

**Wealth Indices of
Investments in the
U.S. Capital Markets**

Year-End 1925 = $1.00

From 1925 to 1994

Index

Small Company
Stocks

Large Company
Stocks

Long-Term
Government Bonds

Inflation

Treasury Bills

$2,842.77

$ 810.54

$ 25.86

$ 12.19

$ 8.35

Year-End

Source: Stocks, Bonds, Bills, Inflation data.
© Ibbotson Associates, Chicago, 1995. All rights reserved.

If a small-cap firm has and continues to generate good earnings, it will grow and reward you in the long run.

I can hear some of you cynics quoting John Maynard Keynes: "In the long run, we are all dead." However, in the stock market the long run is subjective and can be described in terms of months or years. Of course, it's true that after you've held a stock for years without movement, selling it will naturally cause it to soar dramatically within days or weeks of your sale. I have never figured out how stocks know this, but I'm convinced they do. Therefore, it follows that a necessary ingredient for success in the stock market is patience and then, more patience.

Remember: money always follows money. If your stock has continuing positive earnings, and especially if the earnings are improving, it will appreciate in value. Like the arrival of most scheduled airlines, the timing of this will not be precise, but the certainty of it is.

Two Separate Issues—The Stock and the Company

Some of the frustration most stock investors experience comes from not understanding the relationship of the two separate elements of an investment: the stock is one element, and the company is the other. Logically, the stock represents the company, and, therefore, the two should be inseparable. However, the market is not always logical, which is part of its undying fascination.

It often happens that the stock market behaves like the tide and takes all boats with it, rising and falling. For example, even if a company in which you own shares continues to improve its earnings, the stock will probably be hurt if the general market is dominated by fear (about the economy, about an election or about an overseas war or incident) and will go down.

A psychological truism states that when fear enters a room, reason flies out the window. However, in the stock market, when reason flies out the window, perched outside is greed, impatiently waiting for its opportunity. Thus, fear and greed run the markets. As an investor, you are betting on reason, not greed, to win; it always has. Investors buy stocks where earnings keep improving. That's common sense. Your challenge is to buy stocks that fear has thrown away.

Ultimately, there is always a reconciliation between price and earnings because the stock price represents the present value of the future earnings of the company. This is called discounting the future earnings and is the most fundamental premise in investing, accepted by every scholar and investment manager. The only exceptions are the managers who own certain bio-technology stocks. The prices of these stocks seem to discount the future and the hereafter.

This principle is worth repeating: ultimately, the market price of a stock is determined by discounting the future earnings stream. Sometimes, however, the stock market forgets this maxim, usually when fear is rampant. Sometimes, as a buyer of stocks, that's good. Sometimes, as an owner of stocks, that's bad, very bad.

Look at the graph again. Notice the line for small-cap stocks goes down as well as up. Sometimes the line even goes down when the large-cap stock line stays straight or goes up. Notice the painful period from about 1967 to 1975. Notice the wonderful upward movement from 1975 to 1994.

This graph clearly shows the superior performance of small-cap stocks when compared with more conventional investments, but it also underscores the importance of timing and patience, two attributes necessary to offset the additional risk inherent in small-cap stocks.

ONE REASON SMALL-CAP STOCKS OUTPERFORM LARGE-CAP STOCKS

Small-cap companies usually have fewer shares outstanding than large-cap stocks. Some have fewer than 1 million shares. Most small-cap companies have 2 million to 15 million shares outstanding, offer real products or services and have real earnings. These real companies are the focus of my investment strategy, not the small-cap stocks offering hope and concepts but not earnings.

The number of shares outstanding is an important consideration because of the basic laws of supply and demand. If everyone wants to buy something when there is a limited supply, the price moves up sharply. This economic principle works noticeably well in small-cap stocks, especially following announcements of better-than-expected earnings.

Of course, the opposite can always happen. When the earnings disappoint or go down, so does demand for the stock. The price has to adjust downward to the new reality to attract new investors or to encourage current holders to buy more.

At times, a small-cap stock may have no buyers and many sellers, especially after a poor earnings report. Then the price has to drop until it reaches a level at which investors perceive value.

SUPPLY AND DEMAND:
A SMALL-CAP STORY

Let's look at a company that had positive earnings and few shares: Garan, Inc. Garan is an apparel manufacturer that makes sweatshirts and other fleece garments. Its stock price went from $20 per share in December 1990 to $74 in June 1992. The stock trades on the American Stock Exchange. In 1992, Garan had 2.5 million shares outstanding, but half of these were owned by the management of the company and a few institutions; so the "float," the number of shares available for trading, was limited.

The company's management rarely sells its stock, and because the average daily volume of shares traded is only 4,800 shares, the few institutions that own it can't easily buy or sell it in quantity. This is typical of a good small-cap stock, especially the part about management owning a big chunk of the stock.

In February 1992, Garan was trading in the $54–$56 range, going through what chartists, stock technicians who watch the price and volume movements of a stock, call a consolidation period. The stock had run up from $38 in December 1991, appreciating 42% in three months, but the "price-to-earnings ratio" or P/E—discussed later in Chapters 5 and 6—was still somewhat low, often a good investment signal. After the stock had run up, the price held steadily, known in technical terms as consolidating, and then it broke into new-high territory, above $56. I bought the stock then.

A month later, in March 1992, Garan announced its earnings, up 103% from the year earlier. The stock promptly went to $74 per share.

Most institutions weren't buying Garan. Why not? Shouldn't they want a company with great earnings? Of course they do, and there are a few that did own it, mostly growth-oriented mutual funds.

However, because Garan's capitalization was so small, very few could buy it in meaningful quantities. This is the kind of opportunity that you, the small-cap investor, can identify with your computer.

The company split its shares in the beginning of 1993, so it now has about 5 million shares outstanding, still too small for most institutions. And until the stock has a larger number of shares available for the big funds, those funds will not be significantly involved in this stock. Small-cap investors will.

GOING DOWN: DEMAND IS LIMITED
GOING UP: SUPPLY IS INFINITE

Do you ever wonder why some stocks plummet so quickly, but rise so slowly? This phenomenon is especially true with large-cap stocks. Let's use IBM as an example, which at this writing has over one-half billion shares outstanding. Most of those are owned by institutions. If earnings are not up to expectations, a lot of that stock will be for sale, and the specialist on the floor of the New York Stock Exchange where IBM trades can only buy so many shares.

A specialist works for a company that puts its own money at risk to buy and sell shares of a New York Stock Exchange or American Stock Exchange-listed company. All the stocks on the New York and American Stock Exchanges are assigned to specialists. Their job is to maintain an orderly market in each stock they trade, and they operate under various requirements and SEC restrictions.

If there are no buyers for a stock, the specialist is sometimes only required to buy 100 shares and can then move the bid to a level at which other buyers will come in to purchase the stock. The bid is the amount the specialist or anyone else will pay for the stock.

This is something most investors have difficulty understanding. They wonder why a stock can go down so quickly but up so slowly. This concept goes back to supply and demand. When a stock is going up, everyone who owns it is a potential seller. For large-cap stocks, there are plenty of shares available, which tends to control the rise in price. However, when a stock goes down, only the specialist in the stock is required to buy some of it, and the specialist can lower the bid for the stock. If the specialist is the only buyer, the bid will be lowered until other investors come forward to buy the stock. If no buyers appear, the bid will disappear, and the stock will be prevented from trading until a level is found at which buyers finally emerge. Some stocks—even major companies—free-fall a long way after bad news, until that bottom is found.

Now think back to IBM. If IBM announces earnings and they're equal to or above projections, every stockholder is a potential seller of the stock if it moves up. In fact, with that number of outstanding shares, there is almost an infinite supply. Any price increase is spread over a tremendous number of shares.

Compare that with Garan, Inc. with its mere 5 million shares. If the stock advances in price, the supply for sale is severely limited, especially since almost half of those shares are owned by management that rarely sells. If the price goes down, the investors who follow the stock recognize its value and will step in to buy it. In some cases, that level may be lower than earnings suggest it should be, but once found, the stock will stop there. However, compared with IBM or any other large-cap stock, the potential for an upward move in price, when the buyers do enter the market, is much greater because of its limited supply.

Earlier, I described Garan's stock going from $56 to $74 in a relatively short time. In an even briefer time, it went back to $56. I called the company and asked what was new or if there had been any announcements made. The officer at Garan said there was no news and that they were just going about their business.

He also lamented that once again the stock was volatile because of its small float. Almost every day the stock was trading down; there were fewer shares traded than its average daily volume. So, even though the supply factor was quite small, there was no demand on the days the sellers wanted out. The stock finally did find a level that attracted buyers, around $57. The sellers stopped selling, and the stock moved up quickly to $64. Once it started to move up, there was a limited supply of stock, and the price increased nicely.

MAJOR WARNING: PLEASE READ AND HEED

This stock, Garan, and others used in this book are meant to illustrate an idea. They are not recommended for you to buy. Since circumstances change daily, every investor must find out the current numbers and stories about a company.

Garan, for example, was hit hard by the baseball and hockey strikes because it manufactures many professional team shirts. It is still a fine company, but the stock's price has been affected because of the new realities the company faces.

Every stock described in this book will be different by the time you read about it in here. This book is purposely not about recommending specific stocks. Its goal is to teach you how to find good ones and become a better investor.

More Advantages for Small-cap Companies

Just think of the bureaucracy involved in any large company. Layers and layers of management are stacked on top of each other, and most of them are involved in decisions, both small and large. For examples, think of General Motors, any major bank, or for the most part, any of the S&P 500 stocks.

Now try to imagine what it takes to introduce a new product in one of these companies. Think of foremen talking to engineers, suggesting to managers, proposing to committees, submitting the idea to more committees that send memos to everyone before the final committee presents the concept to the board of directors. And most of those directors own little or no stock in the company, reducing their incentive to try anything different: if an idea benefits the company, they are not rewarded, and if their idea fails, they could be out of a pleasant job.

This is one of the problems corporate America has with its boards of directors: most don't own enough shares to have a meaningful stake in the company's future. Look at the prospectus or annual shareholders' announcement of a large company and see how few shares, if any, the directors own. These are the people responsible for ensuring a company's and its shareholders' prosperity, yet many have no personal investment at risk.

Now think about a smaller company in which the management, and especially the founders, own a significant percentage of the shares. They're in the same position as every other investor in the company, only more so. They, like us, want to work in their own best interest and, it logically follows, the best interest of the investors. When senior officers and most of the employees own a large amount of their own stock, look for the stock's price to rise.

It's like a ham-and-egg breakfast. The chicken has an interest in it, but the pig makes a commitment. You want to be the chicken; let the corporate officers and directors be the pigs, so to speak.

But back to new product introductions. A smaller company with fewer layers of management has to compete effectively within an established industry. It has to develop new or better ideas and market them quickly.

For a basic example, look at the success of Ben & Jerry's Homemade Inc. They make ice cream in Vermont, and how long has there been ice cream? Yet here were two men who decided to produce it the best way they knew how, create new flavors and see if people would buy it.

Not only did people buy the ice cream, they also bought the stock. Ben & Jerry's shares went from a low of $4.25 to $29.75. The same phenomenon occurred with Starbucks Corp., a company that sells coffee. Starbucks found a niche in a crowded market by making gourmet coffee readily available to the person on the street and at home. The company's stock also had a meteoric rise.

There are literally hundreds of stocks with similar stories in which an entrepreneur parlays an idea to do or make something better than is currently offered. The first commercial personal computer, the Altair in 1975, was the brainchild of a private entrepreneur, Edward Roberts. Unable to keep up with demand, he sold his company. Then a series of other companies entered the market, including Pertec, Tandy Radio Shack, Commodore International and an upstart home-assembled manufacturer oddly named Apple.

When its two brash young partners, Steven Jobs and Stephen Wozniak, created and marketed the Apple II in 1977, the personal computer industry suddenly went big-time.

After raising their start-up capital by selling a VW van for $1,300, just four years later, in 1980, Apple's annual sales were $117 million, and the two entrepreneurs entered Wall Street with the largest initial stock offering since the Ford Motor Company in 1903. A year later, 1981, IBM lumbered into the personal computer market, confident it would blow this young upstart off the map. While Apple has had its share of success and enjoys the highest customer loyalty of any computer maker, it has also had problems. So many that it has had three CEOs in three years and its market share has slipped to 10% from 15%. But no one expects Apple to just go away; its operating system is the easiest to use. The company will either revive or be purchased.

This is one of the exciting aspects of most small-cap stocks: their involvement in new ideas, products or services. They can execute those ideas without becoming unduly burdened with corporate protocols and committees. Of course, large companies still produce new ideas. A mundane but solid example is Post-It Notes from the 3M Company, a large firm. These now-famous little yellow pads of paper with adhesive on them are quite useful for holding temporary notes. And there are thousands of other innovations brought to market by large companies, despite their internal complexities, because they have plenty of money to develop, publicize and distribute new products.

Nevertheless, the majority of new products and services from which you can profit come from small businesses that don't have a capital cushion on which to sit as they ponder the ultimate success or failure of a new idea. They have to get to the marketplace quickly because their success as a company depends on the revenues their exciting new product will produce. The product or service must be well researched before it is introduced or it will fail, but it can't gestate too long or another firm will fill the gap.

In such a manner, the introduction of a new product or service, or even new management at a large, established firm, can signal an investment opportunity. Just as the first people must have enjoyed their initial ice-cream cone from Ben & Jerry's, you, too, can use your own good judgment when you see, taste or experience something new. If you really like it, and so do your friends, maybe there's a company behind the product or service that deserves your investment consideration.

YOUR COMPETITIVE EDGE IN INVESTING

You have an advantage over institutional investors when it comes to investing in new companies: large brokerage houses don't report on them. They won't send a research analyst to taste the latest ice cream because the company doesn't have enough shares outstanding for the institutions to buy, no matter how good the ice cream. Many ice-cream cones later, and after several splits, or additional offerings of shares, the institutions can buy all they want. That may be the perfect time for you to sell your shares.

Another advantage small-cap investors enjoy is the ability of new companies to exploit certain market niches too insignificant for the larger firms. Whether it is a mature market with limited participants or an emerging growth area, these markets are purposely overlooked by large corporations because they won't produce enough meaningful earnings. Small-cap growth companies aggressively seek these markets and serve them. If an emerging market continues to grow, then the larger firms either buy the most attractive company serving the market or enter it themselves.

A good example of this is the portable computer. Osborne Computer came on the scene with the first one in May 1981. Certainly somebody at IBM had at least thought of this idea, but it probably died sometime between the third and 10th committee meeting. It was Osborne, a new company with a specialty product serving what was then just a niche in a large market, that turned the idea into an overnight success. Then along came Compaq Computer to take it to even greater heights. Apple's recent PowerBook line of portable computers has now outsold all other computers in its history. And IBM has finally jumped into the market with its very successful ThinkPad.

The third advantage small-cap investors have, as alluded to previously, is the lack of institutional following or sponsorship. There is a strong herd mentality on Wall Street: if no one has heard of a stock, no one buys it. In contrast, if analysts and managers are buying and talking about a stock, there is a whole herd of funds rushing into it.

Many excellent small-cap companies are not monitored by any Wall Street analyst, a person from the research staff of a brokerage firm who recommends stocks. Because of this, small-cap stock prices are lower. There isn't as much demand for the stock because no major broker is pushing it as the pick of the day. You can buy these stocks early, because you can find them using your computer and the methods described in this book.

However, if a company expands, receives good publicity and achieves strong earnings, the analysts start to hear about it. It gets their attention, and they investigate. If it is deemed worthy, they recommend it to their money managers, who in turn buy the stock. The managers, once they own it, go to lunch and brag about their new favorite investment. Their lunch companions then rush back before the market closes to buy the stock for their funds. The stock price goes up and soon everyone on Wall Street knows about it.

If you do your research and buy good small-cap stocks, you might soon be able to tell your own exciting investment story instead of hearing about one from your stockbroker.

THE TIME FOR SMALL-CAPS IS NOW

The investment rage of the 1980s was the leveraged buyout (LBO). This strategy is simple to describe but hard to execute: an investor borrowed a large amount of debt and bought an undervalued asset such as a company, often using the company as the collateral for the debt. The investor radically trimmed down the operations, made the company more efficient and then took all the cash flow to pay interest on the money borrowed.

This was a strategy that Drexel, Burnham, Lambert, the now-bankrupt brokerage firm, helped finance with what became popularly known as junk bonds. They believed in the concept and so did a substantial sector of corporate America. As long as the assets continued to hold their value and their cash flows, LBOs worked very well.

The companies most sought after by the so-called corporate raiders were the big ones, with brand-name value, such as RJR Nabisco, the largest corporate purchase ever. Or they had high name recognition and valuable real estate, such as Macy's. Or they had a great franchise and a great product, like Levi Strauss. Most of these LBOs were large transactions and required huge amounts of capital. As these large-cap companies were bought by investors, their share prices went up, and as a group, they outperformed the small-cap stocks for some time.

Then things changed. The issuance of debt, the junk bonds, became impossible. It turned out that the universe for this investment was limited, extremely so. In fact, the once powerful Drexel, Burnham, Lambert went out of business because it kept issuing these bonds without any investors left to buy them.

With not enough buyers, Drexel became the reluctant investor of last resort, and when the junk-bond market collapsed in early 1991, Drexel's large inventory was like a large hole in the side of a submarine. Every day the bonds were marked to market, that is, priced to the current value of the bonds as required by the SEC. The value became so low it wiped out Drexel's capital, which at one time was more than $4 billion. Without Drexel, the dominant player in the LBO game, very little capital was available. Without capital, the game was over.

In addition to less capital, there was the problem of undervalued companies becoming overvalued, as investors sought to pick stocks of companies that were likely takeover targets and drove up prices to artificial levels. Furthermore, in October 1987, there was a stock market correction of about 1,000 points in one week, or about 50% of the market value. To call this a correction is to describe King Kong as a gorilla. While technically correct, it misses the emotional impact completely.

This raised the specter of fear in many investors; actually, it was more like terror. Convinced the sky had truly fallen this time, they moved their money to safe harbors in the forms of money-market accounts or blue-chip stocks. They got out of those risky small-cap stocks, driving prices down.

Another factor helping the large-cap issues on a relative performance basis in the 1980s was the advent of stock indexing. This was a portfolio technique that required a money manager to buy all of the stocks in a major index such as the Standard & Poor's 500 or the Dow Jones Industrial Average—an average consisting of only 30 stocks, but having enormous influence on investor psychology.

The Dow Jones Industrial stocks are much like Rolls Royces: there aren't many of them, but they symbolize some of the best in their industry.

The stocks in most of these indexes were large-cap issues, and because institutions managing index funds were buying these stocks for their portfolios, those stocks did better on a relative basis than small-cap issues. Investors in these funds simply want to do as well or as poorly the indexes, but because it would require more money than most investors have to buy all the stocks in any one index, they can participate by purchasing an index fund. The fund then pools all the money and buys the large-cap stocks in the index and helps support the price of the stocks.

TIME TO MOVE ON

Because of the combination of LBOs, the 1987 market crash and stock index funds, large-cap stocks did outperform the small-cap stocks in the latter part of the 1980s.

But the mid- to late 1990s look like a different story. While there are always lessons to be learned from the past, smart investors acknowledge previous experience and then look forward. The LBO activity will not return until assets are perceived as undervalued. And it will require new wealthy players in the game since several of the old, now poor ones, have gone bankrupt. The senior managers from Macy's wish they had never heard of those three letters. They are now gone due to the bankruptcy of their companies.

Furthermore, even if the will comes back, the way looks difficult because the owners of the previous LBO bonds won't be quite as anxious to lend money. In my experience, however, most investors have weak memories when promised large returns. And if enough time passes, a new generation of self-proclaimed smarter managers will have replaced the current ones, and the concept will seem new. LBOs will be back, but not soon.

With value-investing LBOs out of favor, investors will go back to finding those companies with the best earnings in terms of both consistency and growth. Clearly, the small-cap stocks represent most of the companies with growth potential.

The stock-indexing mutual funds have just about run their course. While these are funds with billions of dollars matching the financial indexes, it seems unlikely that this is a growth area. After all, if an investor just wanted to match the averages, why pay a manager to do that? Managers are supposed to beat the averages or lose the funds they manage. Statistically, it has been proven that no one can consistently beat the averages.

However, some money managers, like Peter Lynch of the Fidelity Magellan Fund during the 1980s, consistently do. The money invested in index funds will eventually be reallocated to maximize returns within certain parameters. Part of that money will go into small-cap stocks, part into large-cap stocks and part into international opportunities.

As for the correction in the market, we can be sure it will happen again. I can't guess what its severity will be, but absolute fear will grip the players in the market; the sky will certainly, positively, be falling. Panic will prevail for a while, and when all of that happens, prices will drop, and you and I will be waiting to take advantage of yet another opportunity in the adventurous world of small-cap stocks.

With or without that market correction, there are always opportunities in the market. You just need tools to find them. For investing, those tools come in the form of a computer and some software. Don't be frightened. Help arrives in the next chapter.

CHAPTER TWO

THE RIGHT WARES: HARD AND SOFT

Before you invest in any stock, invest in yourself. It's the best investment you can make. Don't underestimate your own worth by buying a cheap computer or the daily local newspaper instead of a good stock publication.

To be a desktop stock tycoon, you need good equipment, although not necessarily the best or the most expensive, as well as specialized information. This chapter describes the hardware and software you can use for successful investing. Fortunately, prices for computers are literally dropping every day, and you can buy a complete system for less than $1,500.

Obviously, on-line investing requires a desktop computer. However, the computer must have certain elements in it or attached to it for accessing and analyzing the data you need.

I started using a computer in early 1991. I knew nothing about it, except how to turn it on. I know a little bit more now. I am definitely not a computer expert. However, I have learned how to use it for my investment purposes. I will take you through this part of the book in the simplest terms, and you will learn all you need to know about buying and using computers for investing.

THESE ARE THE BASICS

Robert Townsend, in his book *Up The Organization*, described computers as big, fast, dumb, adding machines. I agree with him, except now they're smaller, faster, and smarter.

A computer is no more than a facilitator, but it facilitates very well and very logically. One of its main functions is to store information and allow you to retrieve it at a later date. You can work with that information, manipulate it and then store it again. All computers do this. The following information will help you decide which computer will be the best for your investing success.

GETTING STARTED

Buying a computer is like buying a car: you pick the one that fits your needs. You may want a Ferrari, but what you need is a van. The answer to this conflict is to find a nice van.

A computer for investing has certain minimum requirements, which I will describe shortly. Your goal is to purchase one that performs all the current tasks you want done and has the power or the expandability to perform future ones.

When buying a computer, there are two truths I have learned. The first is that every 18 months computers double their productivity and go down in price by 50%. This means you get more computer for less money every day. It also means the day after you buy yours, the same model will be cheaper somewhere else. A month later, it will be much cheaper. Within five years, it will be almost obsolete.

The constant rapid evolution of computers is a mixed blessing. It brings down the costs of computers very quickly, but it also makes you reluctant to buy one because a better and cheaper one will be announced tomorrow. You can't fight this. You must simply make the decision to go ahead and purchase one. Even though it's depreciating as you carry it to the cashier, buy the computer, use it and get on with investing.

The second truism is the bigger the number describing most parts of a machine, the better. For example, a 486 chip is faster and better than a 386 chip. A 340-megabyte hard drive is better than a 120-megabyte hard drive. I'll explain both of these next. Keep the element of bigger being better in mind as you shop for your computer. It will help you determine value as you compare machines.

Two exceptions to the rule of bigger is better are retrieval time and refresh time. Retrieval time has to do with accessing stored information, and refresh time measures how long it takes to bring up a screen image. Retrieval time is measured in milliseconds, one-thousandth of a second. Refresh time is measured in nanoseconds, one-billionth of a second. That's with a "b." You can buy hardware that accesses data in seven milliseconds instead of 12 or 15. For large corporate and scientific purposes, that's important. For you and me, it will make absolutely no difference in any of our investment decisions. So when it comes to time, less doesn't matter. In all other functions of the computer, go with the bigger numbers.

THE COMPUTER WORLD IS DIVIDED INTO TWO

There is the DOS world, totaling 85% of computers, which are more commonly called IBM or IBM clones, and there is the Apple world. DOS stands for Disk Operating System. This means you have disks that perform required tasks. The most famous DOS system is the Microsoft or MS-DOS program, which is in the majority of DOS computers. However, there are other DOS systems, including the latest from IBM, the OS/2 program.

Apple computers also use disks, but their operating systems are not based on Microsoft or other DOS programs. Initially, Apple's competitive advantage was its ease of use. You simply pointed with a mouse at a little picture on the screen, an icon, clicked the mouse twice, and the computer gave you the program you wanted. With the advent of Windows by Microsoft, the two systems have become similar and are almost equally easy to use.

Recently, Apple introduced the Power PC, a computer that runs DOS and Apple programs. The ability to use both types of programs is called cross-platforming. Because most software is written for DOS machines, there is little or no advantage for an investor to buy a Power PC. If you own an Apple and want to upgrade your system without losing your Apple data, the Power PC is a great buy. Then you can go both ways, DOS and Apple.

I learned on DOS computers, and because they represent the majority of systems and have the most software programs, I will be using them as examples. Apple has equivalent machines for any of the hardware described, but most of the software is only available in a DOS format.

THE COMPUTER CHIP OR THE MOTOR
IN YOUR CAR

The most important element in your computer is the microprocessor running the machine. It's like the motor in a car. Instead of being measured in cubic inches to determine power, it is described by an X86 chip, such as 286, 386, or 486. These are chips developed by Intel Corporation. The minimum chip you want in a computer is a 486 or its equivalent.

If you buy a computer based on a chip other than Intel (which supplies 70% of the chips for computers), be sure your chip will run the software for your investing program. Not all chips will run all software, but because Intel makes the most chips, almost all software is built around its specifications.

Along with the numeric (486) designation, a chip will have a megahertz number. The configuration looks like: 486/33 MHZ. The second number tells you how fast the machine computes. Here again, the larger the number, the better. The new Pentium chips are being clocked at 200 MHZ. You need at least 75 MHZ, and I would recommend 100 MHZ. Once you experience the efficiency of a faster chip, it's hard to go back to a slow machine, but unless you plan to do a lot of complex spreadsheets or want to estimate the trajectory of a Patriot missile, you don't need a high-speed chip, one above 150 MHZ. Remember, you need a van, not a Ferrari.

A 486 chip has enough power to run most of the software you need in a timely manner, but a pentium chip is a worthwhile investment. And since the prices have been cut dramatically, it's much easier to justify the small increase you pay to get one.

RANDOM-ACCESS MEMORY
OR THE PLAYGROUND

The next consideration for your computer is the RAM or random-access memory. Think of RAM as the playground for your 486 chip. RAM is the area in the computer where your chip runs software programs. The bigger the number of megabytes, or millions of bytes, in RAM, the more room your chip has to play. You will want at least 8 megabytes of RAM, and 16 megabytes is better.

You need large RAM so your chip can run several programs at

once. An initial software program you are using may require 2 megabytes of RAM, but then you might want to look at another program while the first is running. Your new program may also require 2 megabytes of RAM. If you don't have enough playground space (RAM), you always have to exit one program before starting another. You don't want that.

THE HARD DISK DRIVE OR THE STORAGE BIN

The hard disk drive is where all software programs reside. On almost all computers, it's called the C drive. It's a place where all your programs and files of data are stored. This is not the playground (RAM). It's the storage bin. You take programs out of the storage bin (the C drive) and put them in the playground (RAM) to run. After you've played with them in RAM, they return automatically to the C drive.

Like money, you can never have too much hard drive space. You will continue to add programs and data until your hard drive becomes full (or your children will put on games until you have no room for your investment software). Buy plenty of hard disk space even if you think you'll never use it.

Hard disks are measured in megabytes, or millions of bytes, just like RAM. You want at least 850 megabytes for your hard disk. Like most other elements of the computer, less is not more. You will never regret buying a lot of hard disk space. You will eventually fill it.

If you already own a computer and have most of your hard drive occupied, there are new programs that can double your hard disk space by compressing your data, something like taking the air out of your sleeping bag when you stuff it in its nylon sack.

Stac Electronics and Microsoft are two manufacturers offering these programs. Be careful before you run them, however. Many users have lost some of their data when compressing it. The latest versions of compression software are marketed as foolproof, and your data is supposed to be safe. Make a backup of all your data before you attempt to double your hard drive. Then, if you can't find a file or data after you've used the program, you can replace them from your backup disk.

THE MOUSE, THE MONITOR
AND THE KEYBOARD

This sounds like a Disney production, but it refers to the small, rounded, usually white, pointing instrument, the mouse; the TV-like screen, the monitor; and the board full of keys.

The mouse allows you to point at things on the screen, usually icons, click a button and then have the computer go to whatever the icon represents. For example, if you need to use a spreadsheet, you move the small arrow on your screen to the icon, a little picture representing the spreadsheet, and push the left button on the mouse two times. Within seconds, the spreadsheet appears.

You don't need an ergonomically designed, supercharged, high-velocity, take-no-prisoners mouse. You won't use it enough to develop knuckle fatigue or wrist convolutions. Buy a basic mouse, plug it in and use it.

The monitor, however, deserves more consideration. Being at the computer should be fun and colorful if you want to keep coming back to it. A color monitor will go a long way to make that happen. Also, a monitor of at least 17 inches is highly recommended.

The most important characteristic in a color monitor is resolution. This is the measurement for how sharp your text and numbers will be. Resolution is described in pixels or dots; again, the more, the better.

The minimum you want is a monitor called a VGA or Video Graphics Array with a resolution of 640 x 480 pixels. If you can afford to buy one of the better models, which can go up to 1,024 x 768 pixels, you will not regret it. However, these models are much more expensive and not necessary for your investing needs. In fact, you can buy a monochrome (black-and-white) monitor for much less, but it won't be as much fun. Furthermore, spending long hours on the computer will cause eyestrain and/or headaches if your monitor is not clear. Don't buy a cheap black-and-white monitor; remember, investors should have fun, too, and all the best games come in color.

The keyboard has become almost standardized. You need a basic one with all the keys. Be sure you sit and type with it before you buy, to make sure you're comfortable with the keys, the height, the sound and the feel. Because you won't be on it all day, don't worry about the ergonomic properties it may or may not possess. Just get a good standard keyboard.

PLUG IN, TURN ON AND DROP
EVERYTHING ELSE

Once you've purchased your basic computer, you'll need to take it home and put the parts together. One of the brilliant design qualities of the computer is the uniqueness of each plug in the main processor, the CPU or central processing unit. Most computers have three parts: the CPU, the monitor and the keyboard.

Assembling these parts is very easy. You can't make a mistake. You can't accidentally plug your monitor cable into the keyboard slot. No one can. Why? Because the plug won't fit. Each accessory (monitor, keyboard, modem and mouse) has a plug with a unique set of pins and/or shape. You can try to do it wrong, but you can't. It's physically impossible to put the right plug in the wrong place.

You don't need a computer guru to install your computer. You don't even need any tools. Just open the packages and plug each accessory into its appropriate slot.

Put your computer in a safe, quiet place. You'll need to think when you use it. Also, check your wiring because electrical problems can cause loss of files or data. To be safe, I had an electrician install in my home a new set of plugs with new wiring just for my computer.

You'll need a number of plugs because almost every accessory to the system needs a plug: the monitor, the backup device, the modem, the CPU, the printer and anything else you add to it.

Another smart purchase is a multiplug surge protector. This item, which costs less than $20, can save you a great deal of grief. A surge in electrical power can wipe out your hard disk drive, the storage bin of your computer. This will make you very unhappy. Prevent this tragedy with a small investment in equipment.

THE MODEM

This is your personal on-ramp to the information highway. The modem allows your computer to access databases on another computer via a telephone line. Instead of talking like humans, your computer, via the modem, instructs a host computer to give it data. Your computer then stores this data in a file you have created to receive the information. Or the modem puts data or pictures on your monitor and allows you to use the host computer just as you do your own.

Modems can be internal (in the machine) or external (one you buy and plug into your computer). Either configuration works well. The difficulty with having an internal modem is that if and when you upgrade to a faster one, you have to open the computer, take out the old one, and then replace it with a new one. This is not as difficult as you might imagine, but the external modems are simpler to unplug and replace.

In addition, external modems have little blinking lights that tell you if a program is running or if data are flying between your computer and another. My modem has 10 blinking lights. I have no idea what seven of them mean. However, the "RD" and "SD" lights blink when I am receiving or sending data. This is a very helpful feature when you sit and wait and wonder if anything is going on. When those lights are blinking, computers are communicating. An internal modem doesn't show any lights.

However, internal modems shouldn't be immediately dismissed. Because they can be installed for you when you buy a computer, you can use it immediately, and there is one less machine on your desktop. Moreover, if you buy a fast one, you won't need to replace it. But how fast is fast?

Let's look at how fast is measured. Modems are described in bits per second or bps (pronounced bips). A bit is short for binary digit. Each bit carries a signal for the computer, and eight bits together make a byte. The byte is used by the computer as a basic unit. Each letter of the alphabet has its own unique byte configuration, as does each number.

Because your modem will transfer large amounts of data, the faster it works, the more time and money you save. Many of the early modems worked at a speed of 300 bits per second. Now many businesses are using 9,600 bps as a standard, and scientists are working with computers at even faster rates, in ranges beyond 70,000 bps.

You need a minimum speed of 9,600 bps, not only for the speed of delivering data, but also for any fax software you may add to your computer. The 9,600 bps rate is the standard for fax transmission.

Fast modems can always take in data at slower speeds. If you have a 9,600 modem, but the host computer you're using only transmits with a 2,400 bps speed, you won't have any problem. The opposite, however, is not true. You can't transmit data from a fast transmitter (the host computer at 9,600) to a slow receiver (a 2,400 bps modem).

The faster modems represent savings in the long run. If you start using many other on-line features from various vendors, you may have to pay for the time you are on-line receiving data from a host computer. If you have a slow modem, you will be on the line longer and, therefore, pay more fees. It also takes more of your time.

Once in a while, vendors will charge extra for transmitting data at a faster speed. If you don't want to pay the extra charge, receive in the cheaper, slower mode. With that kind of flexibility, you always benefit from the faster modem.

There are two phrases you will see or hear when buying a modem: Hayes compatible and baud. The first modems with the highest reliability were made by Hayes. Just as IBM became known as the standard for computers and was copied extensively by IBM clones, the Hayes modem became the industry leader. Be sure the modem you buy is Hayes compatible and works with your hardware and software.

You may also see the modem described with the word baud, as in 9,600 baud modem. Baud is used interchangeably with bps; however, baud actually refers to the speed between modems, not the rate of data flow from the computer to the modem, which is measured in bits. It's a small technicality, but you'll sound impressive when you make the distinction at your next cocktail party. There's more about modems at the end of this chapter.

RECOMMENDED OPTIONS: A PRINTER AND AN EXTERNAL BACKUP DEVICE

These are options because you don't have to own these to investigate and invest in stocks. However, you'll use both of them extensively once you do own them, especially when you set up your computer for letter writing or spreadsheets.

The printer does pretty much what you'd expect: it prints whatever you see on the computer onto a piece of paper. By printing graphs or your portfolio or data on your stocks, you can take them with you when you travel or put them next to each other on your desk to get a full picture of your work.

There are three types of printers to consider: laser jet, dot matrix and ink-jet. Laser jet is the most expensive and professional in its output. It is also the fastest and quietest of the choices. It works much like a copying machine and can produce graphs in color as well as correspondence in black-and-white. The laser jet printer usually costs more, but is recommended if you are sending business letters or creating professional documents for presentations.

The dot matrix printers are the most common in the computer world. There are two types: those designed for high-speed, high-volume, and those meant for low-volume, letter quality output. Unless you have specific tasks for the high-speed capability, you want the letter quality printer. They make a little more noise than a laser printer, but they cost much less.

The ink-jet printer is also very good at printing with relatively little noise. It literally sprays the ink on to the paper and produces a high-quality letter. The only concern is the ink sprayer sometimes clogs with dried ink. These machines are closer to the laser jet printers in price and give you the option of printing in color.

You should test-drive any printer you want to buy to see the quality of the ink. Bring along the kind of paper you use at home or the office and print on it. Sometimes ink sprayed on certain surfaces doesn't hold. Or if you have stationery with embossing, it may not flow through the rollers of the printer. Also, bring along an envelope to test on the printer. Some printers will mangle an envelope because of its thickness.

Back Up, Back Up, Back All the Way Up

This will be mentioned several times in the book: back up your data, letters, files—everything on your computer. Do it often. Back up means you transfer the data in your computer's hard drive (the storage bin) and store them on a floppy disk or tape drive. If you ever lose any important work because of a power surge or computer crash, you will always back up your files religiously. I want you to get religion now and avoid the pain of losing anything.

Make backing up your work part of your work. Every two weeks, I back up my entire hard drive, and keep that backup tape in a safe place away from the office. That way, if there is a robbery, a fire, an earthquake or an errant teenager on my system, I can replace any lost information. And if my entire computer is ruined, I can buy a new one, plug in my backup device and start up in minutes.

This last scenario is why I recommend an external backup device. They are more expensive, but give you freedom from anxiety. You are no longer reliant on one computer. If your computer goes down, or is destroyed, you may have momentary grief, but you're ready to move on. You can buy a new computer, plug in the backup device, download the data and go back to work. If you use an internal backup device, it can be stolen or burned with the computer.

One backup device is a tape drive with a small cassette that looks much like a small tape for music. The tape plugs into a machine if it's an external backup or a slot if it's an internal one.

You can also back up data by using floppy disks. Initially, floppy disks are fine. However, as your programs and data grow, you'll find it takes more floppies and more time to do the job effectively. If you use floppy disks, be sure to label them with a description of the information on them and the date on which the backup was done. Then store them away from the office. The latest versions of Windows, a software program described later, have backup functions for storing data on floppy disks.

The steps required to back up your data will be described by the software program you use.

A Hardware Summary

When you shop for your computer, you want the following elements as a minimum for the most basic system for investing:

Computer Minimums

Microprocessor or chip	Intel 486 or higher
Speed	75 megahertz
Random-access memory	8 megabytes
Hard drive memory	850 megabytes
Modem	9,600 BPS
Mouse	Any one you like
Keyboard	Any one you like
Monitor (color)	VGA, 640 × 480, 17 inches

Options

Printer	Laser jet, dot matrix or ink-jet
Backup tape drive	120 megabyte

In Computers, It's Caveat Emptor

You can find many computers that give you the minimum standards described. However, if you don't buy from a major computer make such as IBM, AST Research, Dell, Compaq, Hewlett-Packard, Gateway 2000, Packard Bell, and Toshiba (all DOS systems), or Apple, be sure the manufacturer you choose will be around when you have a problem, or, at the very least, that the retailer selling you the system guarantees repairs. Most computer manufacturers will replace any hardware problems within 30 days, but get a warranty for as long as you can.

Assemble; Get a Guru; Keep Sharp, Heavy Objects Away

While assembling the computer and loading the software is easy, making it all work together can be frustrating—make that *will* be frustrating. Nothing encourages you to smash a computer more than one that won't do what you want. The reason it's so maddening is that you know you're only one or two keystrokes away from completing your task. You can spend hours trying to figure out the simplest problem, and oftentimes, never resolve it.

Save yourself a lot of time, hair, ulcers, broken monitors and relationships with significant others, and hire a computer nerd. If you live in a college community, put an ad in the daily college newspaper. Just say "Computer Nerd Wanted by Computer Neophyte," and you'll have plenty of techies calling you. Pay him or her by the hour. They will be much cheaper than replacing equipment or paying doctor bills.

They can get you started by teaching you about files, working with the mouse, backing up, suggesting additional software, arranging your Windows icons and setting up the system the way you want it. Once they know your configuration and your programs, you can call them when you're stuck, and they can quickly tell you how to continue. They're well worth every dollar you pay them.

If you don't live near a college, you can advertise in the local paper. Use the same ad. There are plenty of computer whizzes who have day jobs as accountants, engineers, stockbrokers and secretaries.

When interviewing for your guru, describe your system and ask them if they know how to set it up properly. A good Apple user won't be a good DOS expert. Get at least two references.

While your new guide is directing you through the computer maze, you must simultaneously read about your system and the software. Most of the manuals are frustratingly difficult. The best books for learning how to quickly use software are written by users and have titles like *Idiot's Guide to DOS; Computers, the Plain English Guide*; and the Que books for jumpstarting you onto programs like WordPerfect, a software program for writing letters, books, and presentations. Your goal is to use your guru sparingly and, eventually, compute on your own.

THE SOFTWARE

The instructions for making a computer do something is called the software. Without software, the computer would just sit and hum. It's the way to turn the metal into your obedient servant, crunching numbers, displaying stock quotes and writing eloquent phrases.

For the sake of brevity, I'll limit my description of software to those programs related to running your computer and investing. There are literally thousands of software programs that can help you do millions of tasks. For our purposes, we only want to get the computer running and our investment strategy working.

FIRST THINGS FIRST

The computer needs basic operating instructions to store data, add numbers, calculate your return on investments and perform other assignments. Those instructions are provided by software, and, in particular, MS-DOS or Microsoft Disk Operating System.

If you buy a new computer, the latest version of DOS should be preinstalled. If it's not in your system, you'll need to buy it.

DOS consists of small disks that fit into a slot, called the A or B drives, in your computer. The instructions for DOS installation will guide you through the process in a few minutes. Once loaded into your computer, you can run any other software, back up your data, double your hard drive disk space, undelete data you deleted and accomplish many other tasks. However, the basic operating instructions for doing these are incorporated in the MS-DOS software, and it must be installed prior to any other software.

When buying the computer, negotiate to have the dealer include the DOS software and Windows as a package. You should be able to buy them cheaper, and the dealer can install them, although if you must do it yourself, putting them into your computer is very easy and only requires a short time. The instructions have come a long way from the Neanderthal carvings of original programs. Software vendors have also added wonderful support staff to answer your questions.

Some of the vendors supply toll-free lines, but most do not. Nevertheless, if you spend hours trying to figure something out, it can save you time, money, frustration, alcohol abuse, smashed monitors and maybe your marriage if you call the vendor. You're always just a few keystrokes away from solving any problem. The difficulty is to know which keys to stroke. That's when the support staff shines like a beacon.

The reason I recommend MS-DOS is because almost every software vendor writes its programs to specifications for DOS. In other words, there are other system software programs, many of them very good, but the widest choice of programs is available when DOS is in your computer.

WINDOWS ON THE SOFTWARE WORLD

Let me tell you a story. In the beginning, there was Apple. It was a computer meant for people without pens in their pockets and propellers on their heads. It was much easier to use than the lumbering giants built for commerce. It had little pictures and a pointer that let the user point and click and do wonderful things. The little pictures were neat and so easy to use.

The lumbering giants didn't think much of this little Apple until they noticed its sales were going faster than money in Las Vegas. Then the giants decided to build little computers, too. But they didn't change the way the computers operated. There were no little pictures or pointers. There were very difficult DOS instructions that were similar to a foreign language, say Chinese, only more difficult. Sales of Apples continued to soar. Sales of DOS systems went mostly to the techno nerds.

This was more than Microsoft, the developers of DOS, could stand. And so they invented Windows.

Windows is an operating system that sits on top of the DOS programs, much like a frame surrounds a picture. It puts all the programs in a cohesive unit, and allows the user to more easily access each program or use multiple programs simultaneously.

Each DOS program is represented by a small picture on the screen called an icon. When you move the arrow on the screen with the mouse and place it on one of the icons, you double-click the mouse (push the left button twice), and the program appears. Then you work on the program.

Windows makes your computer easier and more efficient to operate. The second program you want behind DOS is Windows. The version of Windows should be 3.1 or higher.

A neat trick with Windows is moving between programs. If you are looking at your portfolio in your portfolio program and then want to look at the closing price of a stock in another program, Windows allows you to keep your portfolio program active in the playground (RAM) and bring in the quote program. By pressing the "ALT" key and the "TAB" key, you can toggle between several different programs. This is a big time saver. Without Windows, you have to exit one program, bring up the new program, get the information, exit the new program and then bring in the first program again.

ON-LINE INVESTOR SERVICES FOR STOCK QUOTES AND DATA

Because you are going to invest with your computer, you'll need stock quotes and stock data. There are several providers of these services: Prodigy, America Online, GEnie, Signal, Dow Jones, Telescan and CompuServe are on-line services. These allow you to link up with a host computer, receive stock quotes either on a 15-minute delay basis, which will cost you nothing but the base service fees or on a real-time basis, which costs much more. You do not need real-time quotes unless you want to trade the stock market. I don't recommend trading. In fact, I urge you not to do it. I'll go into more detail on trading in Chapter 6, which explains how to buy and sell stocks.

I describe each of these services in detail in the next chapter. My purpose here is to alert you to the need for one of these programs.

THE SPREADSHEET SOFTWARE

There are two dominant spreadsheet programs: Excel by Microsoft and Lotus 1-2-3 by Lotus. Both work well. You can't go wrong with either one. Each program has a complete user's guide for installing and working with the software. Many people find these instructions less than instructive and need outside books, written for novices in simple English to explain how to use the programs. I prefer the Excel software because there's a wonderful book entitled *I Hate Excel* that takes some of the pain out of learning the program. However, there is a very good book printed by Que, which is a shortcut guide for using Lotus 1-2-3.

A spreadsheet program allows you to do calculations over a range of columns and rows. You will find this helpful as you develop your investing skills. You don't need highly refined mathematical abilities to use the spreadsheets to your advantage. In fact, Appendix B shows you how I use spreadsheets to rank stocks for investing. It is not complicated, and I highly recommend you include this in your software purchases.

SOFTWARE SUMMARY

There are only a few programs needed to turn your computer into an investment powerhouse. You will add to these as you get more comfortable with your system.

SOFTWARE REQUIRED

Operating system	MS-DOS, version 6.1 or higher
Macro operating system	Windows, version 3.1 or higher
Stock quotes and data	America Online, or other service, such as Dow Jones, Prodigy, CompuServe, GEnie, Signal, Telescan
Spreadsheet	Excel, Lotus 1-2-3
Portfolio management	See Chapter 7

SO WHAT DOES ALL THIS COST?

Because hardware and software are continuously decreasing in price, it is impossible to give an accurate cost for your computer and its programs. However, for general numbers, you can expect to pay less than $1,000 for the computer and less than $1,000 for the software.

Your costs will depend on the size of the hard drive, RAM, the chip, the monitor and other items. Much like the options on a car, you pay extra for additional power and amenities. And, like a car purchase, you'll find your best deal will be a complete package, especially on last year's models.

Remember, you don't need more than the minimum requirements described in the tables for hardware and software. Buying more equipment won't make you a better or smarter investor.

MORE ON THE MODEM

The modem is your connection to the outside world. It can bring you data and information and turn your computer into a resource of infinite capacity. It can save or cost you considerable money and time. The kind you buy and the way you use it will determine its cost effectiveness. Here are a few helpful tips:

- Buy the fastest one you can afford, but nothing less than 9,600 bps. I've already discussed the reasons.
- Don't install a dedicated phone line just for the computer. Unless you make your living on an on-line system, one where you have to be on the modem continuously, you don't need a dedicated line.
- Don't have call waiting on the line you use. When you're on an on-line service, call waiting will interrupt the data flow and cut you off from the service. You have to exit the program, sign on to the program again, get back to the data page you want and then continue. If you already have call waiting on your phone, push *7 on your phone before you start up your program; this will disable the service for that one call. Or add a second line to your home, and use that one for the computer.
- Don't put your modem on your business line if you work at home. Business lines are usually metered, and if your computer is on that line, you'll be paying for the service you use as well as the business metering rate.
- Always buy services on a flat-rate basis if possible. When you compare information or database services, always pick the one with no metered charges. That means the service bills you on a flat, one-fee rate, with unlimited

access to the program. You can't always get everything you want on that basis, but that's an ideal you're trying to achieve.

Sometimes service charges are based on the time of day that you're on the system. For many stock and news services, that means you can use them on a flat rate when the stock market is closed. If you have a job during the market's hours, you won't use it much any other time, anyway.

If there is a unique service you simply must have and you have to pay while you're on-line, always download your information and read it after you sign off. When you download, you take the information and put it in a file on your hard drive (the storage bin). You then call up that file and put it in RAM (the playground) and spend as much time as you want with it.

The best way to use on-line services that charge for access time is to prepare before signing on by listing everything you want. Don't spend time thinking about what you might need or like while the meter is running. The secret to keeping your costs down is to get on and get off as quickly as possible. The programs I recommend for databases in Chapter 3 have flat-rate charges or timed access only during certain times of the day.

Be sure your access phone number is a local one or toll-free. Most services want you to use their system and have a network system that allows local calls in your area or supply a toll-free number. However, not all of them do. Be sure the phone prefix of the number you are given to access a program is for a local call or an 800 number. You can check the local number prefix in the front of your phone book.

Sometimes, if you live too far from civilization, you have to pay the price for the nearest access number. These charges add up fast, especially if you access the service daily or for long periods of time. Your first phone bill will be a shock. Either move, try to get an 800 number or stop buying some special treat and pay for the phone. The knowledge you get from the service should more than reward you for its expense.

MORE COMPUTER TIPS

Once you have your computer home and set up in a good quiet place, the first thing you should do is play with it. Unless your idea of computer play is throw and catch with King Kong, it's almost impossible to hurt or destroy the computer or the programs in it. Buy some games like Solitaire or Sim City or any other software that looks fun, load it up and play with it before you try any of the serious stuff.

By playing with the various keys and the mouse, you are learning how to use the system, how to point and drag information, how to load and exit the program. After you've used the computer for a while, you'll begin to see the pattern of how programs are written and how most of them use the same format for most of the functions.

You'll discover how resilient these programs are. They keep coming back up even if you've exited them incorrectly, shut the machine off in the middle of a calculation or had the machine freeze up and then had to reset it. All of these calamities and more will happen, maybe even a power outage just as you've finished a great spreadsheet. No need to panic. Especially since you're saving all your work as you go along.

Saving work is different from backing up. Saving is when you take the data from RAM (the playground) and instruct the computer to save it to the hard disk (the storage bin). Every 10 minutes or so, you should make it a practice to save your work. Some programs, such as WordPerfect, have an automatic Save feature, which puts your work onto the hard drive every five minutes.

Playing with your computer will help you discover how easy it is to use and how tough it is to lose data or a program. It will also show you how frustrating a logical, nonthinking machine can be. Do not keep a hammer near your computer. If you have a problem, and you will, first read the guide that comes with the software. If you can't figure it out, and many times you won't, call the company's technical support number. Then, if you still can't figure it out, call your local guru. But get on with using the computer: Play with it; work with it; yell at it; and jump for joy when you make a breakthrough. But get on with it. It's the key to the magic kingdom.

WATCH OUT FOR THIS KEY

There is one key that deserves special attention: the "delete" key. That does exactly what it says. When you direct the computer to delete information or data, most programs will ask you a question like: Are you sure you want to delete this information about Aunt Susie's recipe? The programs take deleting very seriously. So should you. However, even that damage is now sometimes repairable thanks to the "undelete" feature on programs like Windows. I wouldn't rely on the program to fix a deletion. Think it through carefully before deleting any information.

The delete key is about the only way you can hurt yourself and your programs on the computer. And that's totally within your power. I have heard of hard disk crashes where your hard disk, due to a power surge or failure, gets wiped out, everything goes to zero. But you can't control that. You can have a special surge protector, which has been described, and, of course, you will have backed up your system on a regular basis. Even if you were to experience the worst scenario, a hard disk crash, you will be able to reload your backup tape, and within minutes get right back to work.

The message here is: Don't be afraid of the computer or to try different options on a program. You won't hurt anything, and you'll gain more confidence in your ability each time you're on it.

COMPUTER MAGAZINES

One of the best ways to become more familiar with computers is to read about them. There are several excellent magazines which the novice and intermediate user will find of considerable help. The following have articles on what hardware and software to buy, the best way to utilize both and trends in the industry. They are all at the magazine rack of bookstores, computer stores and libraries.

> *Computer Buyer's Guide and Handbook*
> *Compute*
> *PC Computing*
> *PC Magazine*
> *PC Novice*
> *PC World*

After you've bought the hardware and software, you may feel as if you're sitting in the cockpit of a 747. You know it will take you wherever you want, you just don't know which buttons to push. Let's start pushing some of those buttons, and get you where you want to go.

CHAPTER THREE

SMALL-CAP INFORMATION: DISCOVERING STOCKS WITH YOUR COMPUTER

Like the famous forty-niners prospecting for gold, today's investor needs to constantly search for nuggets. However, today's mother lode isn't in the mountains, it's in small-cap stocks.

Good small-cap stocks are found in many places: your computer, local and national newspapers, newsletters, television, neighborhood bars, the backyard fence and your spouse and children. All of these are excellent sources for stock ideas or tips. You just need to keep your eyes and ears open.

The fact is you never know where you'll find the next stock like Snapple, the beverage maker whose share price grew from $5.00 to $32.25 in two years, or American Power Conversion Corporation, the manufacturer of uninterruptible power supplies that rocketed from $1.87 per share to $29.87 in three years. However, you'll increase your odds of success if you systematically dig for treasure while you're waiting for lady luck to find you. And your computer is an excellent shovel.

By itself, your computer will only sit there. You and some software have to make it work. If you buy a program and install it in your computer, you can go after small-cap stocks. Usually, the program is an on-line service such as America Online that sends you a floppy disk which you install, and it has all the instructions for your computer to access the service by means of your modem.

By the way, the term *floppy disk* can be confusing. Most floppy disks are now hard and don't flop at all. But early in the development of the computer, a floppy disk was a thin disk, measuring five and one-quarter inches across. It would fit into a floppy disk drive, which is a small opening in the computer, and it was thin enough that it would flop if not held firmly in the middle.

As with all things related to the computer, this floppy disk format changed. The new standard became a rather thick disk measuring three and one-half inches across. It didn't flop. Now 99% of software is written on the new standard, but they're still called floppy disks. This can be confusing to the novice, especially if you're directed to use something floppy and are holding something which isn't. For our purposes, the floppy disk everyone refers to is the three-and-one-half-inch disk. This is the disk your on-line service will send you. Put it in your computer's A or B drive slot.

You'll also see software on CD-ROMs or compact disks–read only memory. These are the same as CDs you've been buying for music, but they only contain software or data programs, not your favorite melodies. To use this format, you need a CD player in the computer or buy an add-on CD player. Be sure the player is 4X or higher speed rated.

Your on-line service provider has a large host computer, full of data and information you can see on your screen and/or download into your computer (into the storage bin, the C drive). After you download, you can pull up that data (into your playground, the RAM), and use it as you wish.

There are many companies offering various services. Some of them focus on charts of stocks. Others have all the basic numbers on stocks. Still others combine numbers, charts, quotes and news wires. Usually, the more information you receive, the more you'll spend for it.

By using one or several of the following services, you can turn your computer into a mining machine that will dig out small-cap stocks.

THE BASIC SERVICES YOU WANT

Now that you own a computer, have it set up and want to get started, hold on to your software dollars. Before you rush out and buy some floppy disks for a database service which may or may not help you find better investments, consider these factors.

Your ultimate goal is to get as much information as possible, with unlimited access time for a flat rate, and no extra charges for anything. That is an ideal. You won't find it. But keep it in mind as you compare various services.

Also, programs are constantly being revised and/or updated. Vendors change their pricing strategy as competition gets tougher. What I describe for the following services will certainly be different in some aspects when you look at the same program. But the basic elements are:

- Flat-rate fees. This means you don't pay for time you spend looking at data on your screen from the host computer. When you pay for time spent on the system, called access time, you begin to appreciate the old saying, time is money. If you have to pay for your access time, be sure you know what you want to get, request it, download the information into your system and get off.

- A local phone number or a toll-free one. Even if you don't have access-time charges, your phone bill will resemble a smaller version of the national debt if you don't have local access or a toll-free line. You'll be impressed with the length of time you spend on the computer if you have to pay for the phone bill to use it.

- High-speed access to data with a minimum modem speed of 9,600 bps. As discussed in Chapter 2, the higher the bps (bits per second), the quicker you get information, as well as on and off the service. It can be frustratingly slow to use a program at a rate of 2,400 bps. Going from one section to another can take what seems like the gestation period for a baby elephant, especially if you want the information NOW. By using 9,600 bps, you can literally zoom from one section to another in any program, and if you are downloading information, you can get on and off much quicker. Look for a service that doesn't charge extra for the faster rate transmission.

- The program should be Windows-compatible. That means you can put a little icon in the Windows Program Menu on the main screen on your computer, point at the icon with the mouse, click twice and bring up the program. Many services are available only in the DOS format, meaning you need to exit the Windows program, wait for the "C" prompt and then type in the program access code. This becomes very tedious over time and doesn't allow you to use several programs at once, which the Windows program does. Many of the

DOS-only programs will eventually go to a Windows format or they will not be able to sell their product. Unless a DOS-only service is unique, get one that is in the Windows format.

- The service should be easy to use. If you need a PhD in physics to run the program, go back to school and get one or buy a simpler program. There is no excuse for vendors to make a service difficult to use, because there are too many easy ones already available. You don't have to be brilliant to be a successful investor or a computer user. Avoid the programs that demand too much from you.

- More stocks are better than few stocks. Your investment focus on small-cap stocks will sometimes take you to places where some databases do not go, namely small companies with little public information. You want a service that covers at least 5,000 stocks and, preferably, many more. The smaller the stock, the harder it is for services to get information to input in their databases. Some of the stocks you discover will be so small no one will have anything on them. Those stocks are too small. However, if you have a service with 5,000 or more stocks in its database, your chances of finding information on a particular stock are greatly improved.

THE DATA SERVICES

There are on-line services and disk-based or off-line services. The on-line services use a host computer format in which your computer dials up the company through the modem, uses the host computer while you're on-line or downloads the information for your use after you've exited the program. Dialing the service is done automatically by the computer. It's part of the software you load onto your hard drive. These on-line services update their databases by the minute, hour, day or week, keeping you abreast of all new developments for a stock.

Disk-based services send you a disk full of information on a regular basis, such as weekly, monthly or quarterly. You can manipulate these data as much or as little as you want without worrying about access time because there is none. You download the disk onto your hard drive and then use the information as often as you want. While these offer excellent data for many stocks, and some services have many more stocks than others, there is a time delay between disks. You can get excellent fundamental information from these services, but don't expect them to give you news in a timely manner. Only an on-line service can bring you up-to-the-minute items.

THE ON-LINE SERVICES FOR STOCKS

The following companies are the major on-line information services. If you buy one of these programs, they will send you a packet that will include a floppy disk to load into your computer and instructions on how to use their system. Once you've loaded the disk, your computer can automatically dial into the service. On-line services vary as to the depth and amount of news, stock quotes, stock information, stock screens for picking stocks and stock charts.

The following are the best-known and largest of the current on-line services. There will be new ones appearing, but it is very expensive to buy the data or create the database needed to compete in this market. The following, current vendors serve as excellent examples of what you need to discover good small-cap stocks.

Most of these companies will send you a demonstration disk to test their programs. No one is perfect in the sense that it gives you everything you need in one place, but one, Prodigy, comes very close. All prices and phone numbers are as of this writing.

- America Online (800-827-6364)

  Charges $9.95 per month for ten hours of usage, then $2.95 per hour. Has a 30-day free home trial with up to 10 hours of usage. Works with DOS, Windows, and MacIntosh computers. Provides business and financial news supplied by UPI, Business Wire, PR News, and international services. Market news is updated daily after the close, all stock quotes for the New York, American, and Over the Counter Exchanges on a 20-minute delayed basis. Has portfolio management capability, on-line investing and offers investment advice. See Chapter 9 for more on America Online.

- CompuServe (800-848-8199)

  Introductory membership is free. Charges $9.95 per month for ten hours of unlimited service (10 the first month) with a charge of $2.95 per hour thereafter. Also has an alternative program charging $15 per month for 15 hours and $1.95 per hour thereafter. There are also available several premium services that charge for an inquiry or on an hourly basis. Has strong general and business news, economic news and data, company news, financial statement data, SEC filings for companies, analyst reports, earnings estimates, charting, technical studies, screens for fundamental factors, technical factors and mutual funds. Offers on-line brokerage and message and mail areas. Runs on any computer.

Includes MicroQuote II, which provides over 12 years of pricing history on more than 160,000 publicly traded securities, plus 20 years of dividend history. *Money* magazine's FundWatch On-line provides information on more than 1,900 mutual funds. Detailed company data are provided by Standard & Poor's, Value Line, Disclosure, and Institutional Brokers Estimate System. Bulletin board for investors. Databases on international companies. Global Report, a business and financial information service from Citibank, is on-line, and stock brokerage firms are available 24 hours a day. Data can be downloaded.

- Telescan (800-324-8246)

Charges start-up fee of $199, monthly fee of $45.00 for unlimited non-prime time use; standard database usage during prime time is $0.75 per minute, $0.33 per minute of non-prime time, and 25% surcharge for 2,400/9,600 bps access. Works on the DOS system. Combines software program and on-line database, allowing users to perform technical and fundamental analysis on more than 74,000 stocks, mutual funds, industry groups, options and market indexes. Updates every 15 minutes; data goes back 20 years. Has more than 80 technical and fundamental indicators; reads and plots insider trading information; shows quarterly reported earnings and Zack's Estimate Service for projected earnings; and offers updated news stories and historical news, company fact sheets, and investment newsletters. Can display up to four graphs on a single screen. Accesses Standard & Poor's Marketscope, Morningstar Mutual Fund data, MarketGuide Reports and SEC Online.

- Prodigy (800-776-3449)

Prodigy offers good financial information. The basic service costs $9.95 per month with ten hours of use. Extra hours are billed at $2.95 per hour. They also have a heavy user program that allows 30 hours of use in a month for $29.95. Hours in excess of 30 are billed at $2.95 per hour.

There is a very good financial program called Strategic Investor available on Prodigy at a premium cost of $14.95 per month. Let's look at what you get for the money.

IT'S NOT FREE BUT IT'S VERY GOOD

OK, you have to pay extra but here's what you get:

When you order Prodigy (America Online or CompuServe), you receive a kit that includes a floppy disk and a booklet with instructions on how to load the information from the disk to your computer. It will also give you a unique code number. You must use that code number and a secret word or set of numbers, which you choose, much like the secret number you have for your ATM card.

First, take the Prodigy floppy disk and insert it into the A or B drive of your computer. At the prompt on your computer, type "install," and the computer will start to make little noises, meaning it's taking information off the floppy disk and putting it on your hard disk, the C drive. During the installation, you will be asked questions such as what is your name and other challenging items. It is very simple.

Once the program has been installed, you are ready to sign on to Prodigy. Be sure your modem is turned on if you have an external one. If the modem is internal, the computer automatically instructs it to go on-line.

If you have a Windows version of Prodigy, you simply point the arrow to the Prodigy icon, double-click on it, and a screen will appear. Type in the number you were given by Prodigy. Below that type in your secret code word or number. Then put the arrow on the "View Highlights" box and double-click. The computer will then start to put you in touch with the host computer.

The software you installed will instruct the computer to dial the phone number you supplied for the nearest hookup for the Prodigy service. That number is in the booklet Prodigy sends you. You will hear your modem dial a number, hear a phone ring, then some loud, static noises follow. When you've connected, your modem goes silent, and your screen will change to the Prodigy Highlights page, which has the latest news headlines. On the right side will be several choices such as "Business/Finance," "News/ Weather," "Travel," "Shopping," "Computers," "Reference," and "Entertainment."

For our purposes, move the arrow to the "Business/Finance" line and double-click on it. This will put you on a page of business and financial news headlines. These headlines are updated throughout the business day. Each is numbered in a box to the left of the headline.

If one of the stories is of interest, move the arrow to the numbered box, double-click on it and the screen will change to provide the story requested. When you finish reading the story, move the arrow back to the "Menu" box at the bottom of the screen, double-click on it, and the screen will change to the "Business/Finance" page.

A FLOWCHART FOR PRODIGY NEWS AND INVESTMENT INFORMATION

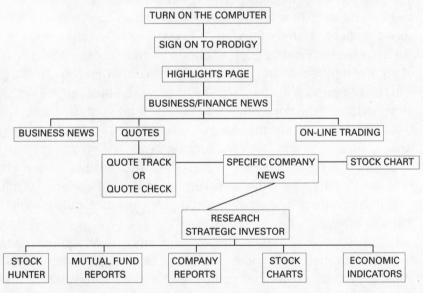

On the right side of this screen are several boxes, each one will take you to another feature in the service. By moving the arrow to a box, then double-clicking the mouse, you will pull up a new screen of information.

The first box is "More News." When highlighted with the arrow, a new menu appears with several choices: Business News, Company News, Market News, International News, Economic Indicators, five advisors' comments and Home Business.

For our purposes, the Business News feature is the most useful. It contains more headlines, but these focus on companies. Announcements of mergers, sales of subsidiaries, earnings releases and resigning presidents are all part of the everyday business news. The full stories behind the headlines are available and can be retrieved by placing the arrow on the headline and double-clicking the mouse.

Prodigy uses the Dow Jones News Service for its financial information, one of the best sources for company news. Because the *Wall Street Journal* and *Barron's* magazine are published by Dow Jones, any story containing company information or a reference to a company is available to Prodigy subscribers. These are in addition to the breaking news of the day.

Specific company stories are found by going to the Company News choice on the pull-down menu. By double-clicking the mouse on this feature, the screen changes and you are asked to type in a company symbol or name. If there are any stories over the last three weeks on the company, the screen will change, and the latest story will appear. This is an excellent way to keep up with the news on any company in your portfolio.

GRAPHIC PARK

By double-clicking on the Menu box, we return to the Business/Finance page and can choose "Markets." This feature shows how the markets are doing graphically. Double-click on the box, and the screen changes to four graphs: the Dow Jones Industrial Averages for the day, the price of gold, the price and yield of the 30-year Treasury bond and the U.S. dollar index. This last graph displays the value of the U.S. dollar compared with all other major currencies. When the graph is going up, the dollar is increasing in value.

These graphs provide a quick and easy visual summary on how the various markets performed for the day. If you check during the trading day, each graph is updated about every 15 minutes.

STRATEGIC INVESTOR OR THE GOLD MINE IN YOUR COMPUTER

If we return once again to the Business/Finance page by double-clicking on the Menu box and look on the right side of the screen, the box below Markets is labeled "Research." By double-clicking on it, a new box appears with several choices: Charts/Price History, Company News, Company Reports, Consumer Reports, Economic Indicators, Investor's Glossary, Mutual Fund Analyst, Stock Hunter, Strategic Investor and Wall Street Edge.

Four of these choices, Mutual Fund Analyst, Charts/Price History, Stock Hunter and Strategic Investor, cost extra. If you buy the Strategic Investor for $14.95 per month, it includes Mutual Fund Analyst and Stock Hunter along with many more features. If you want to use only the Stock Hunter, you can purchase it separately for a daily cost.

Let's assume you've purchased the Strategic Investor and want to use the Stock Hunter feature. By double-clicking on the Strategic Investor icon, the screen changes, and you go into a different world. You're entering the gold mine. There are definitely nuggets in here, but you have to uncover them.

The new screen has a number of headlines on it, referring to articles about companies that have appeared in *Investor's Business Daily* in the last week, as well as "hot" stock charts for the New York Stock Exchange, the NASDAQ, and the American Stock Exchange. On the right of the screen are several boxes, one of which says Stock Hunter. Move the arrow to that box and double-click on it.

The screen changes again, and on the bottom are eight titles: Graham and Dodd, CANSLIM, One Up On Wall Street, Wallflowers, Sustainable Earnings Growth, Consistent Dividends, Low Price-to-Book and High Price-to-Book. Each title represents a unique method of analyzing stocks. In other words, by using a particular mathematical formula, these analytical tools go into Prodigy's database of 6,000 stocks and give you a list of issues fitting their investment criteria.

I'll describe the screening methods each of these models use, although four are best-suited for small-cap investing: CANSLIM, One Up On Wall Street, Sustainable Earnings Growth and Wallflowers. However, I urge you to look at every screen because, from time to time, there are great small-cap ideas in each of them. Again, small-cap stocks are everywhere, and you need to constantly look for them, just like the nuggets in a mine.

When you double-click the arrow on the number to the left of each investment methodology, the computer screen changes to a list of stocks that meet the criteria for that investment philosophy. A complete explanation of how the stocks are chosen is given in the "Model Info" box. Sometimes, there are only eight or nine stocks on a list. At other times, there are as many as 100.

Each week these screens are updated by 9:00 A.M. Saturday morning and are unchanged until the following Saturday. In fact, all data for the 6,000 stocks are updated on a weekly basis by 9:00 A.M. on Saturday.

When the stocks are chosen by the computer for each investment methodology, they are listed on your computer screen, starting with the best stock in that category. Each stock is in its own rectangular box, and when you see the page, the first stock is highlighted by a flashing frame. If you want to look at the data for that stock, you simply put the arrow on the box, click the mouse once, and the screen changes to the first page of data on that stock. In Chapter 6, I'll explain how to use these data.

When you've finished with that stock, return to the list of stocks by putting the arrow on the Menu box and double-clicking. You're then back to the original list. Any other stock from the list can be chosen by placing the arrow on the stock and double-clicking the mouse. Once you've done this a few times, you'll get into the rhythm and be bouncing back and forth. By using the strategy in Chapter 6, you can quickly determine whether a stock is worth pursuing.

Let's look at the eight investing methodologies or screens and see how they can help you invest. Remember, the idea here is to present one on-line service's ability to help you find small-cap stocks. You can see what Prodigy offers and then compare that with any other service to determine if you are getting more or less value.

THE FIRST SCREEN: GRAHAM AND DODD

Benjamin Graham and David Dodd were the first to suggest that the value of a stock should be determined by the expected future earnings and dividends—the basis for fundamental analysis.

The theory states that if you can find stocks selling for less than this intrinsic value, you have a good investment. Graham and Dodd focused on large, mature companies for their database, and at the time of their research, AAA corporate bonds yielded 4.4%. Current users of the model adjust for today's yields.

Graham and Dodd recognized that their calculations were only an approximation of a fair price for the stock. Therefore, to reduce risk to the investor, they recommended that stocks should only be considered if their actual price was 80% or less than their theoretical price.

This model is best used for evaluating mature stocks that have experienced several business cycles, such as public utilities, life insurance, food processing, medical supplies, beverages and household products. A complete description of the model is given in the program and is taken from the book *Security Analysis*, fifth edition, by Benjamin Graham and David Dodd.

By Popular Demand: *One Up on Wall Street*

Peter Lynch literally wrote the book on this investment methodology. Its focus is to find undervalued stocks. Basically, the approach says, a stock is fairly priced when there is a one-to-one relationship between its expected future return (earnings and dividends) and its current price-to-earnings, or P/E, ratio, net of long-term debt.

The P/E ratio is a number derived by dividing the price of a stock by its previous four quarters' earnings. For example, if a stock has a price of $20 and has earnings for the last four quarters that added up to $1, the stock has a P/E of 20.

This model, to be conservative, considers a stock for investing only if expected future return is more than twice the adjusted P/E ratio and the company has a strong balance sheet, which usually means that the company has little debt. Also, long-term debt cannot be more than 25% of total assets, and if a company uses financial industry accounting practices, such as a Savings and Loan, that company is not included in the model because long-term debt cannot be determined. One last criterion: the stock price must be less than or equal to 10 times free cash flow per share. (Free cash flow is the earnings of a company plus depreciation.) This gives you, the investor, the potential for at least a 10% return, a minimum reward one expects from owning stocks.

As with all models, there are limitations because you are only using numbers. Peter Lynch believes that isn't enough. The original model also considered important factors such as hidden assets, inventory levels and changes in inventory levels. There is a full discussion of the model in the program, and for further understanding, the book *One Up on Wall Street* by Peter Lynch is highly recommended.

This model is one of the best for finding small-cap stocks. However, don't blindly buy the stocks on this list or any other. You have to investigate each stock, determine if it fits your level of risk and then diversify your portfolio properly. You will learn these important elements of investing in Chapters 6 and 7.

Also, any of the terms used in the above description, such as P/E ratio, that you don't understand now will be explained in Chapter 6.

CAN YOU CANSLIM?

William O'Neil, founder and chairman of the *Investor's Business Daily*, wrote a book entitled *How to Make Money in Stocks*. In it, he describes the CANSLIM method of investing, one that picks the innovative, entrepreneurial companies, also known as the best small-cap firms.

The CANSLIM breaks down like this:
C - Current quarterly earnings per share
A - Annual earnings increases
N - New products, new management and new highs
S - Supply & Demand, small capitalization and volume demand
L - Leader in its industry
 I - Institutional sponsorship
M - Market direction

The selected stocks for this model have current quarterly earnings up at least 25% from the same quarter a year ago and annual earnings must be up more than 15%. These choices give you the fastest-growing companies.

In addition, earnings growth must be relatively stable. Stability measures annual deviation from the earnings trend and is ranked from 1 to 99, with 1 being a perfect fit to the earnings trend. Only stocks with a rating of less than 25 are selected.

The current stock price must be within 10% of its 52-week high. O'Neil's research found that stocks hitting new highs typically go higher. Stocks selling near their lows tend to move lower.

The company must have less than 25 million shares outstanding and some of the stock must be held by institutions. The stock must have a relative price strength of more than 85. This means that the price performance of the stock was better than 85% of the more than 6,000 stocks within the Stock Analyst universe.

The model can only measure certain aspects of the full CANSLIM approach. Market direction, for example, is considered at least as important as the other items. Even if you invest in the right company,

"If you are wrong on the direction of the broad market, three out of four of your stocks will slump with the market averages, and you will lose money," O'Neil claims.

You must also exclude one-time gains from all earnings calculations, something the model does not do. For further discussion of this, see Chapter 6. Also, the model does not know how to pick companies that are buying back their stock—a sign that implies the company expects improved earnings.

This CANSLIM screen is a great source for small-cap ideas. There are lots of nuggets in here. And by using this method as a starting point, you can find stocks, evaluate them using the approach given in Chapter 6, list the ones worth following and then buy the best for your portfolio. This screen gives you in seconds what would take you months to find on your own. Check it out and use it!

BEAUTIFUL WALLFLOWERS

These stocks are the forgotten, discarded or overlooked nuggets of the market. For whatever reason, institutional investors don't own these companies or at least own very little of them. This model seeks them out for your consideration. This is another great small-cap nugget finder.

The computer searches for companies with less than 15% of their shares held by institutions. That list is then trimmed by taking only companies with less than $100 million in market capitalization (share price times the number of shares). Then, the model retrieves from this list only the stocks with steady or increasing earnings per share (EPS) during the past two years, and those that don't pay dividends. The return on equity (ROE) for the company must be at least 15%. See Chapter 6 for a full discussion of ROE.

Furthermore, the model doesn't take companies with debt equaling more than 25% of equity. The more debt a company has, the riskier the investment since the interest payments are a constant drain on earnings. Also, stocks using the financial institutional accounting practices are eliminated because debt cannot be properly determined.

The original model for Wallflowers considers factors that cannot be determined from the databases in the Stock Analyst, such as the average daily share volume of a stock. Stocks with high volume are more liquid and will appeal to institutions. (This model is discussed in detail in an article entitled "Beating the Institutions to the High-

Profit Firms," in the November 1987 issue of the *American Association of Individual Investors [AAII] Journal.*)

You can see why these stocks are the smaller, high-growth companies. This model is another excellent place to find the stocks you want. But remember, as with all these methods, you simply can't buy a stock just because it's on a list presented by a computer screen. You need to determine for yourself whether it meets your criteria for investing. All of these investing models are great places to start, not to finish.

One final word about the Wallflowers: if there are no institutions owning the stock, you shouldn't either. A stock needs some sponsorship from larger investors to help the flow of stock trading and research. If it has no such sponsorship, the stock trades more by appointment, and information is almost impossible to find. You should see at least 5% ownership by institutions before considering a purchase.

GROWTH, GROWTH AND MORE GROWTH

The next model is called Sustainable Earnings Growth. This theory states that investors can determine the likely future earnings trend of a company by monitoring variables that might indicate at what level growth can be sustained. If sustainable growth is high relative to actual growth, earnings tend to trend up as a company fulfills its potential.

As the company's actual growth rate approaches its sustainable growth rate, earnings growth will slow and tend to trend down, unless the company improves its return on equity by increasing profit margins, acquires more efficient assets or increases debt to fund increased growth. As already mentioned, too much debt is not good for you or the company.

The model estimates sustainable growth by multiplying return on shareholders' equity by the company's retention ratio. That's not a psychological term. The retention ratio measures the part of earnings not distributed to investors as dividends but reinvested in the company, or simply retained in the company.

The model only selects companies with earnings per share growth rates greater than 10% and debt-to-equity ratios of less than 50%. The companies are sorted by the percent difference between their sustainable growth rates (the ideal) and their actual earnings per share growth rates.

This model is fairly small in variables, but will pull out the growth companies. For a full discussion of it, read "Corporate Earnings

Growth: Can it be Sustained?" in the October 1990 issue of the *AAII Journal*. It's just one more screen for ideas and a good starting place.

THE LAST THREE MODELS

The Consistent Dividends model is great for investors seeking companies with consistent dividends. Since we're looking for small-cap stocks that pay small or no dividends, this model is not for us.

The Low Price-to-Book model isn't very useful for small-cap investing either. It focuses on book value, which is determined from the balance sheet of a company by taking all assets and subtracting liabilities and preferred stock. The theory is that if a stock has a price significantly less than the per-share book value, it may be undervalued and poised for a turnaround. A group of investors called contrarians uses this method.

It works very well for older companies with hidden assets such as real estate held at original cost or trademarks. It doesn't help us find small-cap stocks.

The last model to consider is High Price-to-Book, the reverse of the above method. These stocks can be useful if you're looking to sell stocks short because they may be overvalued. Selling stocks short occurs when investors believe the price of a stock will go down, and they sell the stock even though they don't own it. They hope to buy it back at a lower price.

This model has little use for investors looking for small-cap stocks. If you want to short stocks, check it out. Otherwise, use the CANSLIM, Wallflowers, Sustainable Earnings Growth and *One Up on Wall Street* methods. They'll help you dig and shine light on the nuggets.

A WORD ABOUT THESE MODELS AND ALL OTHERS

Any computer model is only as productive as the numbers it uses. If you have good numbers, you get good results. If you have garbage in, you get a stinking mess. The databases for these models, and other on-line services, are taken from sources that simply report the raw numbers. That is, there is no consideration for extraordinary items that may cause earnings to jump significantly or any other one-time event. That is why it's critical that you use these models and any others as idea generators, not blind investment tips.

You need a method for examining these stocks, determining their merits based on an investigation of the numbers and understanding the intangibles that numbers can't quantify. You'll get that in Chapters 5 and 6.

OFF-LINE SERVICES FOR STOCKS

Many investors like to own the data they use and not worry about access time or a system going down while they're in the middle of running numbers. So, they subscribe to an off-line service that sends them a disk filled with data on stocks. The users then have the flexibility to do research their way, find stocks that suit their needs and work under no time constraints.

The only drawback to off-line services is the timeliness of the information. While it can be mailed once a week (very expensive), month or quarter, the news is never as timely as that of an on-line service since the on-line service is updated daily. Otherwise, the off-line services represent good value.

The following are examples of off-line services. For a more complete listing, see *The Individual Investor's Guide to Computerized Investing*, 13th edition, 1996.

- AAII STOCK INVESTOR (312-280-0170) Provides a quarterly updated program containing fundamental financial data on over 7,000 publicly traded stocks listed on the New York Stock Exchange, the American Stock Exchange, the NASDAQ national market, and the NASDAQ small-cap market. User can screen stocks with 300 variables. Income statement data include eight quarters of earnings and dividends, five years of revenue, cost, cash flow, earnings and dividend data. Balance sheet data cover previous three years. Has over 60 ratios and growth rates and users can create 40 custom variables. Price data included for last five years. Data can be exported to other programs.

    Cost is $99 per year for AAII (American Association of Individual Investors) members, $150 for non-members. Disk is sent quarterly. You need a DOS system, minimum chip of 386, 3 megabytes of RAM, and 25 megabytes hard disk space.
- VALUE/SCREEN III (800-654-0508) Provides financial statement data and earnings estimates. Screens on both technical

and fundamental factors. Transmitted by modem or disk. Fees are $325 per year for quarterly updates; $465 per year for monthly updates; $1,995 per year for weekly disks. System can be DOS or Mac.

Stock screen based on Value Line data. Has over 50 fundamental data items on about 1,600 stocks. User can screen stocks based on up to 25 different criteria. All data can be downloaded to other programs.

BEFORE YOU ORDER

Whether you're considering an on-line or off-line service, you should test run it first. Almost all services have descriptive material available at no cost. Many will send demonstration disks to give you a feel for how the program looks, acts and responds to your commands. Others will charge an introductory fee that includes the software for setting up the program on your hard drive. Then, if you continue to purchase the service, your computer is ready to run the next program or disk.

If you receive a demonstration disk, remember that most of them download to your hard drive and take up space. If you are not buying that service, go into your file manager program, find the name of the program and delete it.

Similar to buying a new car, you have to test-drive these programs to find the one that fits your likes and needs. The degrees of difficulty and information vary tremendously. If you're not comfortable, can't understand it or can't make it work: DON'T BUY IT AND HOPE FOR THE BEST. There are too many good, easy-to-use programs. You have to make some effort, but if your effort is turning into frustration and headaches, you're on the wrong program.

MORE SOURCES FOR STOCKS

While the computer is great for discovering stocks, it isn't the only source. You're limited to the stocks in your database, and those most likely won't include good, small companies in your community. The way in which you computer-search for stocks won't uncover all the good to great investments. You need to do more than turn on the computer and search. Your investment success can come from many different sources.

KIDS SAY THE DARNDEST THINGS

If you listen to kids, they have a lot to say between repetitive phrases, particularly about what's hot and what's history. You know how every little girl has to have a Barbie doll? Or how all the boys want computer games? And how every kid needs the latest hit CD?

Find out which companies make these latest crazes, and look them up on the computer. Analyze them by using the method in Chapter 6 and see if the stock makes sense for you. If nothing else, it's a good exercise in using your computer.

While many of these may be fads and fade, there is often an opportunity to do well if you're nimble, follow the stock closely and carefully watch for warnings of a slowdown in sales or a new direction for the company. Atari comes to mind for its computer games for television that were spectacularly successful, only to be followed by personal computers that were failures. When the management decided to take on IBM and Apple Computer and promised delivery dates that continued to be postponed, it made a decision to go from games to computers, kids to grown-ups. It couldn't make this transition. However, smart investors still did well if they made the decision to get out when the company changed direction.

If your son or daughter wants something, you can bet a lot of other children do. From skateboards to snowboards, from Madonna to grunge, there are trends constantly developing, growing or fading. Find out which companies are making the current craze, see if they have publicly traded stock and then check them on your computer.

TELEVISION IS NOT A VAST WASTELAND
FOR INVESTORS

Business news programs keep getting better and better. Part of your daily investor routine should include watching CNBC's "The Money Wheel" before, during or shortly after the stock market trading hours. CNBC is a cable channel included in a standard cable package. If you have cable, you get CNBC.

Every half hour, there is a synopsis of what the stock market is doing, the latest news headlines, earnings reports, as well as commentary from investment advisors, stock and bond traders and economists. In addition, the bottom part of the screen has the ticker tape running for the New York Stock Exchange, the American Stock

Exchange and the NASDAQ, or over the counter market, on a delayed basis of 15 minutes.

When you watch the program, you will hear the same phrases repeated. Initially, you won't know what they mean. But stay with it. You'll discover there are basic elements of stocks that people always talk about, such as P/E ratios, sales, margins, sequential growth, etc. Chapters 5 and 6 explain most of these. What's not there is in other places in this book or other books, but none of it is a mystery or hard to understand.

Also, through repetition, you will lose any fear you may have about the stock market. The announcers on CNBC are exceptionally good at explaining new concepts or remembering that most viewers are not professional investors. Furthermore, they are experienced, knowledgeable pros who are not just reading pages of information. They have been in the business long enough to ask the right questions when they do an interview, and then interpret it for the viewer.

They also have guests who talk about stocks. Do not buy a stock someone on this or any other show recommends without doing the analysis you'll learn in this book. You don't know if the stock is right for your portfolio unless you know the stock. Just because someone on TV says he or she likes a stock, doesn't mean it's going to go up. In fact, a few of the people on the programs may be selling the stock at the same time they're recommending it because they need more buyers to get out of their position. Yes, that really does happen.

If you hear an enthusiastic tip, write it down, then go to work. Look it up on your database, put it through the paces you'll learn later, get the annual report, see how it might fit into your portfolio and then buy it for the price you want to pay. Don't blindly pick up the phone and buy it no matter who recommends it. Let other people follow the herd or the tip. You follow your knowledge.

More Good TV

Nightly programs that summarize the day's activity in a half hour are very helpful. One of the best is "The Money Line" with Lou Dobbs on CNN. He and the other reporters give the stories on the most active issues for the day, economic news and general business stories. Because of his stature in the industry, his guests are the leaders in their fields. This is a program worth watching for both general information and potential investments.

Another nightly TV show is on PBS, "Nightly Business," which provides a recap of the most active stocks, news events and interviews top Wall Street and Washington experts.

Of course, the most respected program is Louis Rukeyser's "Wall Street Week," appearing every Friday on your PBS channel. Witty, timely comments are the usual fare with the best investment minds in the business talking about their favorite stocks and answering letters from viewers. Like all other programs, you don't watch this for a stock to buy, but rather for ideas worth investigating.

Another weekly program is on Sunday mornings, reported by Dow Jones, which highlights the events of the week, reports on companies and gives you the economic expectations for the coming week.

With so many programs from which to choose, one or two of these is convenient no matter what your schedule. The more you watch and hear the same jargon repeated, the sooner you'll become comfortable with it. As your comfort level increases, your investment decision making becomes easier.

BUYING WHAT THE PROS BUY

There are more than 300 aggressive growth mutual funds. These are mutual funds that specialize in stocks with small or no dividends and great earnings growth. The aggressive growth funds have mostly small-cap issues.

Each fund is run by a professional, someone dedicating 12 hours per day to discovering the best small-cap stocks. These people are serious, and they have the best computers, software and analysts to help them dig for treasure. Wouldn't you like to look over their shoulder and see what they're doing?

While you can't physically be with them, you can see what actions they've taken. Every one of these funds publishes its stock holdings in an annual report. By going through the report, you can see what they own and investigate the issues of interest.

Simply call the funds and request an annual report. When you receive it, look in the back and you'll see each stock the fund owns. However, it doesn't tell you the cost of the stock or when it was purchased. And, of course, it doesn't tell you if the fund is going to sell it or when it will sell it. So you don't know if they still own it. Therefore, as always, you're looking at these reports for ideas, not immediate investments. Appendix D has a list of some of these funds and their phone numbers.

The second way to find out what these funds are buying and selling in a more timely manner is to read *Investor's Business Daily*, a newspaper described in detail in the next chapter.

Every day, in its second section on the mutual fund page, the paper publishes the purchases and sales for the most recent quarter for six mutual funds. It gives the names of each stock bought or sold, and the quantity as well as the top holdings in the fund. It also provides the performance of the fund for the current year and the past two.

This information is much more timely than that of the annual report. It's updated quarterly. However, the paper doesn't feature growth and aggressive growth funds every day. You get the information on these funds when they publish it. But it's worth the wait.

You can quickly see what each fund is buying and selling or whether it's adding to a position in a stock, always a positive sign. There's a graph of each year's performance for the fund and how it compared with an index. There is also a performance ranking for a fund within its fund category.

Remember two things as you feast on these funds: They are actively buying and selling stocks daily and by the time you read what they own, they may have sold the issues you see in their buy list. Second, don't rush and buy any of these stocks without doing your homework and seeing if they fit in your portfolio. Similar to the television or radio shows, these stocks should be noted and investigated, not heard or seen and quickly bought. (For a full discussion on growth mutual funds, see Chapter 8.)

More Information, More Help, More Nuggets

You can see how much a computer helps in your search for investments when you use an on- or off-line service for data. Furthermore, if you watch television and listen to your friends and family, you can pick up more ideas. However, these are only part of the flow of information you need.

While the computer is an essential element of your investment strategy, you'll miss too many stocks if you don't also read newspapers, magazines and investment research reports. Chapter 4 provides the inside scoop on the best of the printed word.

CHAPTER FOUR

INVESTMENT NEWS: ◄----┘
HERE'S THE SCOOP

Reading is like pumping iron for the mind. The more you do it, the stronger your knowledge, and the better your decisions. You can never read or know enough about stocks or the markets. The question for the investor is what to read, especially if the focus is small-cap stocks.

There is no end to possible choices, from magazines to newspapers, from books to newsletters. Every day there seems to be a new entry into the already crowded field, claiming to know some secret that must have eluded centuries of investors and proclaiming results beyond your grandest greed.

MAKE MORE MONEY THAN YOU CAN COUNT!— A NEWSLETTER PRIMER

No one has made that claim, but that's the inference from many investment newsletters. Unless you can't count very high, avoid these. Here are some basics to remember and consider before you buy any newsletter:

- There is no quick and easy way to make money in the stock market. Some people get lucky once in a great while and buy a stock before it has record earnings or is bought out. Some notorious people made quick, easy bucks with inside information, and are still paying for that knowledge since their careers have been ruined. Real wealth is earned over time, both by labor and patience. Don't buy into outrageous, quick profit claims.

- Ask for a free copy of a newsletter to see if it has the information you want. Most publishers will send one.
- Take a short subscription. Many newsletters offer a three-month trial subscription. Try it, see if you really like it, then commit for a longer term.
- Determine the investment philosophy of the newsletter. After reading a newsletter for a few months, you can tell the kinds of stocks the writers like. Are they the ones with which you're comfortable?

    One highly regarded newsletter, *The Cabot Market Letter*, seems to pick stocks with high price-to-earnings multiples and relies strongly on future earnings. These stocks sometimes perform extremely well, but inevitably hit air pockets and sink when those earnings aren't delivered. The editor also trades the market with high frequency. This newsletter's picks are useful if you wait and buy them when they have a setback. The stories behind his picks are usually good, but you need a strong fortitude for those electroshock therapy days when they dive four or five points. Are you tough enough for the ride?

- Sample a number of newsletters by contacting the Select Information Exchange (212-247-7123). This organization will send you about 20 newsletters for $12.00.
- Don't pay too much, especially for a high-profile name. Some people's only claim to fame is that they are well-known. Anyone can get well-known if they exhaustively promote themselves. A good newsletter shouldn't be expensive; it should represent value by being reasonably priced.
- Examine the newsletter's record. It should have a portfolio of recommended stocks, their purchase and sale dates and the performance of those recommendations. Determine how the letter has done over a three-year, five-year and 10-year time period. If it hasn't been around that long, be sure you understand its investment philosophy.

- Nobody has a guaranteed way to make money. If they did, they wouldn't write a newsletter and tell the world about it. They'd just do it. Some methods work well in up markets, some in down markets and some in stable markets. Nothing works well in all markets.
- An excellent book, published annually and dedicated to reviewing and rating newsletters, is Mark Hulbert's *The Hulbert Guide to Financial Newsletters*. He also publishes a newsletter on newsletters entitled *Hulbert Financial Digest*.
- For a listing of some newsletters dedicated to small-cap investing, see Appendix A.

EXTRA! EXTRA!
READ ALL ABOUT IT!

For serious investors, there are two newspapers: *Investor's Business Daily* (IBD) and the *Wall Street Journal* (WSJ). For this section, I highly recommend you buy a copy of each and refer to them as I guide you through their contents.

While the WSJ may be the older and more famous of the two, the IBD is fast becoming the paper of choice for investors, and particularly small-cap investors. Here's why.

The IBD was started in 1984 by William O'Neil, who had successfully built a business from statistical data on the stock market for institutional investors. He took much of that information and put it in newspaper form. The initial response from the reading public was similar to throwing a rose petal in the Grand Canyon and waiting for the echo. But he was patient.

His paper now has a circulation of more than 250,000, and the roar of approval is evident by its growth. Readers became aware of the wealth of knowledge presented daily, and the value the paper represented.

HOW TO READ THE NEWSPAPER

Many investors are overwhelmed by information. They know there's something good in all of those numbers and stories; they just don't know which ones are right for them.

In the IBD, there are lots of numbers. Rather than explain all of them, I want to guide you to the important ones for small-cap investing. There's much more in there, but if you have a method for looking at the paper for one investment approach, you can start the process of understanding all of the data.

THE FRONT PAGE

Designed to save you time, the IBD's front page features an Executive News Summary, short descriptions of companies or political events in the news. If your paper is delivered early, you can quickly scan these stories and be up on the news before you leave for work.

The right side of the page has four feature stories, each concluded on the next page. You don't have to look through the paper to find the end of the article. Topics usually include investment advice, a national issue, a company or chief executive story and one of personal interest.

INSIDE THE PAPER

The Executive Update page, usually page 3, has individual company stories, a briefing column filled with tips for managers and a computer and automation column. These stories often lead to investment ideas.

The next page is entitled The New America and has information on smaller, newly formed companies, and describes the niche these companies fill. At the bottom of the page is a synopsis on new stock issues coming to market. This page is an excellent source for small-cap stock investment ideas.

Of course, you should never read an article and then buy the stock based on that small amount of information. An article in the paper, a magazine or a stock tip should always be the starting point in your investment odyssey. Once you have the name of a good company, your research begins, and when you've determined that it's right for your portfolio, you buy the stock.

THE MOST INTELLIGENT STOCK TABLES

Every day the IBD lists the 60 New York Stock Exchange stocks with the greatest percentage increase in volume. The theory is that if volume is picking up dramatically, something must be happening, good or bad.

These are not the most active stocks. They're the ones with unusually strong buying or selling activity, reflected in the percentage increase from their daily average volume.

They're ranked from the highest to lowest for the advancing issues and similarly ranked for the declining issues. If you own one of these and don't know why there's increased activity, you should find out.

If you don't own one of these, the tables may provide you with a good investment idea. Besides listing the volume activity, the tables also give the stock's relative strength, its earnings per share ranking, its high and low for the last 52 weeks, the symbol, the closing price, the P/E ratio, how many shares are outstanding and the percentage increase in volume. (All of these terms and ratios are explained in depth in Chapter 6.)

A similar table is given for the NASDAQ and American Stock Exchange securities, and there are several ways to use these tables for finding small-cap stocks.

Using the Tables

If you have been watching a stock, waiting for it to reach a certain level, and it suddenly appears in the highest percentage increase column, it can be a signal for action on your part.

By getting on your computer and checking your on-line service, you can pull up any story on the stock appearing that day, if there is one. Sometimes, there is no story, no apparent reason for new activity. Sometimes, there is only one block of stock accounting for most of the trading, but that's impossible to determine unless you watch the tape, or there is a news item reporting the block.

If there is a story, it might be a news release on better-than-expected earnings, or an acquisition by the company or the company being acquired by someone else. This news might be the event that gives you the confidence to buy the stock.

If the news is bad, such as lower-than-expected earnings or the resignation of a principal officer, you can then judge if this is a one-time event that may not affect earnings in the long run. Then you can buy more shares if you own it or start a position if you don't. Or if the news is truly devastating, you can sell your position.

More Tables, Better Information

Below the percentage-gainer tables are the 20 most active New York Stock Exchange stocks and the 20 most-percentage-up-in-price stocks for more than $12.00.

This last feature is helpful because it eliminates the $1.00 or $2.00 stocks that tend to fill these kinds of tables when presented by other publications.

On the NASDAQ tables, the IBD gives the 30 most active issues and the 15 most-percentage-up-in-price stocks for more than $12.00, as well as the 10 most-percentage-down stocks for more than $12.00. The American Stock Exchange also has these tables.

LOOK AT THE CHARTS

Every day the IBD publishes graphs for 30 stocks from the New York Stock Exchange, the NASDAQ, and eight from the AMEX. These are great idea generators.

Each graph represents a stock selling for more than $12.00 that is at or near new price highs or had the greatest percentage increase in volume. The graph shows the closing price of the stock, the number of shares outstanding, volume percentage change, the group's relative strength, P/E ratio, one year of weekly prices, 10-week moving average of prices, relative price strength line and the relative price strength number. The mutual fund sponsorship ranking is also shown. This last is a letter from A to E that tells you if the best- or worst-performing mutual funds own the stock.

All of this looks like a lot. However, if you check the graph in Chapter 6, you'll see that it's visually very easy to understand. Also, Chapter 6 explains each of these terms except the moving average line.

The moving average line is the stock's average daily price for the last 10 weeks, plotted on a weekly basis. Chartists usually like to buy stocks when they go through this average on the upside and sell them when they penetrate the line on the down side.

For our purposes, this line is useful to see if the stock price has dramatically moved away from its average price. If a stock has moved well above its 10-week moving average, it will usually go down and come close to this line before going up again. If the stock has moved well below its moving average line, it may be in deep trouble. In either situation, you would want to know the news, if there is any, behind the stock's moves. You can find the news, if it exists, through your computer and your on-line service.

New Price Highs, New Price Lows

Ever wonder which stocks are hitting new highs or lows? IBD certainly does, and it prints them every day. Furthermore, the tables tell you how many highs and lows are on each exchange; they then go on to list each one of them with their closing prices and the earnings per share rank. This is yet another source for possible stocks to buy or sell.

The Drivers Behind the Stocks:
The Earnings

Every day the IBD publishes earnings as reported by the companies, but it doesn't just give you a number and send you on your way. It puts those earnings in a very usable form.

Most earnings reports in other publications are listed alphabetically with a minimum of information, rather like a plain hot dog. The IBD gives you the dog with onions, relish, mustard, pickles, mayonnaise, catsup and sauerkraut, wrapped in a cloth napkin.

The first and most helpful item is a table with the Best Up earnings and Most Down earnings. You can quickly see which companies are making or losing the most money from this table.

In the Best Ups column, the stocks are ranked by the best percentage gains. Along with the stock name and symbol, the table shows the quarterly change in percent from the same quarter a year ago, the numerical earnings per share for the quarter and the earnings from last year's same quarter, the earnings per share ranking and the relative price strength of the stock.

This portion of the table is one of the quickest and best ways to get an investment idea. If you see extraordinarily strong earnings gain in a stock and the earnings per share ranking is higher than 80 and the relative price strength is also higher than 80, you can be sure that this stock is worth investigating. Thanks to these tables, within a few seconds, you can determine if a stock warrants your time. This feature alone makes the paper unique and a great investment value.

Flash Warning about Earnings Reports

If you look at an earnings report and see only a number for the quarter, say twenty-five cents per share, you don't know enough about those earnings to make a judgment to buy or sell a stock.

The IBD gives you the industry in which the company works, the symbol of the company, the last price, the earnings per share rating, the relative strength of the stock price, revenues for the quarter, the income, the average number of shares outstanding, the income from continuing and discontinued operations, any extraordinary charges or gains, the earnings per share, the fully diluted earnings per share and the percentage gain or loss from the previous year's earnings. Let's go through each of these items and see why they're helpful to paint a full picture.

In one column is the information on earnings for the quarter just reported. In the next column is the information for the same quarter one year ago. This way you can compare equal time periods.

The first item to the right of the name of the company is the symbol and the closing price of the stock from the previous day. Having the symbol makes it very easy to look up this stock or get a quote from your on-line computer service.

The next line has the industry in which the company is grouped. This helps you determine if it belongs in your portfolio or, if you have too much of this industry among your stocks, why you should not consider it or use it to replace one of your holdings.

For example, if I see a large earnings increase in a company's earnings and it's in the airline industry, I don't spend any time on it. This industry is too volatile in its earnings, has too much regulation and constantly tries to put itself out of business by lowering fares. As a traveler, I love this approach; as an investor, I don't.

On the same line is the EPS or earnings per share rank and the RPS or relative price strength rank. The EPS number tells you what percentile the company's earnings rank it over the last five years against all other companies in the database. If the number is 80, it means the company has earnings better than 79% of the universe. The relative price rank tells you how well the price of the stock has compared against the other stocks in the same database. The higher the number, the stronger the stock has performed.

Many professional investors believe strong stocks get stronger. They look for high EPS and RPS as indicators of the best stocks. While these two measurements are very good, they are only two, and as you will learn in Chapter 6, there are many more to consider before buying a stock. However, if you establish a minimum level for each of these indicators as part of your buying strategy, these two numbers can quickly eliminate many of the stocks not measuring up to your criteria and save you time.

The next line down tells the date for the end of the quarter and on what exchange the stock trades—the NYSE, New York Stock Exchange, the OTC, Over the Counter or NASDAQ, and the AMEX, American Stock Exchange. This small but helpful bit of information saves you time in finding the stock in the stock tables.

Sales data come next. In other words, how many dollars worth of groceries did Safeway sell in the last quarter? Also, how many did it sell last year at this time? Investors are always looking for higher numbers in this department.

Net income or loss is on the following line. Cutting right to the quick, going from sales to net income or loss allows you to see if the company is making or losing money. However, you need to know much more.

The next set of data tells you if there was an extraordinary or one-time occurrence that created a gain or loss for the company. You can't count on an extraordinary item to keep happening, so you have to take this element out of the reported income, which IBD does for you.

If a division of a company has been closed and a loss was created, that will be reported as a loss from discontinued operations. IBD also breaks out the loss or income from continuing operations, the most important number for an investor because that's the engine keeping the company going forward.

Of course, each number reported for this quarter is shown alongside its previous year's counterpart. You're looking for income to be going up, losses down.

Average number of shares is also reported. This is the average number of shares outstanding for the quarter. When you look at the earnings per share, you need to know the number of shares used for the calculation because if a company has been issuing shares over the past year and its earnings per share have increased over that time period, it's doing very well.

Another way to look at the average number of shares is to see if there are fewer shares outstanding since last year. This tells you the company is buying back shares in the open market, and there are less remaining shares to divide into the net income. That way, earnings per share can go up, even if net income were to stay the same, because there are fewer shares this year to divide into it.

Income or loss per share is presented next. Income or loss per share gives you a raw number, as if there were no extraordinary losses or gains. If there were no events, then income and net income will be the same number and will be reported as net income. However, if there is an extraordinary event, then the income number has to be adjusted by that amount to show the net income figure. Again, the IBD does this for you. So the next line gives you the net income or loss per share. You're looking for the companies making more income this year than last.

The IBD also gives you the net income figure and the fully diluted net income figure. Fully diluted net income is the income per share that would be reported if all securities that are convertible into common stock would be converted. Because every convertible bond or convertible preferred share has the potential of being common stock, most investors want to know what effect that conversion would have on the common stock's earnings per share. If you see the fully diluted earnings per share markedly lower than the earnings per share, be aware that there is a great deal of stock, much like a large tidal wave, which will come overwhelmingly into the earnings per share calculations in the future. To raise funds in the past, company management may have sold stock in the form of convertible debt. Eventually this debt all becomes stock.

The final and unique item is the percentage change for the earnings. In other words, how much up or down, in terms of a percent, did the earnings for the company change? While a simple number to determine—you divide the difference between this year's earnings and last by last year's earnings—the effort to do it for each reporting company can be very time-consuming. However, IBD does it for you for every stock, saving you the effort and the time.

How to Use This Data

The Company Earnings News reports are some of the most useful information in the IBD. By breaking out the Best Ups and Most Downs, it provides you with the stocks to investigate and those to avoid. The full earnings reports give you more vital information, and from these you can develop a shopping list of stocks to start to monitor.

For example, I will take two or three stocks from the Best Ups list, ones with very strong earnings, and put those symbols on my on-line service for quote monitoring, something on America Online called Quotes and Portfolios. My purpose is to start to get a feel for the price movement of stocks and their volume. I may buy them, but initially I don't know enough about them. I start watching them while I do more homework, a process fully described in Chapters 5 and 6. Then, if all the elements I use for investment decisions agree, I'll establish a price at which I will buy the stock. That price may be at, under or over the market price. That way I control the buying process and feel very comfortable when I buy stocks.

Conversely, if a company I own shows up in the Most Downs table, and it's a total surprise, I need to investigate the stock further by calling the company and checking the news releases, and then determining if there is a good reason to hold the stock. The process of selling a stock is covered in Chapter 6.

THE IBD STOCK TABLES

For each stock exchange, the New York, the NASDAQ and the American, there is a table of stocks showing how they traded the previous day. As with other parts of the paper, more useful, time-saving information is crammed into these tables.

For each stock listed, the following information exists:

- EPS, or earnings per share rank, described above.
- RPS, or Relative Price Strength, also described above.
- Accumulation or Distribution. This is a category rating from A to E, with A the strongest buying interest and E the strongest selling interest. If a stock has an A or B rating, it means it is being accumulated by investors. The rank is determined by multiplying the daily volume, number of shares of the stock traded, by change and direction in the stock price. Strong, upward-moving stocks have an A or B rating; weaker or downward-moving stocks have a D or E rank.
- Fifty-two-week high and low price. These numbers tell how high and low the stock has gone over the past year. Some

investors like to buy stocks when they are at or near their highs, others at their lows. If you use this indicator as one of your buy or sell criteria, these columns are most helpful.

- The name of the stock.
- The symbol for the stock.
- The closing price for the stock from the previous day.
- The change of that price from the previous day's close.
- The volume percentage change from that stock's daily average volume. For example, if a stock trades on average 200,000 shares per day and one day it trades 400,000 shares, then the volume percentage change would be 100. If it's only one day, that may or may not be significant. However, if the next day the stock trades 500,000 shares, and the next day 600,000 shares, there is definitely news or rumors about the company. This is a unique number generated by IBD and tips off the investor that something is going on if the volume percentage change is large. Even if the investor doesn't know what is going on, a large volume change is a red flag, saying look at this stock. If investors own it, they need to find out what's happening. Using an on-line service such as America Online for news or calling the company should help explain what's behind the activity.
- Actual volume. The number of shares traded the previous day.
- Group strength. This is shown on Mondays and gives a ranking from A to E. Whatever industry group your stock is in, such as airlines, automobiles, semiconductors or any of the other 196 categories IBD uses, that group's relative price strength is compared with all the other groups' price movements and the top 20% of the industry groups are given an A rating, the next 20% are given a B, and so on down to E.

Many investors like to concentrate their investment dollars in the strongest-performing industries as determined by price strength. Then they buy only the top-performing stocks within those industry groups. If the top 20% of the groups receives an A, then the investor has almost 40 industries from which to choose stocks, and within each industry group there are usually at least five stocks. Therefore, portfolio diversity can almost always be achieved from the 200 or more stocks that this A group represents. See Chapter 7 for how to build a portfolio.

However, the investor has to keep monitoring the changes in these rankings, selling the stocks that fall below the required price strength and buying the new stocks which are moving up. This can create large turnovers in the portfolio and raise commissions accordingly.

Other investors like to buy the bottom 20% of the industry groups, figuring they have nowhere to go but up. That isn't necessarily true. You, as an investor, shouldn't be doing anything based solely on a stock or group ranking. You need many more reasons than that for buying.

- P/E ratios. Price-to-earnings ratios are given on Tuesday. Because these don't change too much, they're given once a week. The P/E ratio is the price of the stock divided by the earnings for the last four quarters. This is a useful number and is fully explored in Chapter 6.
- Sponsorship ranking is given on Wednesday. This is an A (best) to E (worst) rating for a stock based on the mutual funds that own it. The mutual funds are compared on a performance basis for the last three years; the best get an A, and the worst get an E designation. Investors find it helpful and maybe comforting to know that their stocks are owned by the best-performing mutual funds. I might find it a bit unsettling if a majority of my holdings were only held by the worst-performing funds.
- Percentage of outstanding stock owned by management is reported on Thursday. This tells you if the management has a meaningful stake in the company. The higher this number is, the more stock the management owns. Investors like to know that the management's interests are the same as theirs, and that management is committed to making the stock its vehicle for wealth, not large salaries and bonuses.
- Dividend yield is given on Friday. This tells you how much the stock is paying as a percentage of the price. In other words, if the stock is yielding 5%, and the stock price is

$10.00 then the dividend must be fifty cents. This yield is given on an annual basis.

- Day's high and low prices. These two numbers are shown daily and let you know the range of prices within which the stock traded the previous day.
- Small "k" and "o." To the right of the numbers, there is an extremely small space for two letters, a "k" or an "o." The small "k" means that within a two-week period the company is expected to release its earnings. This can be useful to investors because earnings often move the stock if they are better or worse than expected. Many investors will wait for the earnings to be announced before they buy a stock. Others feel comfortable and buy before the announcement, expecting the company to meet or exceed forecasts. Sometimes these investors are right, sometimes not. In the long run, no one earnings report will be of great consequence. Several quarters sequentially are what establish a trend. However, that doesn't mean the one earnings report in the short run can't cause great price volatility.

    The small letter "o" in the same column lets the investor know that the stock has options that are publicly traded on one of the exchanges. Some investors like to buy or sell the options on a stock, and this small letter lets them know if the stock has them. Options are the right to buy or sell a stock at a certain price. They are beyond the scope of this book, but if you have an interest in them, there are many good books on the subject.

Another feature in the tables is the highlighting of the stocks which made new price highs or moved up one point or more by presenting those in boldface type. If an investor likes to buy stocks hitting new highs or moving up dramatically, this feature almost shines a spotlight on those stocks.

MORE IBD GOODIES

Toward the back of the first section of the paper, there is a page entitled General Market Indicators, and to paraphrase Churchill: Never has so much been jammed into such a small space by one publication. There are graphs for 12 different indexes, investment advisory sentiment, mutual funds cash position, the Federal Reserve discount rate changes, psychological market indicators (14 of these), hourly NYSE volume and market changes, the 30 stocks making up the Dow Jones Industrial and the NYSE block trades (10,000 shares or more).

The three largest graphs are the NASDAQ Composite, the Standard & Poor's 500, and the Dow Jones Industrials. By reviewing these graphs, an investor can quickly grasp what is happening in the whole stock market.

THE NASDAQ COMPOSITE INDEX

The NASDAQ Composite Index graphically shows the movement of most of the stocks on the NASDAQ program. This graph is the one to check for a broad market indicator and specifically for growth companies. These are mostly the small- and mid-cap stocks, as opposed to the S&P 500 and the Dow Jones Industrials, which has only 30 stocks.

Like most graphs, this one shows the high, low and close of the index of each day for the previous nine months. It also has the 200-day moving average line plotted. This is the average of the index over the past 200 days. If the index is currently above this line, it's considered positive for the market; if it's below the line, it's negative.

Also within this box, there is the mutual fund cash position, which shows how much cash the mutual funds have currently and what their positions were for the last 18 months. The more cash the funds have, the more fuel there is to push the market ahead when they start buying stocks. The lower the cash position, the less money there is to spend for stocks. Or, if the funds have investors who want to cash out of the market and the funds' cash position is low, they will have to sell stocks to raise cash, thus pushing the market lower.

The investment advisor sentiment graph shows what percentage of investment advisors, the pros if you will, are bullish or bearish or neutral. When the large majority is of one sentiment, the astute investor will invest in the other direction because these advisors will always vote their position. That means if they own a lot of stocks, they will be bullish (aggressively positive) and probably have spent most of their cash. Conversely, if they say they are bearish (conservative about the market), it usually means they have a lot of cash and are waiting for the correct moment to invest.

You shouldn't take this or any other advice in this book as absolutely right in every circumstance. You can't buy a stock on any one tip. But this investment advisor sentiment is another ingredient for the investment stew you're preparing, and it can be helpful.

THE S&P 500

The next prominent chart is the Standard & Poor's 500 Index or S&P 500. This represents the 500 large corporations taken from the three exchanges and gives you the same information as the NASDAQ Composite, but for 500 stocks.

Also included is the psychological market indicators box, 14 different measurements of the market from the current dividend yield of the Dow Jones Industrial Average (DJIA) to short interest ratios. No one of these is crucial to know for your investment success, but taken as a whole, when they are bullish or bearish, this knowledge adds to your investment powers.

Along with their current readings, each of the indicators is shown with its high and low marks for the last five years and for the last year. You can graphically see if new lows or highs are being made and determine if that means danger or opportunity.

For example, history has shown that when the Dow Jones Industrial Average dividend yield is below 2.7%, there has been a major downward correction in the market. Conversely, if the yield is above 5.5%, there has been a strong rally in prices. Exactly when these corrections or rallies will occur is not easily determined. And just because the index may be at, below or above these levels, doesn't necessarily mean history will repeat itself.

If dividend yields are extremely low, one explanation could be that companies are paying down debt or buying back shares instead of paying dividends because dividends are first taxed as profits at the corporate level and then taxed as dividends to the holder of the stock, the double-taxation dilemma. In addition, while the Dow Jones Industrial Average may appear to be high by this dividend measure, one way of correcting for it is not for the market to go down but for dividends to go up. When corporate earnings improve and management is confident of the future, dividends increase. If the DJIA remains the same, the dividend yield must go up because dividends (the numerator of the equation) have increased and the DJIA (the denominator) has not changed.

Using a rule of thumb like "sell all stocks when the dividend yield is below 2.7%" only increases your commission costs. Many statistics are thrown out by newsletter writers that are certainly true, but you have to keep your head and think through all the possibilities before acting. Don't panic just because one indicator is flashing red, or green for that matter. Never make any investment decision based on one piece of news or data.

THE GRANDDADDY OF THEM ALL— THE DOW JONES INDUSTRIALS

When most people ask: How's the market? or What did the market do today?, they expect an answer based on the movement of the Dow Jones Industrial Average. This is like asking how many car sales there were in America for the day and only checking with the Cadillac dealers.

The Dow Jones Industrial Average (DJIA) is composed of 30 stocks. There are more than 30,000 stocks publicly traded, but these 30 Dow stocks have come to mean the market to the investing public. Of course, the index has been around for decades and is shown every night on the news. It's part of the American way of life. You, as an investor, need to keep it in perspective. The market is much broader than this average.

The graph of the DJIA is helpful as an indicator for how well or poorly the large-cap stocks such as AT&T, Philip Morris and Merck are performing. In fact, the 30 stocks for the index are published daily in the IBD inside the box with the graph of the index. All of the information described for the previous two graphs (the NASDAQ Composite Index and the S&P 500) is also published for the DJIA, in addition to the volume for the NYSE.

The best way to use these three large graphs, the NASDAQ Composite Index, the S&P 500 and the DJIA, is to compare them. Are they all moving together? If there is upward movement in the

NASDAQ Composite Index but downward prices in the DJIA, it means that small-cap stocks are doing well while the large-cap stocks are not. Also, remember the broadest gauge of the market is the NASDAQ Composite Index, and the S&P 500 represents the largest group of large-cap stocks. The DJIA contains some of the best of American enterprise, but all the stocks are from the NYSE. Great companies such as Intel and Microsoft are not part of it because they are too new or don't fit the inclusion criteria. In my opinion, these stocks are more likely to reflect the future of business than Exxon, Woolworth or Bethlehem Steel, which are part of the DJIA.

NINE MORE GRAPHS, SAME PAGE

Below the large graphs of the three major indexes described above are nine more boxes, and six of them include the names of the stocks making up the index:

- Junior Growth Index, a composite of 14 stocks taken from the small-cap sector, representing various newer industries such as software, HMOs and discount retailers. This is a good index for a performance comparison with your small-cap portfolio.
- High-Technology Index, which shows how the computer and software makers are doing, including Hewlett-Packard, Intel, Novell and most of the stellar names in the industries. It's a good comparative index for the high-tech sector of your portfolio.
- Defensive Index. These stocks are for the times in the stock market when you're looking for a safe haven to place your money. Stocks included are grocery stores (Albertsons), cereal makers (Kellogg, General Mills) and consumer brand names (Philip Morris, PepsiCo, Quaker Oats). These are quality stocks with slow but steady growth.
- Consumer Index is composed of retailers such as Nordstrom, Home Depot, Sears, Toys "R" Us and Dayton Hudson. This graph tells you how well the retailers are doing.
- Medical/HealthCare Index is comprised of drug, biotech, and health care stocks.
- Bank Index includes the top banks in the country.

- Dow Jones Transportation contains the train, truck and airline stocks. No names supplied.
- Dow Jones Utilities reflects electric and gas utility stocks. No names supplied.
- NYSE Composite represents the stocks on the NYSE.

Because a picture is worth many words, some say a thousand, this page of the IBD is worth several encyclopedias. By looking at these indexes, you can tell which sectors of the market are doing well, leading, lagging, improving or slumping. They can help you switch from a weak sector to a strong one.

As with everything new and unfamiliar, it takes a while to get comfortable with all this data. But once you get in the habit of looking at this page, you will truly have a feel for where the market is and which stocks are leading it.

AND THE DATA, LIKE LAVA, KEEP FLOWING

There are many unique features in the IBD. Two that are especially noteworthy are in the Friday and Monday editions. On Friday, on the second to last page, there is the Weekend Review section. It graphically features stocks that are at or near their highs. Furthermore, there is a box filled with the stocks with high Earnings Per Share (EPS) and Relative Price Strength (RPS) numbers (85 or better) and the funds with the largest positions in the stocks as well as each fund's performance ranking. This page is worth the price of the newspaper. More good small-cap ideas can come out of this page than any other.

The big plus about the IBD Monday edition is you can get it on Saturday if you buy it on the newsstand or if you have it delivered by mail. This gives you an investing head start for the upcoming week.

One last feature I'll mention is Companies in the News. This, too, is reason enough to buy the paper. Every day on the third to last page of the paper is a full-page article on a company, usually a small-cap company with a new service or product. Along with an extensive write-up on the firm, there are graphs and statistical data, which give you a very good understanding of the company and its performance in the stock market. This page is definitely where you'll find good small-cap stocks for your portfolio.

There is so much more to the IBD that a book could be devoted to its contents. However, with the above descriptions, you should be able to pick it up and begin to get great ideas the first day you read it. As you become more familiar with it, you can exploit the paper for all it's worth, from options to fixed-income securities. This paper is truly the best value for the investment dollar for small-cap investors. With this paper and your on-line service, you can make big bucks.

MORE GREAT PUBLICATIONS

Who hasn't heard of the *Wall Street Journal*? Constantly quoted and seen on every investing pro's desk, it is the daily Bible of the investment industry. It has been around forever, and there's good reason for that.

Nobody writes more stories about personalities, politics, economics, corporations and human interest than the WSJ. It's filled with timely in-depth pieces, well-researched and often honored. However, it's very similar to the Industrial Averages: It hasn't fully evolved to reflect all the markets.

Only recently has the paper added a column entitled Small Stock Focus, and it's short, usually recapping the previous day's most-active NASDAQ issues and giving the reason for the activity. That's all the space dedicated to small-cap investing.

The earnings reports are given in alphabetical order, leaving you to do the math for percentage gains or losses. The stock tables give you the most-active stock issues and the largest price movers, but there aren't any screens or limits for inclusion. Many of the lowest-priced stocks continually appear on the largest percentage price mover lists because going from 2.5 points to 3 points is a 20% move. Most investors wouldn't buy a stock that low in price.

My purpose is to contrast these two papers and suggest that the strength of the IBD is its statistical data as well as its focus on small-cap stocks and the new American industry groups. The WSJ, on the other hand, is very set in its ways with a broad range of topics from movie reviews to dog custody battles during divorce to strong investigative reporting on Wall Street practices or White House policies. The WSJ is a great paper and should be read if you have the time.

Furthermore, no one else reports so much news on so many companies pertaining to management changes, new products introduced or trends in an industry. This is where the WSJ shines. It helps investors get the big picture as well as much of the details on most industries and companies.

How to Read the *Wall Street Journal*

One warning about the WSJ: it can be so interesting, you can spend hours on it. You don't have time during the week for that. You need to get to the relevant data and get to work. The following is a synopsis of the layout of the paper and where you should focus your attention for small-cap stock information.

The first page has six columns. The outside two columns present stories on companies, leaders, politics and social and economic trends. Check these to see if a stock you own is featured or if there is a company presented which might be of interest to you.

The middle column is always interesting, usually humorous, but has no relevance to investing. It's devoted to human interest stories, and if you have the time, you'll enjoy reading it. You don't have the time in the morning.

The What's News section is two columns. This is a synopsis of company news on the left and world news on the right. A great place to quickly tell what's happening. Always read these.

The fifth column is dedicated to a specific topic for that day of the week. For example, on Tuesday, it's entitled Work Week and discusses issues affecting workers. On Monday, the Outlook reports on the economy; Wednesday it's about taxes; Thursday it's entitled Business Bulletin; and Friday it features goings on in Washington, D.C. Most columns are filled with short paragraphs, each with a different idea or fact. These are always interesting and a fast read.

Like Gaul, the *Journal* Is Divided into Three Parts

The first section contains the major stories about companies, the reviews of books and movies, and the editorial pages. Check the headlines of the stories to see if any of your stocks are there. Also keep up with the industry trends in these stories. There's an international section in here as well, covering the political leaders of countries, the economic trends and the major companies. Watch out for this first section, it can really eat up your time. Try to stick to the important investment stories during the week, then on the weekend or after work, catch up on the rest.

The second section is entitled the Marketplace, and on the second page is a listing of all the companies written about that day in the WSJ and the page of the article. You can use this feature to find any of your stocks. This is a great timesaver.

The remainder of this section is broken down into categories such as Travel, Computers, the Law, Marketing and Media, Advertising, Technology, Business Briefs, Corporate Focus and Who's News. All are self-explanatory. If you are working within one of these groups, you can stay abreast of your industry through these columns. And the Business Briefs does an excellent job of reporting new contracts, discoveries, and press releases of most companies. This section gives you short and important information on many subjects. Always scan through it.

The last section is entitled Money and Investing. It holds all the data on stocks, bonds, futures, options and mutual funds. The front page, on the left side, has six graphs: the Dow Jones Industrial Average, the Lehman Brothers Bond Index, fed funds interest rate levels, the U.S. Dollar index, and the Commodities index. The sixth graph changes every day and features other charts or indexes. These graphs will not keep you up on the stock market because the only index representing stocks is the Dow Jones Industrial Average. Remember, there are only 30 stocks in this index. However, the other indexes are helpful for levels of interest rates, commodity prices and the value of the dollar compared with other currencies.

Inside, on the second page, there are two columns: Abreast of the Market and Heard on the Street. Both are worth reading. Abreast of the Market is a good overview of the most-active issues and their stories, and presents general comments on where the market has been and where it might be going. Usually, professional money managers or economists are quoted in this section.

Heard on the Street can be a powerful column. It used to be that a positive mention here was all any stock needed for success. Conversely, if the news was bad on a stock, the opening of that stock would be much lower than the previous day. Always check this column to see if one of the stocks you are following or own is featured.

Also on this page are statistical data on the market, gainers and losers and trading volumes. Then the tables begin for the New York Stock Exchange stocks, showing the high and low prices for the last year, name of the stock, its symbol, dividend yield, the P/E, volume of share traded on the previous day, the high price for the day, the low price for the day, the close and the change from the previous day. Useful information, but not as detailed as the IBD tables.

The Small Stock Focus column is on the fourth or fifth page. As mentioned above, this is a recap of the previous day's most active small-cap issues. Sometimes these issues will strike you as possible investments, so go to your on-line service and check them out by using the method described in Chapter 6.

The remainder of the paper has statistical data on stocks, options, bonds, futures and mutual funds. All are reported in a straightforward manner and show the price movement from the previous day.

The WSJ is an excellent financial newspaper with great stories and extensive coverage around the globe. Its primary purpose is to report on large corporations, and it does that very well. However, if you are focusing on small-cap stocks, you won't get the kind of investment information that the IBD presents. Also, the WSJ takes much more time to read than the IBD.

If I had to pick just one paper, I couldn't. They both give the reader valuable information. If you want only small-cap stock data, the IBD is the paper for you.

BUSINESS MAGAZINES TO KNOW AND READ

There are many business news publications. These are some of the best:

- *Forbes*: In-your-face reporting, opinionated, sometimes funny, confrontational, excellent coverage on small and large companies, pulls no punches. Every year has a listing of the best small-cap firms, a treasure trove to explore on your on-line service. Also does an annual review of mutual funds with a unique ranking system. The bonus here is the new quarterly entitled *ASAP*, which focuses on technology, and it's included with your subscription. Excellent choice for all investors.

- *Barron's*: Another great one. A weekly newsprint with more statistics than any other publication. The writing can be very funny, and the magazine has in-depth articles on stocks or industries. Plenty of ideas presented every week for you to investigate on your own. Again, just because a stock is touted by a portfolio manager or highly praised in an article, do not, repeat, *do not* buy it the next day. Use the method described in Chapter 6 to find out if you're comfortable with it. *Barron's* is the most respected of the investment weeklies, and if you have the time, this is a great read. Also, you can buy it on Saturday and be ready for Monday.
- *Business Week*: Another very good magazine, with a straightforward style. Trying to shake its stodgy image, loosening up a little. Has an excellent annual survey of the best small companies and mutual funds. Another good digging ground for the investor.
- *Fortune*: This is geared for the senior managers of large companies. While there is always an interview with a portfolio manager, most of the articles are on personnel concerns, managing growth, and other big-picture topics. Not a good one for small-cap ideas.

ANOTHER GREAT PUBLICATION:
The Value Line Investment Survey

While there are many good investor services in print, the best value is *The Value Line Investment Survey*. None of the others give the historical and current data found in this weekly.

The survey covers 1,700 stocks. Because there are about 1,000 large corporations, that leaves at least 700 mid-sized and small-cap stocks for you to investigate. Each stock receives a write-up of about 250 words, surrounded by statistics for the last 15 years.

Also included is a weekly synopsis of the stock market and economy, ample data on each, and a summary and index for all the stocks in the survey. Each stock is given a rating for its safety as defined by its financial position and the *Value Line*'s numerical opinion of the stock's expected performance, with 1 being the highest rating and 5 the lowest. The results from buying the stocks rated 1 have far exceeded the performance of buying the S&P 500 or the Dow Jones Industrial Average.

The publication's cost ($575 per year) seems expensive at first glance. However, all you need is one or two good stocks to pay for it. It takes a while to get familiar with all the numbers and how to exploit all the data, but it's all explained. Once you get into the flow of this weekly, you'll look forward to your Friday mail and the weekend to review this information. Highly recommended.

Getting Control of All This Information

Obviously, you can't spend all your time reading about the market, the economy and individual stocks. Otherwise, you'd be an investment advisor. No, you've got a real job, and probably don't have time for all the reading you want to do already. All the above newspapers, magazines, newsletters and books sound interesting, but you can't possibly read every one of them.

I recommend the following approach. Buy the Hulbert book on newsletters and order a trial subscription for every one that looks interesting. Read them, then decide which ones to renew.

Take both papers for three months, the *Investor's Business Daily* and the *Wall Street Journal*. See which one you read the most and gives the best information for your investing dollar.

Take every business magazine mentioned, and any others you see or hear about, for a few months. Even if you have to subscribe for a year, you can cancel and receive a full refund for your remaining issues on most magazines. Again, see which ones you read the most and have the best ideas for you.

You get the formula: Try everything, find out what you like and use and let the rest go. You will winnow your choices down within three months. Then try those for a year and repeat the process.

The cost for all of these publications will seem expensive initially, but remember, you're not going to find all of them useful. Those you cancel. After you find one or two great stocks in the ones you keep, you'll think their prices are trivial.

When you do find that one stock you think you have to own, what do you do next? Do you rush out and buy it and hope for the best, relying on the wisdom of the source where you read about it? Don't you dare. You need to analyze the stock and understand it so you know that it's right for you.

The next two chapters will walk you through the steps needed to understand a stock and determine its potential. Like baby steps, these can be a little difficult at first, but once you get walking, there'll be no stopping you.

CHAPTER FIVE

STOCK EVALUATION: ANALYZING YOUR TREASURES

You pick up a shiny jewel: Is it a diamond or cubic zirconium? Unless you have the training to analyze the stone, you can't know.

If you get a hot stock tip, is it really a winner? Or if you see a stock rocketing up day after day, should you buy it? Unless you can analyze a company's financial information, you can't know.

So let me walk you through a financial report, show you what's important, and give you the knowledge to make good decisions on your small-cap investments. Again, no need to come from the deep end of the gene pool to understand and use this material. You can do it.

Your main source of information will be the annual and/or quarterly reports of a company. You don't need to use your computer when looking at annual reports unless you want to set up a spreadsheet for that purpose. I find it easier to use my calculator because I'm mostly looking at percentage growth (or lack of it) from year to year.

It sure would be pleasant to do without this effort, but successful investors have to analyze a company. For a little work, they can reap enormous rewards. The data for analysis have to come from the annual report or other reports, not from a synopsis in a database. The computer can help, but you have to get into the numbers. It's the only way to know the company.

FINDING A STOCK

Let's say you're driving down the highway in Minnesota, and you see a large, clean, blue truck with the word MARTEN prominently displayed on its side. You're impressed with the truck. It looks like it might represent a good company. Maybe it's a good investment. Remember good stocks come to those with their eyes and ears open.

What are you going to do about it? Well, first you have to find out if the company has issued stock. The fastest way to do that is to go to your computer, get into your selected database provider (let's use America Online), go to the stock section and type in the name of the company.

On America Online, that means you sign on to the service, click on the Keyword icon in the upper right, and the screen will appear asking to do a keyword search. Type in the words: Stock Reports.

When the screen changes, the box will ask for the symbol or name of the stock you want to analyze. You type in the word "Marten" and click on the OK button. Within seconds, the computer will give you a name highlighted in a box. Double click on that highlighted line, and you'll soon be looking at a great deal of information on the company. The next chapter will walk you through all the important numbers and what they mean (the example there uses the Prodigy program). Our purpose right now is to determine if this is a company with stock outstanding and to get its annual report.

Marten is indeed a public company, one that has stock trading on the NASDAQ program. On the screen, you'll see the symbol for the company: MRTN. Because it has four letters, you know the company trades on the NASDAQ. Companies trading on the New York or American Stock Exchanges have one, two, or three letters unless the stock represents a series "A" or "B," then the symbol will be four letters, three letters for the company and one for the series the stock represents.

Where this small bit of stock symbol trivia is helpful is when someone tells you the name and symbol of a stock, or you ask for the symbol of the stock. If it's three or fewer letters, you know to look on the New York or American Exchange listings in the paper to find it. If it has four letters, you immediately go to the NASDAQ section.

Let's go back to the computer screen on America Online. This page will give you enough initial information so you can see quickly if you want to pursue investigating the stock. By using the tools described in the next chapter, you will be able to determine in a few seconds if a stock meets your criteria for investing.

For now, let's assume Marten makes the cut, and you want to look at its annual report. On the AOL Stock Reports, you will see a description of what the company does, and the telephone number of the company.

How to Get What You Want

After deciding to investigate this investment prospect, you want the annual report and every piece of information the company can provide such as the 10-K and 10-Q reports, brokerage firm analyses and descriptions of their products and services. The 10-K report is an annual filing every public company must make with the Securities and Exchange Commission (SEC). It contains all the numbers in an annual report, sometimes additional important tax information and a very informative section called Management Discussion, in which the management must describe the current business environment and its plans for the company.

The reason it's so complete is that the SEC requires full disclosure from a public company. In other words, as long as a company tells you what it has done, the SEC is satisfied. That's why the SEC should not be viewed as an advisor for the investor. The SEC doesn't say the company is good or bad. Its purpose is to get public companies to tell the investor what they are doing.

The 10-Q is the quarterly edition of the 10-K with fewer details but much more information than the normal quarterly reports that are sent to shareholders.

There are two ways to receive 10-K and 10-Q information. The first is by going to the Internet and using the EDGAR (Electronic Data Gathering And Retrieval) site, found by the address: http://www. sec.gov/edgarhp.com. It has all the reports filed with the SEC for public companies. You can access the Internet by an on-line service like America Online. In fact, AOL has an icon which is linked to the EDGAR site on the Company Research Page, making it very easy to get the reports.

The other way to get 10-K and 10-Q information is to pick up the phone, call the number given on your computer screen, and ask for the investor relations department, shareholders' relations or the treasurer's office. Many small firms don't have a full-time department, so don't be surprised if the operator asks if he or she can be of help. It doesn't matter with whom you speak, it's the information you get that's important.

Tell whomever responds to your questions that you're interested in making an investment in the company and are seeking more information about it. Specifically ask for the annual report, the latest quarterly report, the 10-K and 10-Q reports and any brokerage firm analysis. Also ask which brokerage firms follow the company's stock.

Companies are happy to send you the material, and within a few days, you'll receive a heavy envelope with as many of the reports as the company can produce. The companies want you to make the investment because most of the officers may be significant shareholders, and when more investors buy the stock, the price goes up.

Let's assume you called Marten Transport, Ltd., and the company sends you all the information you requested. Open the envelope and take out the annual report. This is the first step to understanding a company.

Most annual reports will have the same or very similar information to the one we're going to dissect. Some will have different wording or new entries, but the majority will categorize their assets and liabilities just as this company does. If you see strange entries that don't make any sense, a very handy reference guide to reading the annual report, *Keys to Reading an Annual Report*, is published by *Barron's* and is available at most libraries and bookstores.

A Very Good Small-Cap Company

Marten Transport, Ltd. is a great example of a small-cap potential investment. The reason I say potential is because whenever you read this, circumstances within the company will have changed. It happens every day: the company buys another company; a senior officer leaves; or a new contract is signed, doubling sales. Therefore, the purpose here is to give you the guidelines to look at this and every company objectively and determine if you should invest in it. Pages 93–100 have the financial highlights, balance sheet and income statement for Marten for 1993.

ABOUT THE COMPANY

Marten Transport, Ltd., with headquarters in Mondovi, Wisconsin, provides time- and temperature-sensitive truckload motor carrier services to customers nationwide. Marten serves customers with more demanding delivery deadlines or those who ship products requiring modern temperature-controlled trailers to protect goods. Founded in 1946, Marten became a public company in September 1986. The company's common stock is traded on the NASDAQ National Market System under the symbol MRTN. Marten employs 1,128 people, including office personnel, mechanics and drivers.

Financial Highlights

(In thousands, except per-share amounts)	Years Ended December 31, 1993	1992	Percent Increase
Operations			
Operating revenue	$112,180	$98,194	14%
Operating income	11,359	7,678	48
Income before extraordinary item	5,462	3,434	59
Net income	6,345	3,434	85
Income per share before extraordinary item	1.58	1.00	58
Net income per share	1.84	1.00	84
Financial Position			
Current assets	27,088	21,987	23
Current liabilities	30,789	24,792	24
Property and equipment, net of depreciation	69,563	59,229	17
Total assets	96,776	81,434	19
Long-term debt and capital leases, less current maturities	21,117	20,523	3
Shareholders' investment	34,729	28,384	22

Operating Revenue (In millions)

$87.8	$98.2	$112.2
1991	1992	1993

Net Income Per Share

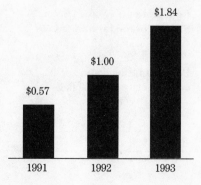

$0.57	$1.00	$1.84
1991	1992	1993

BALANCE SHEET

(In thousands)	Years Ended December 31,	
	1993	1992
Assets		
Current assets:		
Cash and cash equivalents	**$5,339**	$5,875
Receivables:		
Trade, less allowances of $540 and $422	**12,444**	10,692
Other	**2,769**	683
Prepaid expenses (Note 1)	**4,626**	2,912
Deferred income taxes (Note 5)	**1,910**	1,825
Total current assets	**27,088**	21,987
Property and equipment (Notes 1, 2, 3 and 4):		
Revenue equipment	**99,129**	88,012
Building and land	**2,999**	1,969
Office equipment and other	**3,144**	2,633
Less accumulated depreciation and amortization	**(35,709)**	(33,385)
Net property and equipment	**69,563**	59,229
Other assets	**125**	218
	$96,776	81,434
Liabilities and Shareholders' Investment		
Current liabilities:		
Accounts payable	**$2,626**	$1,898
Insurance and claims accruals	**8,863**	7,906
Accrued liabilities	**4,147**	3,785
Current maturities of long-term debt and capital leases (Notes 2 and 3)	**15,153**	11,203
Total current liabilities	**30,789**	24,792
Long-term debt and capital leases, less current maturities (Notes 2 and 3)	**21,117**	20,523
Deferred income taxes (Note 5)	**10,141**	7,735
Total liabilities	**62,047**	53,050
Commitments (Notes 1, 3 and 9)		
Shareholders' investment (Notes 1 and 6):		
Common stock, $0.01 par value per share, 10,000,000 shares authorized, 3,429,950 shares issued and outstanding	**34**	34
Additional paid in capital	**10,865**	10,865
Retained earnings	**23,830**	17,485
Total shareholders' investment	**34,729**	28,384
	$96,776	81,434

The accompanying notes are an integral part of these balance sheets.

STATEMENTS OF OPERATIONS AND RETAINED EARNINGS

	For the Years Ended December 31,		
(In thousands, except per share amounts)	**1993**	1992	1991
Operating revenue	**$112,180**	$98,194	$87,763
Operating expenses:			
Salaries, wages and benefits	**40,873**	36,030	31,216
Purchased transportation	**3,963**	2,761	3,137
Fuel	**18,896**	17,294	16,141
Supplies and maintenance	**10,889**	9,180	8,009
Depreciation and amortization	**12,530**	11,430	10,701
Taxes and licenses	**4,386**	4,110	3,584
Insurance and claims	**5,246**	5,438	5,151
Communications and utilities	**1,137**	1,012	1,123
Gain on disposition of revenue equipment	**(1,208)**	—	—
Other	**4,109**	3,261	2,855
	100,821	90,516	81,917
Operating income	**11,359**	7,678	5,846
Other expenses (income):			
Interest expense	**2,447**	2,330	2,771
Interest income and other	**(186)**	(261)	(373)
	2,261	2,069	2,398
Income before items below	**9,098**	5,609	3,448
Provision for income taxes (Note 5)	**3,636**	2,175	1,340
Income before extraordinary item and cumulative effect of change in accounting principle	**5,462**	3,434	2,108
Extraordinary item—proceeds of life insurance policy (Note 8)	**883**	—	—
Cumulative effect of change in the method of revenue recognition (Note 1)	**—**	—	(143)
Net income	**6,345**	3,434	1,965
Retained earnings:			
Beginning of year	**17,485**	14,051	12,086
End of year	**$23,830**	$17,485	$14,051
Earnings per common and common equivalent share data:			
Income before extraordinary item and cumulative effect of change in accounting principle	**$1.58**	$1.00	$0.62
Extraordinary item	**0.26**	—	—
Cumulative effect of change in the method of revenue recognition	**—**	—	(0.05)
Net income	**$1.84**	$1.00	$0.57

The accompanying notes are an integral part of these statements.

NOTES TO FINANCIAL STATEMENTS

1. Summary of Significant Accounting Policies

Nature of business: Marten Transport, Ltd. (the company) is a long-haul truckload carrier providing protective service transportation of temperature-sensitive materials and general commodities pursuant to operating authority, both contract and common, granted by the Interstate Commerce Commission. The company derived approximately 14 percent of its revenue from a single customer in 1993, 13 percent in 1992 and 14 percent in 1991.

Cash equivalents: The company invests available funds in short-term cash equivalents, principally mutual funds containing U.S. government-backed securities which have an original maturity of three months or less. These investments are stated at cost, which approximates market value.

Prepaid expenses: As of December 31, prepaid expenses consisted of the following:

(In thousands)	1993	1992
License fees	$1,521	$ 612
Tires in service	1,302	1,189
Parts and tires inventory	654	539
Insurance	255	326
Other	894	246
	$4,626	$2,912

Property and equipment: Additions and improvements to property and equipment are capitalized at cost, while maintenance and repair expenditures are charged to operations as incurred. Gains and losses on revenue equipment dispositions are included in operations. Certain facilities are leased from entities owned by its current and former chairmen of the board (see Notes 3 and 4).

Depreciation is computed based on the cost of the asset, reduced by its estimated salvage value, using the straight-line method for financial reporting purposes and accelerated methods for income tax reporting purposes. Following is a summary of estimated useful lives:

	Years
Revenue equipment:	
Tractors	5
Trailers	7
Satellite tracking	4
Building	20
Office equipment and other	3–15

Tires in service: The cost of original equipment and replacement tires placed in service is capitalized. Amortization is computed based on cost, less estimated salvage value, using the straight-line method over a period of 24 months. The current portion of tires in service is included in prepaid expenses in the accompanying balance sheets. The cost of tires amortized beyond one year, along with the estimated salvage value of tires in service, are included in revenue equipment in the accompanying balance sheets. The cost of recapping tires is charged to expenses as incurred.

Insurance and claims: The company self-insures for property damage and self-insures, in part, for losses related to workers' compensation claims, auto liability, cargo and employees' group health benefits. Insurance coverage is maintained for per-incident and cumulative liability losses in amounts the company considers sufficient based on historical experience. The company provides currently for estimated self-insured and partially self-insured losses. Under arrangements with its insurance carriers, the company has provided approximately $7.5 million in letters of credit to guarantee settlement of claims.

Revenue recognition: In January 1992, the Financial Accounting Standards Board Emerging Issues Task Force reached a consensus on Issue 91-9, "Revenue and Expense Recognition for Freight Services in Process." To comply with this consensus, the company changed its method of recognizing revenue and related expenses from the date freight is received from the customer to the date shipment is completed. The change was effective in the first quarter of 1991. The cumulative effect of the change on prior years was a non-operating charge of $143,000, or 5 cents per share, and was included in net income for 1991.

Earnings per common and common equivalent share: Earnings per share have been computed based on the weighted average number of shares outstanding during each period as adjusted for the effect of the issuance of stock options to certain employees and directors. Weighted average common and common equivalent shares outstanding were 3,451,932 in 1993, 3,434,538 in 1992, and 3,423,364 in 1991.

Reclassifications: Certain amounts in the 1992 and 1991 financial statements have been reclassified to conform to the 1993 presentation. These reclassifications had no effect on previously reported net income or shareholders' investment.

2. Long-Term Debt and Capital Leases

Long-term debt and capital leases consist of notes payable and capitalized leases (see Note 3) collateralized by specific revenue equipment. The notes and leases are payable in monthly principal and interest installments. Interest rates range from 5.0 percent to 9.2 percent.

The debt agreements contain various restrictive covenants which, among other matters, require the company to maintain certain financial ratios. The company was in compliance with all debt convenants at December 31, 1993.

Maturities of long-term debt and capital leases at December 31, 1993, were as follows:

Year	Amount
	(In thousands)
1994	$15,153
1995	10,961
1996	7,619
1997	2,537
	$36,270

3. Leases

The company acquired certain revenue equipment in 1990 under the terms of capital leases which are included within long-term debt and capital leases (see Note 2). The leases provide for 48 equal monthly payments and a guarantee of the residual value by the company at the end of the lease term. Payments made under these leases amounted to $2,488,000 in 1993 and $1,644,000 in 1992. The cost of revenue equipment under capital leases included in the accompanying balance sheets at December 31, 1993 and 1992, was $4,360,000 and $6,149,000, respectively. The related accumulated amortization at December 31, 1993 and 1992, amounted to $2,242,000 and $2,355,000, respectively.

The company also leases facilities and office equipment under operating leases with terms ranging from one to 10 years (see Note 4). Under most of these arrangements, the company pays maintenance and other expenses related to the leased property.

Minimum future obligations of leases in effect at December 31, 1993, are as follows:

Year	Capital Leases	Operating Leases
	(In thousands)	
1994	$1,427	$370
1995	—	207
1996	—	4
Total minimum lease payments	1,427	$581
Less amount representing interest	(65)	
Present value of net minimum lease payments	$1,362	

Lease-related expenses were as follows:

(In thousands)	1993	1992	1991
Capital lease amortization	$867	$925	$925
Capital lease interest expense	288	374	464
Operating lease rentals	493	482	535

4. Related Party Transactions

During the three years ended December 31, 1993, the company engaged in the following related party transactions:

(a) Leasing equipment, office and terminal facilities under a non-cancelable operating lease with a partnership in which its current and former chairman of the board are partners. Total rental expense charged to operations relating to this lease was $175,000 during 1993, $185,000 during 1992 and $200,000 during 1991. Future minimum rental payments under the lease with the partnership are $175,000 for 1994 and $73,000 for 1995.

(b) During 1993, the company made payments of $629,000 to a construction company owned by a director of Marten Transport for additions to the Mondovi, Wisconsin, headquarters and a maintenance facility in Ontario, California.

(c) During the three years ended December 31, 1993, the company has maintained checking, savings and investment accounts at banks controlled by its former chairman of the board and a non-shareholder/officer of the company.

5. Income Taxes

Effective January 1, 1991, the company implemented the provisions of Statement of Financial Accounting Standards No. 109 (SFAS No. 109), "Accounting for Income Taxes." SFAS No. 109 utilizes the liability method whereby deferred taxes are determined based on the estimated future tax effects of differences between the financial statement and tax bases of assets and liabilities given the provisions of enacted tax laws. As permitted by SFAS No. 109, prior years have not been restated to reflect the change. The cumulative effect of the change on 1991 net income and financial position was not material.

The components of the provision for income taxes consisted of the following:

(In thousands)	1993	1992	1991
Current:			
Federal	$1,150	$1,116	$612
State	165	230	223
	1,315	1,346	835
Deferred:			
Federal	1,909	700	502
State	412	129	3
	2,321	829	505
Total provision	$3,636	$2,175	$1,340

The statutory federal income tax rate reconciled to the effective income tax rate as follows:

	1993	1992	1991
Statutory federal income tax rate	34%	34%	34%
Increase in taxes arising from:			
State income taxes, net of federal income tax benefit	4	4	4
Permanent differences	2	1	1
Effective tax rate	40%	39%	39%

As of December 31, the net deferred tax liability consisted of the following:

(In thousands)	1993	1992
Deferred tax assets:		
Reserves and accrued liabilities for financial reporting in excess of tax	**$4,004**	$3,415
State income tax deduction for financial reporting in excess of tax	**348**	212
Alternative minimum tax credit	**83**	—
	4,435	3,627
Deferred tax liabilities:		
Tax depreciation in excess of depreciation for financial reporting	**10,489**	7,947
Prepaid tires, licenses and use tax expensed for income tax purposes and capitalized for financial reporting	**1,930**	1,460
Other	**247**	130
	12,666	9,537
Net deferred tax liability	**$8,231**	$5,910

6. Shareholders' Investment

The company maintains an Incentive Stock Option Plan and a Non-Statutory Stock Option Plan providing for the grant of options to purchase up to an aggregate of 250,000 shares of common stock to officers, directors and key employees. Grants can be made until August 7, 1996, as determined by the board of directors, at a price of not less than 100 percent of the fair market value on the date of grant, except that in the case of any shareholder owning 10 percent or more of the common stock of the company, the exercise price of an incentive stock option is to be not less than 110 percent of the fair market value. The term of the options under the Incen-tive Stock Option Plan may not exceed 10 years after date of grant, except that in the case of options to any shareholder owning more than 10 percent of the common stock of the company, the term may not exceed five years. Options under the Non-Statutory Stock Option Plan may be granted for terms of up to 10 years and one month.

As of December 31, activity under the Incentive Stock Option Plan was as follows:

	1993	1992	1991
Outstanding, beginning of year	**41,500**	41,500	41,500
Granted:			
$6.75/share	—	—	15,000
$13.25/share	**15,000**	—	—
Exercised:			
$3.75/share	**(9,000)**	—	—
Terminated:			
$6.00/share	—	—	(15,000)
Outstanding, end of year	**47,500**	41,500	41,500
Exercisable, end of year:			
$3.75–13.25/share	**17,500**	20,500	14,500

The company also has granted options under the Non-Statutory Stock Option Plan to purchase 23,500 shares of common stock. During 1993, options were exercised for 10,000 shares at $5.00 per share. At December 31, 1993, options for 13,500 shares were outstanding, including 10,166 shares exercisable at $7.00 to $8.67 per share.

The company repurchased, at fair market value, the 19,000 shares of stock issued in 1993 upon exercise of the options noted above. In 1992, the company issued 14,340 shares of common stock as compensation to certain employees. There were no transactions in the common stock and additional paid-in capital accounts in 1991.

7. Retirement Savings Plan

Effective January 1, 1993, the company adopted a defined contribution retirement savings plan, in accordance with Section 401(k) of the Internal Revenue Code, covering all employees who meet a minimum service requirement. Each participant can make contributions of up to 15 percent of compensation. The company's contribution of 25 percent of each participant's contribution to the plan for up to 4 percent of compensation vests at the rate of 20 percent per year from the second through sixth years of service. In addition, the company may make elective contributions which are determined by resolution of the board of directors. No elective contributions were made in 1993. Total expense recorded in connection with the plan was $166,000 in 1993.

8. Extraordinary Item

On August 9, 1993, the company's former chairman and chief executive officer, Roger R. Marten, passed away. The company was the beneficiary of a $1 million life insurance policy on Mr. Marten. These proceeds, net of previously recorded cash surrender value of $117,000, were recorded as an extraordinary credit with no income tax effect.

9. Commitments

The company has commitments to purchase approximately $13.5 million of additional revenue equipment, net of trade-in allowances, in 1994.

10. Quarterly Financial Data (Unaudited)

The following is a summary of the quarterly results of operations for 1993 and 1992:

(In thousands, except per share amounts)	1993 Quarters				
	First	**Second**	**Third**	**Fourth**	**Total**
Operating revenue	**$25,844**	**$28,260**	**$29,079**	**$28,997**	**$112,180**
Operating income	**2,146**	**3,182**	**3,499**	**2,532**	**11,359**
Income before extraordinary item	**934**	**1,562**	**1,761**	**1,205**	**5,462**
Extraordinary item	**—**	**—**	**883**	**—**	**883**
Net income	**934**	**1,562**	**2,644**	**1,205**	**6,345**
Net income per share before extraordinary item	**.27**	**.45**	**.51**	**.35**	**1.84**
Net income per share	**.27**	**.45**	**.77**	**.35**	**1.84**

(In thousands, except per share amounts)	1992 Quarters				
	First	Second	Third	Fourth	Total
Operating revenue	$22,998	$24,014	$25,176	$26,006	$ 98,194
Operating income	1,395	2,095	2,185	2,003	7,678
Net income	517	995	1,006	916	3,434
Net income per share	.15	.29	.29	.27	1.00

WHERE TO START

First, what does the company do and do you understand what it does? Peter Lynch, the very successful mutual fund manager who steered the Magellan Fund with spectacular results in the 1980s, believes that this is one of the most fundamental necessities for investing. In this example, Marten Transport, Ltd. provides time- and temperature-sensitive truckload motor carrier services to customers nationwide. In other words, it's a trucking company shipping products such as milk and other perishable products. This company I understand. For me, the first hurdle has been overcome.

I recently passed on a company that had many outstanding attributes because I didn't have a clue as to what it really did. The annual report described the company as one providing total design and manufacturing capability for complete systems, including multilayer boards, backplanes, and surface mount assemblies. I know these are computer applications, but that's it. While the numbers looked very good, I rejected it as a stock for my portfolio because I didn't have a good grasp of the industry. Other portfolio managers who know the product may make a fortune on it, but unless I can understand what I'm buying, I don't. You shouldn't either.

HOW ARE SALES DOING?

No company has ever gone broke because it had too many sales. It might have too many computers, too many chiefs or too many private jets, but too many sales has never been the reason a company goes out of business. Of course, if the sales are fictitious or sales are reported in an illegal way, the company and its investors have problems, but assume a company's sales are legitimate until you learn differently.

By opening the 1993 annual report for Marten we can see on the first page under Financial Highlights in the operating revenue bar chart that sales for Marten in 1991 were $87.8 million; in 1992, $98.2 million; and for 1993, $112.2 million. These results are reported as operating revenue.

This is a good beginning. Notice that sales are increasing every year. From 1991 to 1992, they increased $10.4 million, and from 1992 to 1993, they went up $14 million. More important than just increasing, they are increasing each year at a greater percentage than the previous year.

The sales increase from 1991 to 1992 was 11.85%. To determine this number, find the difference between the two sales years and divide it by the first year: (98.2 minus 87.8) divided by 87.8. Using a calculator (a Hewlett-Packard model 12C or 13B is highly recommended—they're financial calculators), the answer is 11.85%.

The 1992 to 1993 increase is determined by dividing the difference between the two years by 1992 sales: (112.2 minus 98.2) divided by 98.2. The percentage gain was 14.26%.

Sales are increasing each year, and they are growing at an increasing rate. This is a good indication to look further into the company.

How Are Earnings Doing?

Revenues are important, but it's the earnings, or net operating income, that shareholders can claim as theirs. After the interest has been paid, the wages, the new plant and equipment and all other expenses, the earnings are reported on the bottom line. What you want in earnings is a growth rate faster than that of revenues.

Let's see how Marten Transport did by this measure. On page 93, in the bar charts, the net income per share, also known as earnings per share, for 1991 was $0.57; for 1992, $1.00; and for 1993, $1.84.

On a percentage basis, the earnings grew 75.44% from 1991 to 1992, and by 84% from 1992 to 1993. The math for the first period is ($1.00 minus $0.57) divided by $0.57 = 0.7544, and for the second period, it is ($1.84 minus $1.00) divided by $1.00 = 0.84, simple percentage gains calculations.

What's impressive about this growth pattern is that the percentages have increased over the years, and *the earnings have increased at a faster rate than the sales*.

Look back at the sales increases. Sales were up 11.85% and 14.26%. While that was impressive, the way the company efficiently used those revenues created earnings that grew 75.44% and 84% during the same time period. This means that the company is getting more profitable as it is growing.

Check It Out

When earnings have moved that dramatically, you must check to see how they were attained. You can't read an isolated number and accept it. You need to know if the earnings were from continuing operations or if the company had an extraordinary event such as the sale of a building or a subsidiary, which gave it a one-time profit. You can find the answer in the income statement.

In this example, the summary of the income statement on page 93 tells the story. Income per share for 1993 before an extraordinary item was $1.58, and after the item, it was $1.84. There was a one-time event that influenced earnings by $0.26 ($1.84 minus $1.58 = $0.26). In this example, the chairman of the firm passed away, and an insurance policy paid the company $883,000. This is explained in note 8 of the financial statement. This was definitely an extraordinary, one-time item.

What does that mean to us as investors? It means we have to look back at the numbers without the extraordinary item, and see how the firm is doing on an ongoing or operational basis.

Take out the extraordinary payment, and the earnings are $1.58. Compared with the $1.00 from the previous year, the improvement is 58%. That falls short of the 75.44% from the previous year. The growth in earnings has slowed, but it is still ahead of the growth in revenues (14.26%). And earnings are increasing at better than 50% per year. Ideally, like the revenues, the earnings would increase as a percentage each year. However, these are strong earnings, and the stock deserves more investigation. Let's look at the balance sheet and income statement (pages 94 and 95).

THE BALANCE SHEET

The balance sheet is a financial snapshot of a company on the day the information is gathered, usually December 31. It tells you what the company looks like on that day. For Marten, the balance sheet is on page 94. We'll go through each item and determine its relevance.

ASSETS

The assets of a company are what it owns. The first item is usually cash. Cash is good. Cash gives comfort. Cash, like rain and sunshine to flowers, makes companies grow. Marten had $5,339,000 in cash on December 31, 1993. On the same day in 1992, it had $5,875,000. A little less in 1993 than 1992 but not much, about 10%. There is no dramatic difference, so we can assume that amount is about how much the firm needs to run its business.

The next item on the income statement is receivables, the amount of money customers owe the company. In 1993, it totaled $15,213,000, up from $11,375,000 in 1992, or a percentage increase of 33.74%. This increase has to be considered in context with the revenue growth already calculated. For the same time period, revenues grew by 14.26%.

Receivables are growing at a faster rate than revenues. This is the first red flag to consider. You would want to watch this Receivables number in the quarters ahead. If it continues to grow, this means that customers are slow in paying or that new business is being financed by the company. While receivables should increase with revenues, they should do so at about the same rate.

PREPAID EXPENSES

These are items like insurance premiums, license fees, parts and tire inventory and tires in use, just as it's explained in note 1 to the financial statement. In 1993, they were $4,626,000, up from $2,912,000 in 1992. You would expect higher expenses as the company expands. In percentages, prepaid expenses were up 58.86%. These, too, can be compared with revenue growth. These went up more (58.86% versus 14.26%), but prepaid expenses are items that you want at a higher rate than revenues because these are necessary items that must be paid.

DEFERRED INCOME TAXES

Because these taxes are on the asset side of the balance sheet, these are taxes already paid. This usually occurs when revenue and expenses are reported differently on the income statement from the company's tax return. For Marten, they are $1,910,000 for 1993. That was up from $1,825,000 in 1992, not a meaningful increase.

If the deferred items are on the liability side of the balance sheet, they must be paid some time in the future. It's not uncommon for growing companies to defer paying their taxes and have this figure increase as the company expands.

TOTAL CURRENT ASSETS

This number is a total of all the above items and represents everything that can be turned into cash within one year. In the case of Marten, it had total current assets of $27,088,000 in 1993, up from $21,987,000 in 1992. The increase came mostly from receivables, not too good, and prepaid expenses, which is a positive.

You'll need the current assets number to calculate the current ratio, which is the total current assets divided by the current liabilities. This tells you if the company has enough current assets (money) to cover its current liabilities (bills). We'll get back to this in a moment.

PROPERTY AND EQUIPMENT

This category contains the long-term assets such as the trucks, buildings, land and office equipment. The first category for Marten is revenue equipment. That would be its trucks.

For 1993, the company had $99,129,000 worth of trucks, up from $88,012,000 in 1992. It is buying new trucks to keep up with new business. This $11,117,000 increase in trucks as a percentage increase (12.63%) is right in line with the revenue increase (14.26%). If the increase were too far ahead of revenues, the company would be adding capacity it doesn't need. If it's too far behind revenues, the company would be pushing its current trucks beyond their capacity and wearing them down too quickly. By reading the notes to the financial statements, the firm disclosed it has a commitment to buy $13,500,000 of new trucks in 1994. Revenues, in the opinion of management, must be going up.

The next category is building and land, which was $2,999,000 for 1993 and $1,969,000 for 1992, up about $1 million. By reading the footnotes, we learn that the company has added to its headquarters and a maintenance facility in 1993. Again, the company is growing with its revenues.

Office equipment is the next sector. This means typewriters, furniture, computers, telephones and copy machines. The total value for 1993 was $3,144,000, up from $2,633,000. More equipment was needed as the company added more computing power for tracking its trucks.

The last number in the property and equipment category is accumulated depreciation and amortization. This number tells you how much the company is writing off on an accumulated basis as its assets are depreciating. For example, if you buy a computer for $100 and the computer has a life of five years, you can write off the expense, on a straight-line basis, at the rate of $20 per year ($100 divided by 5 = $20). Similar calculations can be made for the trucks, furniture, buildings and every other asset.

For 1993, the number grew by a small amount. This means that the company is adding assets at a reasonable rate. If amortization jumps significantly in any one year, the company may have changed its accounting methods. This will be noted in the footnotes. Companies sometimes do this to boost earnings in a year when the operating profits haven't been there. However, it can only do this one time without raising suspicion.

Manipulating amortization schedules isn't the purpose of a company. If any stock you're considering is getting earnings from accounting manipulation, stop considering it.

The summation of this category is called net property and equipment. This number gives you the current book value of the assets. By comparing the two years, you see that it has increased by a little more than $10,000,000. Most of that increase came from new revenue equipment.

One interesting sideline to this number was its use in the corporate buyouts of the 1980s. When there was a company with a large holding of valuable properties which had been amortized over a long period of time, it showed on the books at a very low value. However, the astute investor recognized that with the inflation of the 1980s, that number was nowhere near the true value of the property. So the raiders bought companies based on the value of the properties they owned, not the value of the earnings.

One final category is other assets. It's a small number for both reported years. If it were to grow large in one year, find out what other means.

LIABILITIES OR WHAT THE
COMPANY OWES

The liabilities of a company are the bills it has to pay. There are two elements to liabilities: current and long-term.

It helps to keep in mind what the company is: a unique entity with a life of its own and managed by people. The company can borrow money (liability), buy equipment (assets), make stuff (assets), sell it for more than it cost to make (profit) and then add the profit to the shareholders' equity. As the firm earns profits, the shareholders increase their wealth.

Everything is not that simple because there are many games management can play with the numbers, most of them blessed by the accounting profession. For example, there are usually two sets of books a company keeps. One for the shareholders and reported in the annual report. The other is for the IRS and tax-reporting purposes. Eventually, both of these books will reconcile. However, don't think the annual report or any report tells the whole truth about a company. The best we can do as investors is to investigate as thoroughly as possible, and question the company on any numbers that seem inappropriate or suspicious.

Realistically, most investors won't go that deep. You have to be an accountant of some skill to discover the tricks. Let me emphasize that most firms don't play tricks with the numbers. However, if management of a company has had previous disreputable accounting practices, you should avoid the company. My experience has been that these managers have no regard for the shareholders. There are too many fine stocks with solid management for you to consider. Avoid any with questionable characters at the helm.

Fortunately, these people are the ones making the business headlines because of shareholder suits or prison sentences. A little digging in business magazines will let you know if the president or chairman or other senior officers have management skills or questionable reputations.

But I digress. On to the liabilities side of the balance sheet.

CURRENT LIABILITIES OR WHAT'S DUE NOW

The current liabilities are bills due within one year. They are, in the case of Marten: accounts payable, insurance and claims accruals, accrued liabilities and current maturities of long-term debt and capital leases.

ACCOUNTS PAYABLE

These are the bills for today. In 1993, they totaled $2,626,000, and in 1992, they were $1,898,000. There was an increase of 38.36%. Comparing this again with the revenue increase of 14.26% for the same period, you can see accounts payable are growing faster than revenues. As a company owner, you don't mind seeing this figure grow, as long as it isn't too large.

By delaying payment of a bill, you are helping finance the company with that money instead of paying your creditors. You can't do this for long because there are usually penalties for paying late (much like with your credit card), but good cash management requires bills to be paid in a timely manner, not ahead of time.

INSURANCE AND CLAIMS ACCRUALS

Insurance bills to cover liability for the drivers is one of the expenses of doing business as a trucking company. That's what these are. For 1993, they were $8,863,000, up from $7,906,000 in 1992. This is a normal cost of business, and these numbers are in line with the increase in business.

What you are seeking in analyzing all of these numbers is the extraordinary jump or decline on a year-over-year basis. This is a flag signaling that something is different and needs attention. When numbers grow with the business, you can breathe easy for that category and go on to the next one.

ACCRUED LIABILITIES OR SOMEDAY I'M PAYING THESE BUT NOT NOW

These are bills being postponed for whatever reason. The most common is the concept of revenue recognition versus when expenses occur. For our purposes, because we know these bills have to be paid at some point, look at the magnitude of the numbers and their growth.

In 1993, they totaled $4,147,000, a small increase from 1992's $3,785,000. This liability has grown less than revenues (9.56% versus 14.26%). It's under control.

CURRENT MATURITIES OF LONG-TERM DEBT AND CAPITAL LEASES

Eventually, all debt must be paid. If you borrow money for 15 years, at the end of 15 years, you have to repay your loan. Companies do the same thing.

They borrow money for five years, 10 years, 15 years or longer. Then, as time goes by, certain debts become due. In terms of the balance sheet, that moves the debt from the long-term debt category to the current liability section.

Leases are similar to debt in that the company pays for equipment it uses in its business by using the equipment as collateral, and pays the leaseholder of the equipment a monthly payment until the equipment is fully paid for or is returned to the leaseholder.

In the case of Marten, there is a combined payment due for debt and leases of $15,153,000 for 1993. That's an increase of almost $4,000,000 from 1992. And by looking at note 2 of the financial statements, you can see that the next three years will require payments of $10,961,000, $7,619,000 and $2,537,000.

These numbers tell us that the debt payment is peaking this year and may go down over the next three. That could mean more profits if interest payments decrease.

TOTAL CURRENT LIABILITIES

This is the sum of all the debts due this year: $30,789,000. In the previous year, they were $24,792,000. The majority of the increase comes from the debt payment due. The remainder is explained by the increase in business.

What you need to do now is calculate the quick ratio and the current ratio. The Prodigy service does this for you in the Strategic Investor section, but you should know how to do it in case you find a stock that isn't on your database service.

The quick ratio, also known as the acid test, is found by dividing the amount of cash plus receivables by the current liabilities. In the case of Marten, that's $5,339,000 plus $15,213,000 divided by $30,789,000 or 66.75%.

That percentage is a little lower than you would like. You can feel comfortable when it's 100% or higher. The company then has enough cash to pay its bills.

The second ratio is the current ratio, which is all current assets divided by all current liabilities. In the case of Marten, it's $27,088,000 divided by $30,789,000 or 87.98%.

In general, you're looking for 200% or better on this ratio. However, you need to look at the industry average to determine if this is out of line. In addition, the one-time debt payment this year will not occur next year. In fact, there will be a reduction of more than $5,000,000. While the firm may be short this year and probably borrow the necessary funds from a bank, or issue new debt to pay for the old, it will increase its financial strength in the coming years as debt and lease payments diminish.

LONG-TERM DEBT AND CAPITAL LEASES

These are debt and lease obligations that extend beyond the current year. For 1993, they were $21,117,000, up from $20,523,000 in 1992. The difference is small and raises no red flags.

Where this number can be important is when the long-term debt expands significantly from one year to the next. Taking on too much debt, whether as an individual or as a company, can sometimes be severely damaging. Unless the company has specific projects that require debt and will return more than the cost of the debt, avoid the stock.

There's an old saying on the Street: What's good for debt is bad for equity, and vice versa. In other words, debt has a cost in terms of covenants, which are demands the lender puts on the company, usually in the form of restrictions as to what the company can do with its money.

For example, the company may not be able to increase or even pay dividends on the common stock unless there is enough cash to pay for three interest payments on the debt, or some such other restriction. Some debt is necessary to effectively run a company. Too much debt will sometimes bury a company. Keep watch on the long-term debt number.

DEFERRED INCOME TAXES

Because these are on the liability side of the balance sheet, they represent taxes that are payable in the future. This occurs when income reported on the income statement is not yet taxable, but will become so in the future. Monitor this category for any large increases because management might be postponing the inevitable while still reporting good earnings.

For Marten, deferred income taxes increased from $7,735,000 to $10,141,000, about 31%. You would certainly expect an increase along with higher revenues. Also, in note 5, the company explains that there was a one-time change in reporting income taxes and that prior years have not been restated to reflect those changes. Part of the increase can be attributed to this one-time event.

SHAREHOLDERS' INVESTMENT OR WHAT YOU OWN

The final part of the liabilities side of the balance sheet is the residual owned by the stockholders, or the net worth of the company. For Marten, the shareholders are entitled to $34,729,000. This number is calculated by adding the par value per share of the stock, the additional paid in capital and the retained earnings.

The par value of a stock is usually a penny or less per share. Its origins go way back to the beginning of issuing stock and have become meaningless in today's market. For Marten, the par value is a penny per share. There are 3,429,950 shares outstanding. Multiply the two, and you get $34,000.

The additional paid in capital is the value over par the company received when it issued stock. For this company, it was $10,865,000.

Finally, there is the retained earnings component. This is all the profit retained over the years. This number should be growing every year. For Marten, in 1993, retained earnings were $23,830,000. That was an increase from 1992 of $17,485,000, or up 36.29%. This is how much better off shareholders were in one year. That's a very strong return on your investment. In fact, it's the kind of return most people only hope for.

That improvement of $6,345,000 comes from the operating or income statement. It is the net income for the year. Let's take a look at the statements of operations and retained earnings.

THE INCOME STATEMENT OR HOW MUCH DID THE COMPANY MAKE OR LOSE

The income statement tells you how profitable or unprofitable a company is. It gives you an item-by-item reporting of all the revenue and expenses for one year, the year just ended. Most companies are on a calendar year from January 1 to December 31. The annual report, containing this and other information, is usually released to the shareholders in March or April.

The income statement tells you what happened in a 12-month period. If a company has a different year, say from April 1 to March 31, it isn't significant. It only means, for whatever reason, the company chose to use those 12 months as its tax-reporting year instead of the calendar year.

REVENUES OR HOW MANY DOLLARS WERE BROUGHT IN

Revenues are also called sales or the top line. Revenues are how much product or service the company sold in a year. For Marten, as we already know from page 93, the revenues for 1993 were $112,180,000, up from $98,194,000 in 1992. That increase came on top of 1991 revenues of $87,763,000.

The percentages were done earlier, and the main objective is to determine if revenues are increasing and increasing at a faster rate than previously. These do, and that's a good sign.

OPERATING EXPENSES OR WHAT IT COSTS TO GET THOSE REVENUES

Operating expenses are the cost of doing business. The first item for Marten is salaries, wages and benefits. In 1993, these were $40,873,000; in 1992, $36,030,000; and for 1991, $31,216,000.

Once again, you want to look at these relative to the revenues, and ideally, these will be decreasing as a percentage of revenues because that means the company is becoming more efficient.

The first comparison is to sales: for 1993, $40,873,000 divided by $112,180,000, or 36.44% of revenues, went to salaries, wages and benefits. For 1992: $36,030,000 divided by $98,194,000, or 36.69%. Only a very small percentage difference here, but at least incremental costs were not incurred for the additional revenues. For 1991, the percentage is $31,216,000 divided by $87,763,000, or 35.57%, which means that the company was a little more efficient in 1991 than 1992 or 1993.

Because these are such small differences, they are not meaningful. However, if this category of salaries, wages and benefits begins to eat up more of the revenues, it means that management is increasing its own well-being at the expense of the shareholders. Keep an eye on this item.

PURCHASED TRANSPORTATION

This is using outside trucking companies or subcontractors to haul shipments for Marten when the company was short of trucks. Because this item is so small, less than 3% of revenues, it doesn't need exploration. If, however, it becomes significant, say 10% or more, it may mean that the company is not investing enough in trucks and trailers to keep up with its business. And outside truckers will cost the company much more than handling the shipments internally.

FUEL

For Marten, this basic ingredient has increased incrementally with the business. Again, by calculating the cost of fuel as a percentage of revenues, we discover in 1993, fuel was 16.84%; in 1992, 17.61%; and in 1991, 18.39%. You can see that the firm is using more efficient trucks each year and has brought fuel costs down 8.43% in two years: (18.39 minus 16.84) divided by 18.39 = 8.43%. This is always positive when costs are going down, and revenues are going up.

Supplies and Maintenance

This is stuff needed to keep the trucks moving. By looking at their respective percentages of revenue, we can see how well this cost is being managed: for 1993, this category totaled 9.71% of revenues; for 1992, 9.35%; and for 1991, 9.13%.

No cause for alarm here, but these numbers would look better if they were descending rather than ascending. Looked at from the perspective of cost increase compared with revenue increase, we can see that the company is doing relatively worse on this cost than improvement in the revenues. The revenues have gone in 1991 from $87,763,000 to $112,180,000 in 1993, or 27.82%, while supplies and maintenance have increased from $8,009,000 to $10,889,000, or 35.96%. This, again, is not a cause for alarm, but when a cost is increasing faster than revenues, it means that the profit margins of the firm are being hurt.

Depreciation and Amortization

When a company buys an asset, such as a truck in the case of Marten, it has to depreciate it over its useful life. That means if a truck costs $100 and can be used for 10 years, the company can write off the cost of the truck over the 10-year period, or in this case, $10 per year.

This year, the depreciation and amortization is $12,530,000, up from $11,430,000 in 1992, and $10,701,000 in 1991. This number should be increasing as the business expands because the company needs to buy new trucks and equipment to handle new orders.

In fact, if this number isn't increasing with an improvement in revenues, it means that the company isn't adding new equipment and is running its old machinery longer and more frequently. This will wear out the assets faster, and without new ones, the company will not be able to serve its clients, and then the business suffers.

This is one cost that should be increasing in line with the revenues, but not more so. If you have too many assets and not enough business to pay for them, you end up with a lot of shiny new equipment being auctioned to pay for itself.

Amortization is the writing off of an intangible asset, usually goodwill, over a specified period of time. It is defined as the assignment of the historical cost of an intangible asset to production periods as expense.

The short, easy version: Company A buys Company B for $1,000. Company B has a book value of $900. Company A has paid $100 more for the goodwill of the company, an intangible asset, usually attributed to the value of the company's reputation.

Because that $100 cannot be directly attributable to any asset, it must be shown as goodwill and amortized over a specified period of time. The faster the time period, the more the expense, the lower the earnings. The longer the time, the higher the earnings. This is true for all amortized expenses, whether goodwill or research and development or any other.

The more conservative companies will expense (write off a cost in the year it is incurred) as much as they can because the money has been spent, and they feel the sooner the cost is gone, the quicker the earnings will improve. Less conservative companies will want to draw out the life of the expense, charging earnings less, and making their bottom line look better. Watch out for companies with increasing amortization charges without corresponding actual expenses, such as buying new companies. They may be changing their accounting method to improve the bottom line.

TAXES AND LICENSES

These expenses are self-explanatory and should increase with revenues. Marten's are. Not many games are played in this arena by any company.

INSURANCE AND CLAIMS

These have stayed about the same for the three years. If there had been a marked increase or decrease, you would want to delve into the reason why. These expenses are standard costs of doing business. If they dropped dramatically, you would think the company is taking too much of a risk by not being insured.

COMMUNICATIONS AND UTILITIES OR COME IN, GOOD BUDDY

CB radios, telephones and electricity are in this category. Every year they're about the same. Again, any large increase or decrease would need investigation.

GAIN ON DISPOSITION OF REVENUE EQUIPMENT

This shows a number in parentheses of $1,208,000 for 1993 and nothing for the prior two years. The company probably sold some old trucks for more than it had depreciated them, resulting in a gain for the company.

Usually, numbers in parentheses represent a loss. But this number is in the expense column; therefore, it's a gain. If it had been a loss, the number would have been shown without parentheses.

This is a one-time gain, which will flow through to the profitability for the year. When doing a calculation for earnings per share, this number should not be included because it is a one-time event.

OTHER

This is a catch-all category, and your guess is as good as mine. It has gone up about 44% in two years, faster than the revenues, but is not a number large enough to be significant. If it keeps moving up, you'd want to know what it represents.

OPERATING INCOME

After you deduct operating expenses from the revenue, you arrive at the operating income. In 1993, it was $11,359,000, up from $7,678,000 in 1992, and $5,846,000 in 1991. It has almost doubled in two years. This is good, very good. Remember, however, that 1993 income was helped by the one-time sale of trucks.

As we already discussed above, you are always looking for increased performance from a company, and the revenues are the benchmark for judging. Revenues increased from $87,763,000 to $112,180,000 or 27.82% in two years. Operating income increased from $5,846,000 to $11,359,000, but you must deduct $1,208,000 for the gain on the sale of trucks in 1993, which still leaves a very strong 73.64% increase: ($11,359,000 minus $1,208,000) minus $5,846,000 divided by $5,846,000.

This company just keeps on truckin', and it does so more profitably each year. In 1991, its operating income was 6.66% of revenues ($5,846,000 divided by $87,763,000); in 1992 it was 7.82%; and in 1993, it was 9.05% ($10,151,000 divided by $112,180,000). Again, I have deducted the $1,208,000 from reported income because of the one-time event of the truck sales.

While revenues were increasing at a healthy clip, the operating income was even healthier. Put another way, the management is operating more efficiently as the company grows. This is very good, but we're not down to the bottom line, or net income. There are more expenses to deduct.

INTEREST EXPENSE

When you borrow money, you pay interest on it; so does a company. If this expense keeps climbing every year, the company could be borrowing too much. When a firm gets into too much debt, or overleveraged, the interest payments become overwhelming and can put the company out of business. That's what the business headlines of the 1980s were describing when discussing Federated Department Stores, Macy's and many other bankrupt entities.

Marten's borrowing isn't excessive, and it isn't increasing. No need for concern.

INTEREST INCOME

When companies invest money for short periods until they pay their bills, they earn interest on the funds. That's where the interest income is made. If a company were to have a majority of its earnings come from interest income, and that portion continued to increase yearly, the company would be getting out of its basic business and turning into an investment company. Very few companies do this, but be aware of the possibility. You would then be looking at an entirely different industry group and would have to question if the management is qualified to compete in this new industry.

INCOME BEFORE ITEMS BELOW

This is the income flow from the normal course of business. If you look below this, you see a provision for extraordinary items, events that do not recur every year.

For the 1993 year, Marten made pretax income of $9,098,000, an increase of 62.2% from 1992 ($9,098,000 minus $5,609,000) divided by $5,609,000. However, income increased by $1,208,000 because of the truck sales. The 1993 increase was in addition to a 62.67% increase in 1992 from 1991. This income is growing at an annual rate, before extraordinary items, at 62% a year. This is excellent growth.

PROVISION FOR INCOME TAXES

Just like us, the company has to pay taxes on its income. There is a note (note 5) explaining the details of the taxes paid.

For example, note 1 in Marten's financial statement explains that 14% of its revenues came from a single client, 13% in 1992 and 14% in 1991. You know from this note that the company has a diverse revenue base and isn't dependent on any one customer for its survival. If one client comprises more than 25% of a business' revenues, the company will have extreme hardship if that client goes away.

Look for a broad customer base. If you can't find it in the financial statement, look for it in the 10-Q or 10-K report. If you still can't find it, call the company and ask.

EXTRAORDINARY ITEM

This only happens once. They are out of the ordinary items for the company. You couldn't count on these events happening every year. This year for Marten, the proceeds from an insurance policy contributed $883,000 to the profits.

CUMULATIVE EFFECT OF CHANGE IN THE METHOD OF REVENUE RECOGNITION

This means that the company changed the way it paid taxes based on how it recognized revenue. Because it occurred in 1991 and was a one-time event, the company reports it as an extraordinary item that cost it $143,000.

NET INCOME OR THE BOTTOM LINE

For 1993, the company made net income of $6,345,000, which was up 84.77% from 1992. However, you have now learned that the net income was increased by an extraordinary item of $883,000 from a life insurance payment and $1,208,000 from a gain on the sale of trucks. You know those didn't come from the ongoing business and cannot be counted on to occur in the future.

This is why you must scrutinize the net income reported in the papers or a database service. Simply having a number isn't sufficient. You must know what that number represents, and when you do comparisons, such as year to year or quarter to quarter, you must know how the previous year's or quarter's numbers were calculated.

There's an excellent book entitled *Quality of Earnings* by Thornton O'Glove. It tells you how to analyze certain aspects of the balance sheet and income statement. More important, he describes in greater detail than I have the land mines awaiting in several categories, including inventory build-up. If you really want to dig into earnings, this book will help.

RETAINED EARNINGS OR WHAT THE SHAREHOLDERS OWN

Retained earnings are earnings held in the company. They are increased or decreased by the net income or loss and are decreased by dividends. For 1993, retained earnings were $23,830,000, an increase of 36.29% from 1992. Because we've looked carefully at the net income number, we know this increase didn't come only from the operating earnings. There was some help from extraordinary items. The careful investor knows not to give full credit for the retained earnings increase just to the business. It wouldn't be appropriate to say the retained earnings grew 36.29% without also saying that part of the growth came from nonrecurring events.

Without the insurance payment ($883,000) and truck sales (an after-tax gain of $725,283), the retained earnings or net income would have grown by $4,736,717, not the reported $6,345,000. The after-tax gain for the trucks is computed by taking the gain on the sale ($1,208,000) and multiplying by 1 minus the tax rate (1 − 0.3996). The tax rate is derived by dividing the provision for income taxes ($3,636,000) by the income before items below ($9,098,000) or 39.96%.

All this means that net income from the ongoing business was $4,736,717, while retained earnings increased by $6,345,000 because of the two extraordinary items. Remember it's the ongoing business that counts. All your calculations for performance ratios should use only the ongoing business numbers.

On a year-to-year basis, using the net income number of $4,736,717, the company increased net income by 38% from 1992. The calculation: ($4,736,717 minus $3,434,000) divided by $3,434,000. That's still an impressive number.

While it isn't overly significant in this example, there are many times when extraordinary items will bail out a company with terrible operating results. If you don't look carefully at the reported numbers, you won't know this.

Marten doesn't have this concern. It's growing at a very respectable pace and has a clean balance sheet and income statement. The growth rates are impressive.

EARNINGS PER SHARE

This is the final calculation for the balance sheet and income statement. We did it earlier, but it's worth looking at how Marten reports it.

The first line is earnings per share (EPS) before extraordinary items: $1.58 in 1993, $1.00 for 1992, and $0.62 for 1991. We now know that 1993 is overstated because of the truck sales. By taking the after-tax gain of $725,283 and dividing it by the number of shares (3,451,932—a number given in the report), we can calculate how much the truck sales affected the earnings per share: twenty-one cents. Therefore, before the insurance payment or the truck sales, in 1993, Marten earned $1.37 per share, a 37% improvement from 1992.

When extraordinary items are considered, the reported EPS are: $1.84, $1.00 and $0.57. The increases in terms of percentages are now: 84% for 1993 and 75.44% for 1992. However, these numbers overstate the business.

Things look better when the extraordinary items are added. But the investor should take those out of the calculations for EPS comparisons. Look at a business for its earnings, real earnings from operations, not a combination of operating income and extraordinary items.

STATEMENT OF CASH FLOWS OR MONEY IN, MONEY OUT

All annual reports will include a statement of cash flows, which tells you how much cash actually flowed through the business. This kind of analysis gives you the ability to see how the company is using its cash, if it's generating a lot of it, or if it doesn't have enough to meet its obligations.

Many of the leveraged buyouts (LBOs) of the 1980s were based on a company's cash flow statement. If an investor saw tremendous cash flow, and hence the ability to pay interest on debt if the investor used bonds to buy the company, a company would be bought for prices that made no sense from the usual methods of evaluation.

Yardsticks like earnings per share or book value were completely ignored if the cash flow from the company allowed the buyer the money needed to service debt. In some cases, the cash flow was strong enough to pay for additional debt so the acquirer could borrow more.

What you want to look for in the cash flow statement is any item that is significantly greater or diminished on a year-to-year basis. If long-term borrowing jumps, the company may be leveraged too much, or it may be looking to buy more equipment or land. It's worth finding out by calling the company if the report doesn't talk about new debt.

The cash flow statement should always be part of your investigation into a company. If you see an item jump dramatically in one year, look at the footnotes for an explanation, read through the report or call the company. An ongoing, expanding business should have incremental cash flow requirements, filled by bank borrowings, bonds or stock issuance. More debt isn't bad if it's used for making the business grow, and the interest payments don't overwhelm the company's cash flow.

All of the above information on annual reports is based on the numbers of a company. There's a lot more to learn from those reports.

MORE ANNUAL REPORT INFO

When reading an annual report, keep a few things in mind. It is the company's main public relations piece. More people will read or look at the annual report than any other corporate publication. If you were a company, how good would you want this to look? You'd obviously want it to be the best, most polished, most flattering description possible.

Therefore, be aware how carefully crafted the report is. Also, remember that companies must disclose everything in the report or they get in trouble with the law. The truth is in the report, but all the good, wonderful, happy things are in the front, usually with color photos. My favorite reports are the ones done on recycled paper with no photos. It saves the shareholders money.

Most of the bad news is buried in the footnotes to the financial statements. Read the whole report with an understanding of how it was composed.

The letter from the chairman or president of the company is always up front with a synopsis of the previous year and a plan for the new one. Read this statement. If all the focus is on the past with very little on the future, the writer doesn't think there is much of one. If mistakes are not admitted, or dismissed with little explanation, watch out. They will probably be repeated.

Look for elements of the business that aren't quantifiable, such as labor relations. If you read the Marten annual report, the chairman's letter discusses the main problem of the trucking industry: keeping drivers. It also describes the programs the company has developed to overcome the problem. That gives Marten a great competitive advantage. You won't find that information in the balance sheet, the income statement or the statement of cash flows.

Read the annual reports from cover to cover, dig into the numbers and the descriptive narrative. Both have valuable information.

AFTER THE ANNUAL REPORT INVESTIGATION— BUY OR NOT?

So should you buy Marten Transport, Ltd. based on what you learned in the annual report? Not yet, because you don't know enough about the company. You have to take all those numbers from the annual report and begin to use them, develop ratios and compare the performance of the company with the industry in which it operates. That's what the next chapter will teach you.

Before we go into buying and selling stocks, however, there is one more sector of the stock market I want to discuss: the IPO market, or new stock.

INVESTING IN IPOS

An IPO is an Initial Public Offering. Another viewpoint, supplied by Ken Fisher, a columnist for *Forbes* magazine and author of *Super Stocks*, defines IPO as It's Probably Overpriced. I like his definition.

The problems with IPOs for average investors are twofold: if the stock is really a buy, a hot new issue, you won't get any of it. The institutional buyers such as mutual funds, trust funds and investment advisors will get most of the stock. A few individuals will get a few shares, but the majority of the stock will go to the big investors.

The second problem is the reverse: if the stock is a dog, you can have all of it you want. In fact, the broker bringing the issue, also called underwriting the issue, will keep telling you how great the stock is. You should ask yourself: If it's so great, how come I can buy as much as I want?

My favorite story on new issues: It was a Friday afternoon, about 15 minutes after the close of the stock trading day. On any other Friday at this time, a branch office of a brokerage firm would be empty. Not on this day. The company had underwritten a new issue, and it wasn't selling well. There were thousands of shares left. The branch manager put out the word this way: Lock the door, we've still got stock for sale. The brokers weren't allowed to leave until all the stock was sold.

Remember that the next time your broker calls with a hot new issue. You may be listening to a pitch that has nothing to do with investing but everything to do with getting a door unlocked.

I avoid new issues and recommend you do the same. I certainly have missed some great opportunities, but I've also saved money. Investors are better served by watching new issues spend time in the market. The market efficiently determines whether the stock has been attractively priced, underpriced or overpriced.

If I like a stock that has just gone public, I'll watch the price action on it, investigate it by carefully reading the prospectus and be ready to buy it if it gets to the level I believe represents value. If it never gets there, I miss out. Because I have a large wish list of potential investments, I don't curse the wasted time. I've got other stocks to take its place.

Be wary of IPOs. Instead, buy stocks with a good history of earnings and public trading. You can get more information on seasoned stocks that will help you make the right decisions.

ONWARD TO THE BUY AND SELL DECISIONS

It's time to take action. You've looked through an annual report, decided the company deserves your investment dollars and you want to buy the stock. Hold on a little longer. You've just begun the process.

As mentioned above, the next chapter is going to integrate the numbers you've investigated in the annual or quarterly reports into a method for buying and selling stocks. You need more numbers, more ratios and more historical information before you can intelligently buy a stock. And you can use the computer for all the number crunching. Turn the page for the next step in investing.

CHAPTER SIX

BUYING AND ◄---┘
SELLING STOCKS:
SEASON TO
YOUR OWN TASTE

Successful stock investors are like accomplished chefs: They study for years, learn the ingredients of success and then create their own masterpieces by experimenting and modifying. They've also had their fingers burned a few times.

As an investor, you have to know what has worked well in the past, learn as much as you can, incorporate the previous, most successful techniques and then create your own winning strategy.

ONLY GUIDELINES HERE, NO RULES. SORRY.

What follows is a way to develop your own framework for buying and selling stocks. These are good guidelines to know, but they are not rules. There are no absolute rules for buying and selling stocks except the ones you establish for yourself. If you are the kind of person who needs rules and has to know everything about an investment before you buy it, you will probably never own stocks. Like creating a great dinner, buying stocks is neither an art nor a science, but has elements of both. What follows are the main ingredients for successful investing.

KNOWLEDGE IS POWER. IGNORANCE
IS INEXCUSABLE.

You can never know enough about a company before you buy a stock. Accept this. Even the president of a company doesn't know everything necessary before buying the company stock. The president may be thoroughly informed and have absolute corporate control, but the president can't foresee or predict external factors such as interest rates, price competition or a war. These are events beyond the control of the company president, but they affect the economy and the industry in which the company competes.

As an outside investor, you certainly know much less than the president or other officers about a firm. However, this is often to your benefit. You can bring an objectivity to the company and its competition. Your outside sources of information such as America Online, Prodigy, *The Value Line Investment Survey*, *Investor's Business Daily*, and the *Wall Street Journal* will greatly enhance whatever publications you receive from the investor or public relations departments of a company. On the other hand, corporate officers will have inside information, such as the future plans for the company because they are the ones making and executing the decisions.

BIG INVESTING PLUS: MANAGEMENT OWNERSHIP

One of the most positive signals and a good indicator for buying a stock is when the corporate officers start purchasing their company's stock in meaningful amounts. For the investor, it's strong evidence that the company, in the view of the people who run it, is moving to higher ground.

Studies have repeatedly shown stock purchases by company officers correlate strongly with the upward performance of a stock. When three or more officers buy stock in one month, the price of the stock goes up over 70% within three years, according to one research paper (Professors Shannon Pratt and Charles DeVere, Portland State University, 1968).

Management stock purchases are reported in the *Wall Street Journal*, *The Value Line Investment Survey*, *The Insider's Report*, and numerous other publications, and by the SEC.

HANG ON TO YOUR WALLET A LITTLE LONGER

Before you charge out and spend all your money on a stock with this one characteristic, please wait. This is only one piece of evidence. Even if some indicator positively screams at an investor, no *one thing* ensures an investment will perform well. There is always a *combination* of positive factors, and the more of these factors you find in a stock, the better your chances of success.

It's like making the perfect meal: Having a great rack of lamb isn't enough. You need to complement it with fresh vegetables, a good red wine, the right spices and a light dessert before it becomes a meal worth savoring.

EARNINGS, EARNINGS, WHO'S GOT THE EARNINGS

A good meal has a main course, the entree. Similarly, in a stock there is a main ingredient that makes it stand out and look irresistible: growing quarterly earnings.

In his excellent book, *How to Make Money in Stocks*, William O'Neil describes the one common characteristic of the best-performing stocks: "In our models of the 500 best-performing stocks in the 38 years from 1953 to 1990, three out of four of these securities showed earnings increases averaging more than 70% in the latest publicly reported quarter *before* the stocks began their major price advance. The one out of four that didn't show solid current quarter increases did so in the very next quarter, and those increases averaged 90%!"

It can't be stressed enough: Earnings drive stock prices. In particular, look for increasing earnings by comparing one quarter with the same quarter of a year ago. It's important to compare on the basis of the same quarter because of the seasonality factor in business. Retail stores, for example, traditionally experience a strong final quarter because of holiday shopping. Various quarterly influences affect other industries similarly; so compare apples with apples by looking at this year's quarterly earnings with the same quarter of last year.

When examining those earnings, take into account any extraordinary items such as a gain from the sale of a subsidiary, or other one-time event; anything that won't happen again. Take those away, and you have operating earnings. They tell you how strong the company is. The operating earnings come from the continuing business, and they're the engine for future growth.

Look for earnings that have increased *significantly* from last year, applying your own definition of what is significant. I like to see increases of at least 25%. You may want to demand more before investing your money. Why not get the best? Of course, the more you demand of the earnings increase, the smaller the universe of stocks for your consideration. There will be stocks producing the increase you require, within reason, but you may have to look a long time to find them.

Be careful of only looking at percentage increases. If a stock has operating earnings of a penny one quarter and a nickel the next comparable quarter, the earnings growth is 400%. While it looks great statistically, it is highly unlikely that the company will continue to show growth of that magnitude.

To simply buy a stock based on one quarter's percentage earnings growth is not the purpose here. A stock with continued growth, quarter after quarter, is what you are seeking.

Corporate earnings are published in the *Wall Street Journal* and *Investor's Business Daily* and are on the Dow Jones and Reuters news wires on the day the company releases them. Most earnings are announced in January, April, July and October because most companies operate on a calendar-year basis. That means their year-end is in December and their quarters end in March, June, September and December. For comparing earnings, I like *Investor's Business Daily* because it calculates the earnings increase or decrease for you, placing the earnings into Ups and Downs columns that are easy to read.

To repeat, earnings are just the beginning. However, like your rack of lamb, they are the entree of your investment meal. And if a stock has accelerating earnings, say up 25% in one quarter and then up 40% the next, you can start getting excited.

Great companies get better and better as they venture into new markets, increase efficiency, or expand their market share. Their earnings surprises are joys instead of jolts. Such gemlike companies, like real jewels, are scarce but not impossible to find.

Remember Garan, Inc. from Chapter 1? Its earnings grew 41% per year from 1987 to 1991. In September 1991, quarterly earnings increased 62% from the year-earlier quarter. Then in the next quarter, the earnings were up 81% ahead of the prior year's quarter. Two quarters later, in March 1992, they were up 103%. This is the kind of earnings increase you're seeking. While the company was reporting these earnings improvements, the stock went from $38 to $74.

Earnings are the first and most important indicator for buying a stock, especially strong, improving earnings. Pick your stocks from the earnings reports in *Investor's Business Daily*, the *Wall Street*

Journal or other publication, with the minimum gains you have set for yourself, say 25% improvement, and then put them in a spreadsheet to start comparing them.

THE SPREADSHEET FOR POTENTIAL PURCHASES

Using a spreadsheet for comparing and evaluating stocks is a highly recommended practice. If you are unfamiliar with the use of computer spreadsheets, it is worth learning how to use them, and it isn't too difficult. You can purchase one of many financial software programs with spreadsheet capabilities, or obtain a free or inexpensive shareware version from a computer bulletin board or user group. The most common spreadsheets are Lotus 1-2-3 and Excel by Microsoft.

Set up your spreadsheet in columns: label the far-left column "Company" and put the stock symbol of each company down the column. Then across the top of the page, label each of the other columns with the information categories you will use to monitor a stock. Some were described in Chapter 5 and others will be explained in this chapter.

Use these as core statistics and column heads:

1. Cash flow per share
2. Profit margin
3. Return on equity
4. Return on assets
5. Earnings growth rate by quarter and by year
6. Percentage of stock owned by management and by institutions (two separate numbers)
7. Relative price strength (RPS)
8. Earnings Per Share Relative Strength (EPS)
9. Debt-to-equity ratio
10. Price as a percentage of book and of sales (two separate numbers)
11. P/E ratio
12. Target level to buy the stock

Once you've labeled your columns, you can start entering data about your chosen stocks. Most of this data is in the Strategic Investor on Prodigy, America Online in the Stock Reports section or in *In-*

vestor's Business Daily or *Value Line*. You'll have to determine which column should have priority so that the spreadsheet can display the stocks in the order in which you want to see them. Later in this chapter we'll use these data and more to develop an evaluation sheet for each stock. The purpose of this spreadsheet is to quickly compare all stocks you might buy.

Let's say you want earnings growth as the highest priority. This doesn't mean earnings are always the dominant reason for buying a stock. Never forget it takes a mixed menu of qualities to create the proper investment feast. Similar to the allegorical meal we're cooking, you have to decide on your recipe: what ingredients will be included, excluded, emphasized and in what combinations.

Before getting into these spreadsheet numbers, let's look at three other characteristics of stocks.

LOOKING AT CHARTS

In stocks the recipe for success isn't always the same, and there is no mathematical formula that works every time. In fact, one of the ingredients for finding good stocks is the graph or chart pattern of a stock. This is a visual rather than a mathematical tool. A chart is a graphic record of past price movement and stock volume plotted against time.

A good chart can tell you many historical facts about a stock, but it will not predict the future. Some people argue that charts are predictive, but I've never met a chartist, a person who gets paid to create and interpret charts, who would take the following wager: From a number of charts cut in half and randomly ordered, match the first half of any chart with its true second half. It's not possible except by random guesses. This doesn't mean charts are useless. It does mean that charts have limitations, but there's still plenty to learn from them.

The first is the stock-price action. Look at the chart on page 130. It tracks a company called Cognitronics Corp., a manufacturer of computer-related products.

Look at the succession of tiny crosses. Each vertical line represents a range of prices for one week. The horizontal line represents where the stock closed that week. In this graph, there is a period of accumulation between August 1991 and March 1992. The stock's

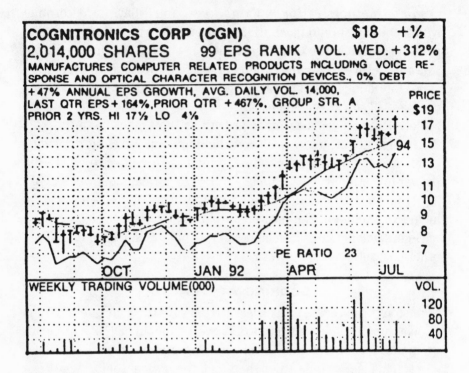

COGNITRONICS CORP (CGN)	$18 +½
2,014,000 SHARES 99 EPS RANK VOL. WED.+312%	

MANUFACTURES COMPUTER RELATED PRODUCTS INCLUDING VOICE RE-
SPONSE AND OPTICAL CHARACTER RECOGNITION DEVICES., 0% DEBT

+47% ANNUAL EPS GROWTH, AVG. DAILY VOL. 14,000,
LAST QTR EPS+164%,PRIOR QTR +467%, GROUP STR. A
PRIOR 2 YRS. HI 17½ LO 4½

PRICE
$19
17
15
13
11
10
9
8
7

PE RATIO 23

OCT   JAN 92   APR   JUL

WEEKLY TRADING VOLUME(000)   VOL.
120
80
40

share price is trading within a range of $7.50 and $10, and there isn't much volume every week as indicated on the bottom of the chart.

Now look how the volume increases dramatically at the beginning of March and the subsequent rise in price. There is another level of accumulation around $13, another increase in volume at the be- ginning of June, and another increase in price. The stock stabilizes again around $16, and the volume starts to increase in the last week reported.

There is definitely a pattern here, and one you can profit by: When you look at a stock chart, find one with a period of accumu- lation, that is, a time during which buyers and sellers have had the opportunity to move in or out of the stock. When the volume begins to increase dramatically and the stock breaks out of its accumulation phase, that is often the best time to buy. However, remember it's like our national motto: E Pluribus Unum. It's only one of many buying factors to consider.

With the addition of a chart, you now have three criteria for buying stocks: management purchase of the stock in meaningful quantities; strong, accelerating earnings; and a chart pattern with upward price movement and increasing volume.

Charts are published in *Investor's Business Daily* and *The Value Line Investment Survey*. There are also chart books by Standard & Poor's and software services such as Prodigy, Signal and Telescan, which create graphs on your computer screen. One of the advantages of America Online when it comes to graphs is that they're free. Most services charge a fee for a requested chart.

BUYING AT THE BOTTOM—MAYBE

Many investors make the mistake of trying to buy stocks at the bottom or trough of their chart pattern. The problem with this strategy is that you don't know how long the bottom is going to last or if in fact the stock has gone as low as it's going.

There's an old saying on Wall Street: "Bottom pickers turn into cotton pickers." Unless there is an impressive increase in volume and the stock has broken out of a period of stabilization, don't buy it. You will still make plenty of money buying the stock after it has lifted if the company is truly moving from its bottom.

BUYING AT NEW HIGHS

Don't be afraid to buy stocks that are registering new highs, especially if those price moves are fueled by improved earnings. Look at the chart on Cognitronics again. Over the time period in the chart, a new high occurred every three months, along with outstanding earnings.

Buying at a new high is probably a new concept because most investors are afraid of stocks at higher levels, preferring instead to buy when a stock has supposedly hit a new low.

Still working on our allegorical meal, think of the cost of the foodstuffs and particularly the wine you purchase. You know you have to pay the price for the finest victuals and viands. If you're buying a good-to-great stock, you also have to pay the price.

On the other hand, do not chase a stock while it is on a dramatic and continuously upward move. If you buy too late in the stock's ascent, it will usually do one of two things: stabilize where you bought it or go down. Chasing stocks is frustrating and expensive.

My advice is: *Don't* chase a stock. They're like buses: there is always another one coming to take you where you want to go. Besides, if you've developed a good prospective list of stocks from which to choose, missing one or two won't matter.

HAVE A PIECE OF P/E

The price-to-earnings ratio (P/E) is one of the most common measurements for a stock. Conventional wisdom holds that the lower the P/E ratio, the better the investment potential. If investing were that simple, everyone would buy those stocks.

As with other criteria, P/E ratios must be viewed within a broader context, as just one more factor to consider. It's like the Caesar salad with the rack of lamb we're preparing: a delightful addition, but only one course in our full and perfect meal.

The P/E ratio is derived by taking today's price of a stock and dividing it by the last four quarters' earnings. If a stock is selling at $20, having earned $2 per share in the last four quarters, its P/E ratio is 10. Peter Lynch, the famous Fidelity fund manager, suggests that investors think of P/Es as a measurement of the number of years it will take them to recover their money. In the above example, if the stock earns $2 per year, it will make back the $20 you spent for it in 10 years.

A P/E ratio by itself doesn't tell you much. If it is low, say 5 or less, it usually means that investors seriously doubt the earnings power of the stock and have dumped it. Most stocks have low P/Es because their earnings are slowing down. However, if the majority of investors who sold the stock are wrong, and earnings improve, then having a low P/E is a positive.

When a stock has a high P/E, it usually means that investors really, truly have faith in the stock. They believe that the earnings will be better than previously reported and will grow at some accelerated rate. A high P/E ratio is usually 25 and above. In February 1995, the average P/E of *The Value Line Investment Survey*, which covers about 1,700 issues, was 13.8 for all stocks with earnings. The highest estimated median P/E for the Value Line group was 16.9, recorded in September 1987, a month before the Great Correction. The lowest P/E level for the group was 4.8 in December 1974.

Many small-cap stocks achieve very high P/Es, and I don't know who buys them. This can be especially true of new issues. At one time, the casino stocks were hot. There is one called Grand Casinos, Inc. Its market niche is the management of Indian gambling clubs. The stock in one quarter reported a loss in earnings of three cents. The previous three quarters combined were a total of 19 cents earned. For the trailing 12 months, the total earnings were 16 cents. The stock was selling at $31. That's a P/E of 193, or about two centuries of living to recoup your investment.

The story on the stock was that most of the gamblers that went to the clubs liked them so much they wanted to own shares in the company. The gambling public was buying it while a large number of Wall Street professionals were "shorting" the stock, meaning that the pros thought it was going down because no stock maintains a P/E of 193 for long. Either earnings jump or the price drops. The stock bottomed at $12. This is the kind of stock to avoid.

So far, we've only looked at P/E measurements as they've applied to past earnings. However, most investors are buying stocks for the future. Research analysts and investors always try to estimate next year's earnings with some confidence, and then calculate a P/E based on that earnings estimate. In that way, a company may look cheap. If it has a new product or just signed a major client, the company's earnings will probably increase. Thus, although the stock seems expensive based on a P/E ratio of the last 12 months' earnings, it may look cheap based on the forecasted earnings.

There are several services that collect analysts' estimates for a company's earnings. One is Standard & Poor's ACE service. Another is Zacks Corporate Earnings Estimator, which forecasts earnings for 3,500 companies and 100 industries. This service is available on its own or as part of a package through Dow Jones News/Retrieval. Another company is Institutional Broker's Estimate Service (IBES) in New York, which is included in the Strategic Investor on Prodigy.

America Online has an excellent service from First Call that gives Earnings and Estimates for stocks. By entering the name of the company or its symbol, you can see what analysts are predicting for the next quarter, the next year, even the next five years for the company's earnings. As with all the services on AOL, there's no extra charge for this one.

A word of caution, however, on using analysts' projected earnings: They're wrong more often than right. Use them to gauge what expectations are, not as facts. Compare announced earnings with previous expectations, and then, sometimes, you'll know why the stock has moved.

RELATIVITY BUT NOT EINSTEIN'S

Another important aspect of the P/E ratio is how a company's P/E ratio compares with the market as a whole. In other words, if the P/E of your selected stock is 20, and the P/E for the S&P 500 Index is 10, then your stock has a *relative P/E* of 2. This means that the stock market believes your stock will grow at twice the earnings rate of the stocks in the index.

The point, for purposes of buying securities, is that by monitoring its relative P/E, you can determine if you are buying a stock at a low or high level within its own history. By using this method of valuation, which *The Value Line Investment Survey* does for each year a stock trades, the absolute P/E, in this example 20, is viewed within a useful context. By comparing its average annual relative P/E ratio, a stock can be historically cheap to the market even if the current absolute P/E ratio seems high.

To illustrate using the above example: if the average annual P/E ratio for a stock has been 15 and the average annual P/E ratio of the S&P Index has been 7 (it hasn't, but this is an example), then historically the relative P/E of this stock has been 2.14 (15 divided by 7). However, with the P/E of the stock at 20, is it expensive? It might be. However, it also might be *relatively* cheap because if the comparative index, the S&P 500, has a P/E of 15, that makes the relative P/E of our stock 1.33, much less than its previous relative level. A low relative P/E ratio is one more positive element to consider if the other buying attributes are present.

As mentioned above, relative P/Es are listed in *The Value Line Investment Survey*. You can develop your own records by keeping track of the P/E of your chosen small-cap stocks and dividing them by the P/E ratio of the Russell 2000 or the NASDAQ Composite indexes. Don't use the Dow Jones Industrial Average because it only represents 30 stocks, and they are large-cap issues.

In summary, the guideline for P/E ratios is that low P/Es do not necessarily mean you are buying a bargain. It's like finding a bottle of French wine on a clearance table and serving it to guests: It could be a steal, but more likely the market didn't want it, and it had to be marked down to sell. Conversely, buying a stock with a high P/E and strong, accelerating earnings could be a bargain.

You also need to compare the P/E of a company you are considering with its historical levels. Buying stocks with relative P/Es close to their historical lows is almost always a good decision if everything else in the buying mix is there.

One rule of thumb the pros use with P/Es: Earnings should be growing at least as fast as the P/E. If a stock is selling at 20 times earnings, it should be growing at least 20% a year. One investment strategy is based on finding stocks with P/Es that have half the growth rate of a stock.

Use the P/E to growth comparison as one way of determining if a stock is too expensive for your investment consideration. In other words, if its P/E is 20 and its earnings growth rate is 10%, the stock better have a great story or you won't enjoy owning it.

EVEN MORE STUFF

If you select a stock with high management ownership, accelerating earnings, an historically low relative P/E ratio and a chart with a price pattern breaking out of an accumulation period with high volume, your odds for success look good. These are proven attributes of the most successful stocks. The future might change this, but for now these are the strong indicators.

However, there are still at least 10 other numbers to consider before buying a stock. Some are important within certain industries, and less significant in others. They're briefly described below, with guidelines as to their importance.

1. INSTITUTIONAL OWNERSHIP

How many institutions own how much of a company's stock? This number can be found in Standard & Poor's *Stock Guide* or obtained from the Company Reports section of Strategic Investor from the Prodigy Service. Too much institutional ownership will throw your stock into the institutional arena, which is where you don't want to be. Too few institutional holders, or none at all, means the stock has no following and limited liquidity.

Ideally, you want at least 5% institutional ownership of a company's stock. In fact, Frank Capiello, president of McCollough, Andrews & Capiello, Inc., an investment advisory firm returning compounded average growth of 17% annually, has said that at least 5% of a stock should be owned by institutions for it to perform well; however, if institutions own more than 30%, there is little buying power left because most institutions with an interest in the stock already own it.

2.   RETURN ON EQUITY

This number is the net earnings of a company divided by the value of the equity. For example, if a company has net earnings of $10 and equity of $100, it has earned 10% on its equity. The return on equity tells you how much money is actually being made for the equity investors. This number shows you how much your investment is earning after all other expenses have been met. A return of at least 10% is what you want. Warren Buffet, the legendary stock investor, believes that return on equity is the most important number for your investment consideration. (Robert Hagstrom, Jr.'s, book *The Warren Buffet Way* is highly recommended.)

You can find the return on equity for a stock in the Stock Reports section on America Online, the Company Reports section of Strategic Investor on Prodigy, in research reports, *The Value Line Investment Survey*, or compute it from the annual report.

3.   RELATIVE STRENGTH

This is a statistic found in *Investor's Business Daily*. It measures a stock's price change over the last 12 months against all other stocks' price changes. On a scale of 1 to 99, the higher the number, the better the stock has performed. This tells you what the market thinks of your stock. If you believe in going with the flow, the relative strength will tell you how strong the tide is for your particular stock.

4. EPS RANKING

Another helpful number in *Investor's Business Daily* is the earnings per share (EPS) rank. The exact definition is given in the paper, but its importance is that it compares a company's earnings with all other companies' earnings in the stock tables. This is also based on a scale of 1 to 99. A stock with an EPS rank of 95, for example, means that its earnings are in the top 5% of all stocks in the tables.

Obviously, this is a helpful number to know when looking for a healthy company. Because earnings drive a stock, you know this is an important indicator. If your emphasis is buying only the best, this ranking helps you stay in the top 10% if that's where you want to be. Be aware, however, that EPS rank is based on earnings over the last five years and doesn't give you any insight into the future earnings prospects for a company.

5. DEBT-TO-EQUITY RATIO

This measures how much a company owes: its debt is compared with its equity. The equity is the amount the shareholders own. Some companies have no debt, which gives them a ratio of 0. Other companies have twice as much debt as equity, or a ratio of 2. Some capital-intensive industries have relatively high ratios because they borrow to buy equipment such as railroad engines or trucks, whereas service industries have little need to borrow.

To put the debt-to-equity ratio into perspective for the company you are considering, look at the industry average. If the company's ratio is higher than the industry average, is it expanding? Is it taking too high a risk with debt? If its ratio is lower than most others, is it too conservative? The individual company and industry ratios are supplied in the Company Reports section of Strategic Investor from Prodigy.

Debt is not necessarily a negative indicator. Many companies use it wisely and well. However, too much debt is like too much of anything: It's not good for you. The leveraged buyout debt of the 1980s has come back to bite many of the senior managers of the companies that issued it. Some of that debt, such as the bankrupt Macy's, did more than bite. It ate those companies.

6.   CASH FLOW PER SHARE

Cash is always good to have, either personally or for a company. This number tells you how much cash each share is generating. The more cash flow a company has, the less likely it will go out of business. In a new company, this number will often be negative because of start-up costs. However, in a service company or less capital-intensive company, cash flow should be positive, and again, the higher the number, the better for you.

If you have invested in a capital-intensive industry, such as automobiles, there may be a huge cash flow during the upward part of a business cycle because sales are strong. However, when the company has to retool and the cycle is on a downward path, the cash flow will quickly turn negative. If the firm is not adequately capitalized for this event, the negative cash flow will drive it to failure.

Look for a cash flow percentage at or above 10%, a general industry standard. For example, a stock selling at $40 with cash flow per share of $4 means that you're recouping 10% cash on your investment. If the percentage is better than this, you are doing well. By the way, this should be "free cash" flow; that is, the cash that is left over after all the debt payments, other cash obligations and capital expenditures have been paid.

The cash flow per share and free cash flow numbers can be found in Prodigy's Company Reports section or in *The Value Line Investment Survey*. Brokerage houses also generate this number in their research reports on a company.

7.   RETURN ON ASSETS

This is the earnings of a company divided by its total assets and measures how efficiently a company uses its assets compared with others in its industry. The higher the number, the better the investment.

Compare your potential stock investment to its industry average. For example, having a 2% return on assets in the banking industry would be phenomenal, but that same return is totally unacceptable in the pharmaceutical industry. You need to look at your company against its competition to see if it is the best in the group.

Return on assets is provided in the Strategic Investor's Company Reports section of Prodigy, and in research reports; it can also be calculated from the annual report.

8. **PRICE AS A PERCENT OF BOOK VALUE**

Book value of a company is defined as all the assets of a company less the liabilities, excluding the stockholders' equity. In theory, you could sell a company's assets for their value as reported in an annual report because the assets have been depreciated. After selling the assets, you could pay off the outstanding debt, and whatever is left you would keep.

The quickest way to calculate this number is take the shareholders' equity value of the company and divide it by the total number of shares the company has outstanding. If a company has a book value of $10 per share, and its stock is selling at $50, the stock is selling at five times its book value. This is an expensive stock. Of course, if a stock has no equity remaining, the book value is infinite, but for purposes of this illustration, assume you are looking at a stock with equity.

Conversely, there are many stocks, particularly in the savings and loan industry, selling well below book value. GlenFed, an S&L in Southern California, at one time sold at 16 percent of book value. That's because investors didn't believe it would survive the economic downturn in California as well as the regulatory environment in which it operates.

Obviously, the lower the price-to-book number, the better your odds are for success, if the company survives. There is a particular group of investors that focuses on buying stocks which have very low price-to-book ratios. They're called value investors. They patiently wait for other investors to determine value in the same way they have. Many of the LBOs in the 1980s were found by using this measurement. Also, value investors thoroughly analyze a balance sheet and try to determine if a company is carrying valuable assets, such as real estate or a trademark, well below their true value and buy the stock based on what they think those assets are worth. Like beauty, value is in the eye of the beholder.

For our purposes, this is just one more ratio or ingredient to consider. Many small-cap stocks will sell at rather high price-to-book ratios. That doesn't make them a bad investment. However, if you find a small-cap stock with increasing earnings and a low price-to-book value, you strengthen your chances for success.

This calculation is made for you or can be derived by using Standard & Poor's *Stock Guide*, *The Value Line Investment Survey*, research reports, or from the Stock Reports site on America Online. Once you generate the number yourself, you'll see how easy it is to calculate.

9.   PRICE-TO-SALES RATIO

This number tells you how much you're paying for the revenues of a company. For example, if a company has sales of $10 million and has 1 million shares outstanding, the sales-per-share ratio is 10. If you pay $20 for the stock, the PSR, price-to-sales ratio, is 2, or $20 divided by $10. If you pay $4 for the stock, the PSR is 0.40, or $4 divided by $10.

Ken Fisher, in his book *Super Stocks*, claims the lower the PSR, the better your chances of making money in a stock. Think of the PSR as a macro way of evaluating a stock: How much are you paying for the sales a company makes? Oftentimes, the less you pay, the higher your returns.

Small-cap stocks have a wide range of PSRs. However, Fisher's studies show that the vast majority of excellent stocks have PSRs below 1, while stocks with PSRs above 3 are odds-on losers.

While the PSR is an excellent guide for buying a stock, it is also a good indicator of when to sell. When a stock's PSR gets too high relative to its industry group, a stock will probably go down in price. If you insist on holding a stock with a high PSR, you should have good reasons for it because a high PSR goeth before a fall.

PSRs are found in the Stock Reports site on America Online, *Value Line,* or can be calculated from the annual report by dividing revenues by the number of shares. Divide the stock's price by this number.

10. PROFIT MARGINS

How much, as a percentage of sales, does a company earn? That's the question answered by determining the profit margin. Divide a company's net income by its revenues to find this number. If the percentage is high, the company is good at earning a profit; if it is low, watch out.

Each industry has a different level of profit margins. For the pharmaceuticals, before the Clinton administration came to office, margins were above 25%. For food supermarkets, margins are closer to 1%. By comparing your stock with its industry average (the Company Reports section of Prodigy does this), you can determine whether you're buying an industry leader or lagger. High profit margins give comfort to the nervous investor.

However, they also encourage competition within an industry. Unless your company has a unique and patented product, be aware that competition will soon enter any market niche where margins are high. Conversely, low margins discourage competition and drive out weaker companies in that sector.

LIVING WITH IMPERFECTION

Finding a stock with all the right ratios is impossible. Many will have low PSRs and low P/Es, but also low earnings and low cash flow. Others will have high earnings and high cash flows, but also astronomical P/Es and off-the-chart PSRs. Your job as an investor is to compromise on certain ratios when the other ratios or the story on the stock are so compelling that they overwhelm the negative factors.

By using your spreadsheet and looking at each stock, you can prioritize the elements you want in your investments. If cash flow gives you comfort, then make that your number one attribute for buying a stock. Or perhaps return on equity is your most important gauge. Whatever it is, rank your stocks by it, then compare all the other ratios. Each stock will be strong in some areas and weak in others.

Then go to the story on the stock. Call the company and ask for its investor relations department. Request the annual and quarterly reports as well as the 10-K and 10-Qs. While you're waiting for their arrival, start following the stock. Don't buy it yet. There are still some factors to consider.

THE BIG PICTURE AND BUYING

Of the many influences affecting the stock market, the level of interest rates is the most profound. When interest rates go down, stock prices usually go up. Conversely, when interest rates go up, stock prices usually go down. I use "usually" because nothing is always the same on Wall Street. Think of a seesaw with interest rates on one end and the market on the other and money flowing between the two.

There is a simple explanation for this relationship: Money goes where it makes the most. As interest rates rise, the return on investing in bonds goes up. Money flows out of the perceived more risky stock market and into higher-yielding, safer bonds. If you are in an economy with rising interest rates, expect stock prices to fall.

However, it is impossible to forecast interest rates. As a wise friend used to say, "Anyone who predicts interest rates and acts accordingly usually has a low net worth."

Your portfolio of small-cap stocks should be driven by earnings, not interest rate forecasting. Even in a down market, you can still see some stocks improve. Good stocks produce good earnings in all markets. Stick with the earnings, and you'll be rewarded even if the market is going down. Sometimes it will take longer than an IRS refund, but you will be rewarded.

To further add to your confidence in buying small-cap stocks with good earnings, look back at the graph in Chapter 1. Notice how investors in this sector always made money, even when they bought at the highs of the market.

To Sum It All Up

On the next page is what I call my stock evaluation sheet. You can use this or create a new one from it. You can put it on your computer or use it on paper. It's a handy way to help you buy and sell securities.

If you decide to put it on your computer, create a directory called EVALUATR (the computer file name can only be up to eight letters) or some other name you like, then input the information. This will create a template for you to use on every company you evaluate. The company's stock symbol can be used to name each file. You can then produce a summary of each stock by simply inputting the data in the correct files and storing them in your computer. It is easily updated when new information is released.

Or you may like to keep a binder filled with this information for each company on this form. It's a convenient way to look at the important characteristics of a stock.

Either on the computer or on paper, the stock evaluation sheet is a useful tool for buying and selling.

Most of these items and the methods to locate or calculate them have been described earlier in the chapter or in Chapter 5.

Using the Evaluation Sheet

For investors interested in one way of using the evaluation sheet, my way, please see Appendix B. It shows you how, by giving numerical weightings to various numbers, you can develop a priority system for investing in stocks.

Where to Find the Numbers

All the information on the evaluation sheet is derived from three sources: Every statistic from the price down to the percent owned by institutions comes from the Company Reports section of the Prodigy Service (most of them can also be found on the Stock Reports site on America Online); *The Value Line Investment Survey* will give you the information from number of insiders buying in last 12 months to average annual P/E; and the final line will come exclusively from *Investor's Business Daily*.

So When Do You Buy?

There is no exact, mathematically correct time to buy stocks. That moment is recognized only in retrospect, after you see on a chart

STOCK EVALUATION SHEET

DATE:	STOCK SYMBOL:
COMPANY NAME:	PHONE NUMBER:
PRICE:	52-WEEK HIGH: LOW:
P/E:	YEAR AGO: INDUSTRY:
PRICE-TO-SALES RATIO:	YEAR AGO: INDUSTRY:
PRICE/BOOK IN %:	YEAR AGO: INDUSTRY:
PROFIT MARGIN:	YEAR AGO: INDUSTRY:
RETURN ON EQUITY:	YEAR AGO: INDUSTRY:
RETURN ON ASSETS:	YEAR AGO: INDUSTRY:
DEBT TO EQUITY:	YEAR AGO: INDUSTRY:
QUICK RATIO:	CURRENT RATIO:
SALES GROWTH 1 YEAR:	3 YEAR: 5 YEAR:
EARNINGS GROWTH 1 YEAR:	3 YEAR: 5 YEAR:

LATEST QUARTER: INCOME GROWTH (%):   EARNINGS PER SHARE GROWTH (%):
                            SALES GROWTH (%):

YEAR-TO-DATE COMPARISON: INCOME (%):   EPS (%):   SALES (%):

FREE CASH FLOW PER SHARE

TOTAL SHARES:

MARKET VALUE

% OWNED BY MANAGEMENT: % OWNED BY INSTITUTIONS:

OF INSIDERS BUYING IN LAST 12 MONTHS: SELLING:

PROJECTED EARNINGS FOR NEXT QUARTER: DUE OUT: FOR YEAR:

RELATIVE P/E: FOR LAST 5 YEARS:

AVERAGE ANNUAL P/E: 1 YEAR AGO: 2:   3:   4:   5:

RELATIVE STRENGTH: RELATIVE EPS:

where the stock hit bottom. Likewise, there is no exact time to sell, except in hindsight at the zenith on a price chart. No loud bells clang when the lows or highs are achieved.

You should buy stocks when you feel comfortable with them. Your job is to gather as much information about the company as possible, watch its stock and get to know it well. Sometimes, particularly if a chart pattern looks promising, you will buy right away and make money. Other times, that same chart pattern will simply be an upward blip followed by a downward trend.

I like to buy a beginning position in a stock, anywhere from 20% to 50% of my target amount, most often 5% and never more than 10% of the total portfolio, and then watch what happens. If the stock goes up, I happily ride it. If it goes down more than 20% without news or a reason for the drop, I add to the position. I buy more because the stock is more valuable at this lower price if nothing has changed at the company. I check on America Online or call the company to make sure there is no news I might have missed.

Many times, I won't buy a stock for a while, but set a target price and wait for it to reach my level. If the stock gets away, I don't chase it. There are plenty more.

Setting a price target has to do with your own comfort level. You may want to buy only at book value or at a slight premium to book. Other times, you may want to buy at the lowest relative P/E multiple. If you rely on a chart, look for the point at which the stock will break out of an accumulation pattern with volume. In that example, you are setting a price target above the current level.

There is no one proven method for buying a stock that works every time. When you feel comfortable with a stock because it fits most of the criteria discussed in this chapter, you will be buying at the right time for you.

SETTING LIMITS

When you're ready to buy, consider using "limit orders." These are simply buy orders with price limits. Often with small-cap stocks, if you place an order to buy more than 100 shares, you might only get 100 shares at one price, and the rest at higher prices. However, if you use limit orders, that is, you specify exactly the price you will pay for a stock, you won't be forced to pay a higher price for it.

The only drawback to limit orders is when others are also buying the stock without limit orders. In that case, your stock can get away from you. However, most of the time, limit orders save you money, and you still buy your stock.

WHEN TO SELL?

This is the hardest part of the investing challenge. Most money managers will tell you this is what gives them sleepless nights. Every day they have to decide whether *now* is the time to sell.

One approach is to automatically sell after taking a predetermined profit, say 20%. The problem with that philosophy is that it limits

stock you want. In that case, you need to pay the offering side of the market or use another firm that makes a market in the stock. When you place an order, ask the broker if the firm makes a market in the stock. If so, try a limit order to buy a stock on the bid side of the market or try to sell on the offer side of the market. You'll save considerable money if you buy or sell the stock.

If the stock market is crashing around you on the day you go to sell, you may be able to sell only a portion of your shares. Then the bid will go lower. If you don't absolutely need the proceeds, be patient, use limit orders (orders with a price below which you will not sell) or wait until the stock comes up again. However, if you determine the stock isn't performing well because of a basic change in its business or industry, simply accept that you must get out at a bad price. If your analysis of the company is right and you're convinced it's not going to improve, get out. Until the stock gets to zero, it can always go lower.

Be willing to take some losses. This is extremely difficult. It means you were wrong. However, you must be able to do this to be successful. You have to accept your mistake and lose money. However, you will get over it, and it will deepen the pleasure you derive from your winners.

INVESTING OR SPECULATING: KNOW THE DIFFERENCE

Benjamin Graham, an acknowledged master investor, in his book, *The Intelligent Investor*, says: "An investment operation is one which, upon thorough analysis, promises safety of principal and an adequate return. Operations not meeting these requirements are speculative."

The emphasis here is on *thorough analysis*, as defined by your own comfort level. I have observed most good investors are thorough and, just as important, patient. Let me repeat that: Good investors are patient. I think that quality deserves almost as much emphasis as analysis.

If you have used the above investing criteria to increase your odds of success, the final requirement is to watch the stock over time. I don't mean minute by minute. You don't need to watch a stock-quote machine to succeed. In fact, Warren Buffet, the most successful investor of our time, doesn't have one in his office.

AMAZING BUT TRUE

To prove that patience is rewarded, the following statistics were generated by Ibbotson Associates over the period from 1925 to 1990 and are based on the S&P 500: The chance of losing money in a stock investment in one year is 24%, in five years is 6%, in 10 years is 1% and in 20 years is 0%.

However, being human, we have a need to watch stocks closely. The best advice I can give you is to make sure you allow plenty of price gyrations while you hold your investments and stay informed on them.

TRUST ME ON THIS ONE THING

As for trading the market, you can't do it. Trading is when you think you can buy and sell stocks on a daily basis and make money. All stock brokerage firms will love to have you as an account because you will generate huge commissions for them. Unfortunately, you'll only generate losses for yourself.

The odds are stacked against you unless you have a real-time stock ticker and a news tape you watch every second and pay no commissions. That's what stock brokerage firms have and if they are right 51% of the time, they're happy. They make a little money. You can't play in that game. You would be back in the big leagues, right where you don't want to be.

But you will trade. So use a small portion of your portfolio, lose it, and then focus on investing. Buy at your comfort level, and sell at your level of discomfort, based on thorough research and thoughtful decisions.

ONWARD TO BUILDING A PORTFOLIO

With the information in this chapter, you're now armed with knowledge and ready to buy stocks. Wait a little longer. You can't just randomly buy stocks and hope for the best. You've got to build a portfolio. And much like building a house, you need to plan carefully, work within a budget and watch the builder. Only now, you're the builder.

CHAPTER SEVEN

DEVELOPING YOUR PORTFOLIO:
SMALL PIECES OF A
BIG PIE

Before you start buying small-cap stocks, you need an overall portfolio strategy. Simply buying a few stocks and hoping for the best will not make you successful. You must have a thoughtful, personal approach that reflects your risk profile. And once you have assembled the stocks, you need to manage the portfolio.

A successful small-cap investor has many stocks, is well diversified across several industries and has limitations on how much is invested in any one company or industry. This chapter will help you develop a portfolio strategy that is comfortable for you. However, before you can build a portfolio, you have to understand yourself and how well you tolerate risk.

YOUR RISK PROFILE

Some investors have no problem if their portfolios have a high degree of risk, while others want no risk at all. Unfortunately, the latter group often interprets no risk as meaning a collection of Treasury bills. There certainly is no risk in that strategy, but after you factor in inflation, there is also no reward, none, zip. Even in a very low-risk portfolio, investors need to incorporate an element of equity investing if they are to keep ahead of inflation over a long period of time.

Part of successful investing requires an understanding of your personality and your tolerance for risk. One of the objectives you should achieve in your portfolio strategy is peace of mind. By knowing yourself, you can shape your portfolio to minimize the anxiety you might feel when investing in small-cap stocks.

Take the following quiz. It helps you determine how much risk you are willing to accept and how to shape your portfolio accordingly.

THE RISK QUIZ

1. I am conservative. True or false?
2. I prefer investments that entail an average level of risk to principal in the pursuit of high asset growth. True or false?
3. I prefer aggressive investments that entail higher-than-average risk of loss of principal in the pursuit of high asset growth. True or false?
4. To what degree is the main purpose of your investment portfolio to provide current income to cover living and other expenses? ___ High ___ Moderately high ___ Low.
5. It is often possible to receive higher capital gains by taking a greater risk of loss of principal. Given that trade-off, how much risk of losing some of your money are you willing to assume to obtain higher profits? ___ Maximum gains/substantial risk ___ High gains/some risk ___ Reduced gains/minimum risk.
6. The total amount of the debts you currently owe is excessive enough to make you very vulnerable to adverse changes in market conditions or personal financial circumstances. True or false?
7. What portion of your annual income are you able to save for investment purposes? ___10% ___8%–10% ___4%–7% ___1%–3%.
8. How much of your investment dollars will you need back for major expenses or other purposes in the following time frame?
   ___ Within two years: Amount _____.
   ___ Within two to five years: Amount _____.
   ___ Five to ten years: Amount _____.

9. Current investments:	Amounts	Percentage of Assets
Savings Accounts	_____	_____
Money Market	_____	_____
Bonds or Income	_____	_____
Funds	_____	_____
Equity Funds	_____	_____
Real Estate	_____	_____
Common Stocks	_____	_____

LOOKING AT YOURSELF

The first three questions are obvious in their intent, but they are only starting places. As you go through the rest of the questions, you may discover you are more risk tolerant than you think, or you may be more risk averse. In addition, your current circumstances may require you to be more careful at the present time than you would like to be, or they may allow you more risk.

That is the intent of the fourth question. If you have high current income needs, the small-cap portion of your portfolio has to be minimal to nonexistent. Most small-cap stocks do not have the capital to pay out dividends. They're too busy growing and require every bit of internal and external capital they can raise. The highest and best use of their money is to fund the expanding company with new people, new machines and new acquisitions, and not to pay out dividends.

That isn't to say there aren't some small-cap stocks with decent returns. Garan, Inc., which is fully described in Chapter 1, has paid generous dividends to its holders over the years. In 1992 and 1993, the yield on the stock was close to 6%. However, the majority of the dividend was paid at the end of the year with a special dividend after the company had earned it. It isn't something an investor can count on every year.

Another stock, Oshkosh Trucks Class B, pays a dividend of $0.50 and is currently selling below $10 per share for a yield of more than 5%.

It is possible to find yield in small-cap stocks, but yield is not the usual reason to buy them. If income is your priority, buy high-quality, fixed-income securities and keep only a small percentage of your investments in small-cap stocks, in the 5% to 10% range.

IS IT REALLY HIGH RISK/HIGH REWARD?

The trade-off of high risk, high reward is not so straightforward in small-cap stocks. While the perception is that all small-cap stocks are risky, the reality is that many are solid, strong companies. To categorize all small-cap stocks as high risk is to dismiss a large segment of the investment universe unfairly. While most of them are higher risk than large-cap stocks, a percentage of your total assets belongs in them. Your comfort level will dictate what percentage that should be. Suggestions are made below for your risk profile.

If you answered question 5 with maximum gains/substantial risk, then your portfolio should contain between 25% and 60% small-cap stocks. If your answer was high gains/some risk, then you should have between 20% and 30%. If you answered reduced gains/minimum risk, you should have between 10% and 20%.

DEBT CONSIDERATIONS

If you need to pay off debts with the money you are considering investing, pay off the debts or at least keep a cushion of savings for monthly payments for the next two years. There is an absolute certainty in the marketplace you don't want to fight: When you need your money the most, your stocks will be at their lowest levels. Then you're forced to sell at a loss. You become unhappy. You swear never to invest again. This attitude does not allow you to win big.

Stay in control of your investments by keeping your debt payments well within your current income with six months of living expenses saved in a liquid investment. Remember, small-cap investing is not always liquid, and the difference between where you buy them (the offer or ask side of a quote) and where you sell them (the bid side of the quote) is often great. It is not unusual for a small-cap stock trading in the over the counter market (the NASDAQ market) to be bid at $6.25 and offered at $7.

As soon as you buy the stock, you are already down 75 cents. If you had to sell it immediately, you lose over 10% of your investment. And that doesn't include the commission charged for buying and selling the stock.

Manage your stocks and debts. Don't put yourself in a position of having to sell stock to pay an interest or principal payment. You won't like the prices.

ALLOCATING YOUR INCOME

The younger you are, the less you have for investment. You have mortgage payments, furniture, cars, clothes to buy, children to feed, the full adult program. Amid all of these obligations, you owe it to yourself and your loved ones to allocate money to buy small-cap stocks. Every month, make it a point to invest in them. Even if it's 1% of your income, make it part of your spending pattern.

If you are older, most of your purchases have been made and a greater percentage of your funds can be invested rather than spent. Be sure you enjoy some of the extra income that this stage of your life provides. However, also put more into your investment portfolio, allocating funds for fixed income, and large- and small-cap stocks. Your portfolio, like your life, should have a balance.

The fact that you are an older investor does not mean that small-cap stocks are inappropriate. It only means they should take up a smaller percentage of your portfolio. You cannot afford to have a small-cap vacuum. When inflation roars back, your "safe" fixed-income portfolio will have the characteristics of Pee-Wee Herman. What you'll need is Arnold Schwarzenegger.

TIME AND MONEY

If you have a major expenditure such as a child going to college or a son or daughter getting married, you should have a minimum of small-cap stocks in the portfolio allocated to fund that obligation. You need time to work through any negative surprises a company might have. Sometimes that's only one or two quarters. Sometimes it's one or two lifetimes. If it's the latter, you should sell immediately.

Small-cap stocks have greater volatility than other investments. This creates opportunities for buying when the stocks are irrationally cheap or for selling when they are too rich. However, the volatility is done when the market wants to do it, not when you are ready for it. Usually two years is enough time to have a good stock recover, and please note the use of the adjective good. In fact, even bankruptcies usually emerge into a new entity after two or three years, if a company emerges at all. However, if you need money in two years, you don't want to rely on small-cap stocks for it. The chances are too great you will have to sell at the wrong time.

If you have two to five years to meet an expenditure, then you should have at least 80% of your small-cap allotment invested. For example, if you had a $10,000 portfolio and you were comfortable with half of it in small-cap stocks, invest only $4,000 in small-caps and put the other $1,000 in a safer place such as a Certificate of Deposit or a Treasury note.

If you have longer than five years, you can assume a full position of small-cap stocks. You have plenty of time to ride out the vicissitudes which will inevitably visit some of your stocks. To use the same hypothetical portfolio described above, you could put the entire $5,000 into small-cap stocks.

CURRENT PORTFOLIO ALLOCATION

The final question in the risk profile quiz gives you an understanding of how you are currently managing your assets. Look at your answers. Is there too much in real estate? You should only count your equity, not the full value of the house or property if you have debt on it.

Or maybe you have most of your investments in bonds or income funds. No well-balanced portfolio has more than 35% in any one of the three major investments: equities, fixed income, and hard assets, usually real estate or gold.

If you have nothing or a small percentage in equities, you need to rebalance your investments. If you have too much in real estate and a recession, such as we saw in the early 1990s occurs, you could lose some or all of your equity. If you have too much in fixed income and there is rampant inflation, such as that of the 1970s and 1980s, you lose some or most of your principal. Depending on the stocks you buy, you can benefit from either of these economic problems. The key is to keep a balance in all of your investing.

Too many people feel they absolutely, positively, know which way interest rates or the economy is going, and put all of their investments to work in the one that will benefit when their economic scenario comes to fruition. Sometimes they are right. However, if they are wrong, that strategy wipes them out.

I like to remind people of how the investors who owned the Titanic must have felt just before it set sail. They must have been feeling pretty good, maybe even cocky. After all, they had just made an investment in something that literally could not go down. The next time you get too excited about any one investment or strategy, remember the *Titanic*.

PUTTING THE PORTFOLIO TOGETHER

It's time to put your stock portfolio together. I am assuming you are balancing your assets among real estate, fixed income and stocks. The portion I want to address is the fixed income and stocks.

IF YOU'RE UNDER 30

If you are younger than 30 years old and have a high risk profile, your portfolio should have 20% fixed income and 80% stocks. Small-cap stocks should be 75% of the stock portion of the portfolio, which means they comprise 60% of the total portfolio.

If you have a medium-risk profile, 30% of your funds should be in fixed income and 70% in stocks. Small-cap stocks should be 50% of the stock portion, or 35% of the total portfolio.

If you are a low-risk taker, 40% of your investments should be in fixed income and 60% in stocks. Small-cap stocks should be 40% of the stock portion, or 24% of the total portfolio.

IF YOU'RE 30 TO 50

You have to be a little less aggressive now, even if your risk profile is high. If you are comfortable with aggressive investing, you should have 30% in fixed income and 70% in stocks. Small-cap stocks should be 60% of the stock portion, or 42% of the overall portfolio.

This book does not address large-cap stocks, but a word of caution is in order: IBM. Everyone knows this stock, and most investors presume it means safety because it is so large. Being large does not make an investment safe. IBM went from $120 to $46 in a little over a year. The collapse came mostly from a shift in the way computers were purchased. Instead of buying large mainframe computers, a market in which IBM dominated, businesses preferred personal and mini-computers. They bought everything but IBM.

A similar story is occurring in the drug industry. Major changes in health delivery systems are eliminating profits, as well as the way drug stocks are evaluated. Don't think big means safe. The market is a dynamic entity and requires your diligence whether you buy small- or large-cap stocks.

If you are more moderate in your approach to risk, you should have 40% in fixed income and the rest in stocks. The small-cap issues should be 50% of the total stocks, or 30% of the portfolio.

If you have a low tolerance for risk, then make fixed income 50% of your investments and 50% in stocks. Put 40% in the small-cap issues, which makes then 20% of the total portfolio.

IF YOU'RE OVER 50

You need to be realistic. Your ability to replace lost capital is impaired by the limited time you have to replace it, not by your work skills. However, this does not mean your money should go under the mattress to be counted every night. Nor does it require you to buy Treasury bills every three months.

You still need to have a balance in your portfolio, but now the fixed-income portion needs to be larger and the small-cap stocks are fewer. Remember, inflation may be dormant while you are reading this, but it will come back. If it doesn't, it will be the first time in all of recorded economic cycles. Don't bet against all those other cycles. Use stocks to fight the certainty of inflation.

If you want to be more aggressive, invest 50% of your funds in fixed income and 50% in stocks. Place half of the stock portion in small-cap issues; that makes them 25% of the portfolio.

For moderate-risk takers, put 60% in fixed income and the remainder in stocks. Make small-cap issues half of the stocks, and you'll have 20% of your total investments in them.

If you want the least risk, put 70% in fixed income and 30% in stocks. Then have small-cap stocks comprise 15% of the portfolio.

DIVERSIFY, DIVERSIFY, DIVERSIFY

Before you buy anything, understand how you want the total portfolio to look when it is complete. Much like a recipe for a pie you want to bake, your portfolio plan should be in place before you make your first stock purchase.

The key to a good portfolio is diversity and balance. Some people believe in buying only a few stocks and watching them closely. You can do that, but if one of your chosen stocks had been Synergen

Incorporated, you could have closely watched it drop 26 points in one day. Bad things can happen and *will*.

However, if Synergen had been less than 5% of your portfolio, even had it gone to zero, your life still would be unaffected except for the emotional wrench that large declines elicit. Realistically, you can afford to lose 5% of your portfolio. However, if you have only three or four stocks and one craters, you are out 25% to 33% of your investments. This would be more than emotionally disturbing.

The first rule, then, is to diversify. That means you diversify across industries as well as stocks. Have at least five to 10 industries in your portfolio, never letting any one be more than 20% of your total investment. And be honest about your industry groupings. Make each one unique.

Also include in your industry groupings your employer, if you have stock in the company. Many people have a disproportionate amount of their portfolio in company stock. I did, and I worked for Drexel, Burnham, Lambert. At one time, the firm had over $4 billion in capital, some of it mine. Now there is no capital or firm.

Trust me on this: Really nasty things happen. Don't believe everything management tells you or that the company's stock can go nowhere but up. Count your company stock like any other, no matter how attractive it may seem. You may find you're overweighted in that one investment. Sell some of your stock and put yourself back in portfolio balance.

Your company also has to be counted in its industry group. Too many people think they know enough about their own industry to have a competitive advantage over other investors. That is probably true. However, no matter how well you know your company or industry, exogenous shocks will hit either or both of them. Again, remember the Titanic.

Therefore, the first diversification is by industry. No one industry should be more than 20% of your portfolio. The second level of diversification is by stocks. Limit yourself to no more than 10% of your investing in any one stock, no matter how great it sounds.

This is one of the hardest rules to follow, especially if a stock has deteriorated in price for no apparent reason, and you just know it's going to rebound. The stock can't go any lower. It's such a bargain.

The stock *can* go lower. Perhaps there is a reason for the decline, but it hasn't been publicly announced. Or maybe there is no specific reason, but, over time, it becomes apparent that the entire industry will suffer from pending legislation. Or maybe there is no reason at all. It doesn't matter. After you have committed to buying the company, limit your purchase of it to 10% of your funds.

One last element of your portfolio structuring: invest all the funds. Any money you have allocated to investing should be invested. When you try to time your purchases, you are usually subject to the human conditions of buying when every one else is and selling with them also. That is not how you make money.

Good investments will appreciate even in bad markets and to try to be a market timer is impossible for most investors. Stay fully invested because you never know when the market will explode on the upside.

However, if you feel the market is close to a top and is too expensive, sell out of your high P/E stocks and go into low P/E stocks, or the safest, high-yielding stocks.

This is not to suggest you don't have any cash for emergencies. You should have cash for debt payments and living expenses. That money isn't counted in your portfolio. Your portfolio funds are for investing, and by being fully invested, you can maximize your returns.

THE STOCKS YOU SHOULD BUY

Start by thinking about the industries you want to own. The following industries and stocks are presented as ideas to investigate before you invest, not as recommendations. Furthermore, because these have prospered previously is no indication they are adapting to the ever-changing needs of the marketplace.

These industries represent the growth areas for the 1990s:

INFORMATION PROCESSING

The major change in computing is the shift from large mainframe computers to smaller, mini-, micro-, or personal computers. IBM was big in mainframes, but it didn't respond to this change soon enough. The stock went from $120 to $46, and there is concern that the mindset that built the company will not be entrepreneurial enough to meet the new world. The president was fired, and a new one hired.

The companies that most prospered in this consumer shift were Dell Computer Corp., Compaq Computer, Intel Corp., Cisco Systems,

Apple Computer, American Power Conversion Corp., Cabletron Systems, Hewlett-Packard, Key Tronic Corp., Sun Microsystems, 3Com Corp., Microsoft Corp., Oracle Corp. and Novell Inc.

These companies focused on providing equipment or software that made smaller computers more productive on a stand-alone basis or through networking with each other. This evolution will continue. The current push is to make computers more portable, more versatile and faster. The companies that give consumers these attributes in their computers will be the solid winners in the 1990s.

ENVIRONMENTAL MANAGEMENT

For lack of a better term, the above is used to include all the environmental industries: waste management, solid and liquid; waste-to-energy conversion; toxic cleanup; and water purification. Unfortunately for the world, there is a tremendous need for these services. As an investor, this need represents opportunity. There will be new companies emerging to solve many of these problems because the old approach of simply burying waste isn't acceptable.

While companies like Waste Management International and Wheelabrator Technologies, Inc. have the economies of scale currently needed, look for the next generation of environmental solutions to come from small, innovative firms. The natural evolution will be collecting trash, separating and cleaning it, capturing the gases emitted from burning it and then recycling most of the by-products.

HEALTH SERVICES

Similar to information processing, this industry is going through changes that require faster, more efficient delivery of health services. While the established, larger firms will be hurt, the newer, more flexible ones will flourish. An example of a prospering company under the new rules is Columbia/HCA Healthcare Corp., which acquires several hospitals in an area and then centralizes the management, the billing and the purchasing while providing most necessary medical services.

Other examples are the generic drug companies, mail-order prescription firms and health maintenance organizations (HMOs). This last group will go through a period of consolidation as the industry requires greater efficiency to compete. As with all investments, the winners will be the lowest-cost producers with the best profit margins. Two of the better ones are Genesis Health Ventures and Mid Atlantic Medical Services. The former specializes in long-term care, and the latter has invested heavily in technology, giving it a cost-efficiency advantage.

Another area of explosive growth will be in biotechnology. Biotechnology companies do research and develop drugs that are biologically-based rather than pharmaceutical-based, which depends on chemical compounds. The strongest advances against cancer, muscular dystrophy, AIDS and kidney failure are coming from this industry. The more famous firms are Amgen, Inc., Genentech Inc. and Biogen.

However, before you simply buy these three firms, none of which is a small-cap firm, beware. Price movement in this industry is extreme. Genentech stock in five years went from $4.50 to $65.25. In the same year (1987) it was at $65.25, it went down to $22. The following year, it went from a high of $47.50 to a low of $14.38. The price histories of Amgen and Biogen are almost as volatile.

You need nerves of steel to be involved in this industry, but you are rewarded if you buy them right. My current favorite is a small firm called ImmunoGen, Inc. It is also duly noted that this company will not generate a profit before 1998. Its competitive advantage is that it has a two- or three-year lead time in the development of the drugs necessary to fight certain cancers.

COMMUNICATIONS

Similar to the Olympic slogan of faster, higher, stronger, the key phrases for communications are lighter, smaller, clearer. You will soon be able to purchase a portable pocket-size telephone that will function anywhere in the world. You will also be able to send and receive faxes through this same phone. The work on this kind of phone is being done by several companies. The investment opportunities will come from the small-cap companies that create the internal chips, manufacture the phones and create the new applications. Don't think only the big firms like AT&T, Sprint and MCI are in the telecommunications business.

And don't think communications only means the telephone lines or cellular phones. Included in this category are the cable industry with companies such as Multimedia, Inc., long-distance line resellers

such as LDDS Communications and telephone equipment manufacturers such as ADC Telecommunications, Inc., Andrew Corp. and
DSC Communications.

If you want to participate in foreign telecommunications, look at
stocks like Telecommunicacoes Brasileiras (Telebras) in Brazil or
Hong Kong Telecom. They could be even more rewarding than Tele-
fonos de Mexico, whose American Depository shares went from $1 3/8
to $60 in five years. Watch out for the hard jolts along the way.

OLD THINGS NEW WAYS

Some of the most successful investments have been basic, un-
complicated stocks. Every big winner doesn't have to be in the
electronics or medical industry. The most powerful example is Home
Depot. Here's a company that is a hardware store, a very big one, but
nonetheless it's your basic hardware store. They took the concept to
its ultimate level by using a warehouse, low overhead and a sophisticated information-systems approach.

The same is true of Wal-Mart stores. These are variety stores. The
first one was very small and in a tiny town in Arkansas. But the
founder, Sam Walton, had a vision that would put these stores all
over America. The key was to keep the shelves constantly stocked
with the right merchandise. So he kept track of every sale on computer and reordered items as soon as a customer bought anything.

Another simple idea is Toys "R" Us. This is a company selling toys,
lots of them. Nothing new or high-tech about it. Some of the toys may
be, but the basic concept is a very large toy store that sells toys at the
lowest prices. Charles Lazarus, the man credited with the firm's success, transformed a bankrupt company by bringing the warehouse
approach to toys. He also used sophisticated computers to monitor
his store sales and for reordering.

These three companies are just a few of the examples of basic
companies applying a new approach to an old business and making
huge successes. One common trait is their use of computers for inventory tracking and orders. Competitive pressure will require that
in the 1990s. The other elements of success for retailers will be lower
prices, better quality and service and greater choices.

Now that you have some suggestions for where growth will occur,
you need to make your stock selections, purchase them and develop
a portfolio.

MANAGING YOUR PORTFOLIO

Once you have purchased your stocks, you need to manage them. That means keeping track of when you bought them, how much you own, what percentage of the total portfolio each represents, how much you paid for them, for how much you sold them, when you sold them, whether you had a long- or short-term gain, how much cash you have in your account, what percentage each industry represents and many more considerations.

You need software to physically manage all of this information, and some guidelines to emotionally manage it. The software available ranges in cost from free to more than $5,000. A description of some of the programs will follow. But first, a few emotional guidelines.

KEEPING IT UNDER CONTROL, EMOTIONALLY

Expect the unexpected. Change is constant in the market. I did my homework on a stock, called the company to verify everything, received all the information from the company and then bought the stock. Two days later, it went down 33% because its earnings were below expectations. Furthermore, because it is in the water business as a purifier and a drilling company, the heavy rains in California that year rendered the company's services unnecessary. Its contracts in the Golden State were canceled. Therefore, the future earnings of the company were expected to be flat for the next two years.

I called the company again, and the CFO was most accommodating, answering every question professionally. Naturally, he couldn't give me any inside information, but I didn't hear any positive reasons to buy more of the stock nor any strong negative reasons to sell except that earnings were expected to be flat. Given my growth requirement for investing, I had to sell the stock even though the company would survive. There are too many other stocks with growth in earnings to sit on one that will be flat for two years.

Even though the earnings in this company had been growing nicely, and it had the dominant position in its industry, the future earnings didn't appear to be there. It had to be sold even though I had just bought it.

Expect change, deal with it rationally and move on. If a stock goes up after you sell, it might be because of a pleasant surprise. If you find the stock attractive given that new information, buy it again.

Don't buy a stock and think you are done. Buying and holding stocks forever rarely maximizes your wealth. It can if the earnings continue to grow, but few companies have ever done that. You have to monitor each stock for news and every quarterly earnings release. Companies change, for the good and the bad, and each stage of their evolution requires you to make a new decision to either buy, sell or hold. Stay on top of your stocks by checking your on-line service for news every day. On America Online, look in the Company News or Dow Jones sites.

DON'T JUST SELL

It's only human to want to get out of a stock when it drops dramatically. When it does, you have to keep your head while all others around you are losing their assets. Look at your stock again. If the stock market has collapsed because of program trading, does that mean your investment is terrible? Look at your reasons for buying the stock. Are they still valid? If so, this is a buying opportunity, or at the very least, it justifies your holding the stock.

If the company has changed fundamentally, use this downdraft in the market to sell the stock and buy a strong one at an attractive price.

Any of the three choices of buy, sell or hold is a good one as long as you have taken the time to reexamine your stock and objectively come to a decision. To simply sell because a stock is down is a sure way to lose money.

Recently, I bought stock in a computer company after it had dropped 12 points in one day. I had been following the company and felt comfortable in buying its stock. Soon after my purchase, the price drifted down another eight points. The usual emotional wrenching ensued. I looked again at all the data I had, reread all the articles on the company and decided to hold the stock. Within four months, I sold it with a 15-point profit.

It was a tough several weeks to endure, but one of the company's so-called problems was that it couldn't ship product fast enough; its backlog was building. I thought this was a positive because the sales were obviously going well, and the company had taken steps to remedy the supply problem. I bolstered my confidence by rechecking the facts and waited for the market to get back to the basics of earnings. It did. And it always will.

HISTORY REPEATS ITSELF,
SO WILL YOU UNLESS . . .

You're reflective. You need to look back on your mistakes and learn from them. When you sell a stock for a loss, think about what caused it. What was wrong with your analysis? Was there a surprising shock that was unpredictable or were there warning signals in the corporate quarterly or annual reports? Could you have been more thorough in your analysis? Are you doing enough research on the companies?

If you've lost money in an investment, don't try to buy two or three times as much of another stock and increase your risk. And don't beat yourself up for losing money. That's part of investing. Also, don't lose your ability to make investment decisions. You need that confidence to buy when everyone else is selling. Accept losses as part of the cost of doing business. You'll find when you look back on your profits and losses that the pain has diminished. In fact, every day you move away from the loss and get more involved in your new investments, the better you'll feel.

KEEPING IT TOGETHER, PHYSICALLY

The sooner you buy software to manage your stock portfolio, the easier your life will be. Appendix C gives the names, approximate cost, a brief description, and addresses of some manufacturers of portfolio software. This list does not include every possible software company because there are new ones arriving continuously. However, by studying the attributes of these systems, you can determine how much of a program your budget allows and what benefits you will derive from each one.

WHAT YOU WANT

There is a minimum level of information you need from your portfolio management program. A history of your purchases and sales is vital. When you buy a stock, you need to keep a record of the purchase date because when you sell it, the IRS wants to know if it is a long-term or short-term capital gain. Oddly enough, the purchase date is often the most frustrating statistic to find, especially if you've owned a stock for years and can't find the original confirmation. Also, the brokerage firms will generate an annual report of all your sales and their dates, but they don't give you the purchase dates, especially for stocks you've bought prior to having an account with them.

Obviously, they can't know that information, but it is frustrating they don't supply the purchase dates for your transactions with them. The software you buy will do that.

You need to categorize your stocks by industries. So the program should give you the option of categories such as Automobile, Airlines and Aerospace, Information Processing, Manufacturing, Biotech, etc. Allow yourself about 45 to 50 different industries. And your program should let you create your own industry headings.

Your program should calculate the percentages of each stock and industry. For example, if you have 10% of your funds in Chrysler Corp., 10% in General Motors and 10% in Ford Motor, then your program should show that and also indicate that you have 30% of your portfolio in the automobile industry. This is a very helpful tool for keeping your portfolio balanced.

You need to know how much cash you have in your account. To do that effectively, you need to keep your portfolio on a trade-date basis rather than on a settlement-date basis. The difference is that the trade date is the actual date you buy or sell a stock; the settlement date comes three business days later. If you are an active investor, you'll need to keep track of your available funds, and the best way to do that is by trade date.

Lastly, you have to be able to generate a yearly report that gives you the profits and losses of your trades as well as the income from dividends and interest in your account. This feature alone will pay for the program and is greatly appreciated around April 15 of each year. Also, if you generate most of your income from your portfolio, you'll need a quarterly report so you can send the IRS your quarterly tax estimate payment. A good program will allow you to specify the beginning and ending dates for any time period. That way, reports can be generated by any quarter, month or year.

MORE THAN THE BASICS

More sophisticated programs will allow you to track and automatically download your dividends and stock splits, break out your brokerage commissions, always an eye-dilating number, and performance by security. They'll also track your performance against any index such as the Dow Jones Industrial Average or the S&P 500 Index.

The best indexes for a measurement of small-cap stocks are the Russell 2000 or the NASDAQ Composite Index. As the names imply, they track thousands of small-cap issues. You can measure your small-cap investing performance against them by noting the level of the indexes on the day you start your portfolio. Then, every quarter determine how much the indexes have moved as a percent versus how much your portfolio has increased or decreased. Sometimes, you will be pleasantly surprised. Other times, you'll feel different. Again, the more sophisticated programs will do these calculations for you.

PORTFOLIOS TAKE TIME

Portfolios take time to build and to monitor. You shouldn't take all your funds and simply throw them at 20 different stocks. You need to watch your selected issues. See what happens to them on major down-swings in the market or on days when the market surges upward.

An old adage on the Street says that price is an investor's best friend. It means you can do a lot of research and find the right stock, but if you don't buy it at the right price, you can wait a long time to be rewarded. Be patient to buy your stocks at the right price, and be patient to sell them.

Also take the time to monitor what you own. If you have a data service like America Online, make a daily check for news or earnings reports. The AOL Portfolio site is linked to many news services by an icon called News By Ticker. Just double–click on the icon, enter the symbol of your stock and you'll see the day's news for the company. Check your stocks daily for price movement and news.

At least quarterly, look at the performance of your portfolio and each stock. How are you doing against the indexes? Have your stocks performed to your expectations? If they haven't, should you keep holding them, sell them or buy more shares?

Try to cut out the stocks that are vegetating because of lack of earnings growth. If the earnings are down for two straight quarters, sell a stock unless there is a compelling story. However, if manage-ment is cutting costs and therefore incurring one-time expenses for severance pay, or the company has introduced new products that have high marketing costs initially, then give the stock an opportunity to absorb these one-time events. If these changes don't improve the bottom line in the following quarter, sell the stock.

THE SOFTWARE ITSELF

As previously mentioned, Appendix C lists software programs, their contents and their prices. You will find a good variety but not every manufacturer is represented. This list is a good place to start and will give you a benchmark for comparing any other software that is not on the list. As with most software, the simpler it is to use, the more you'll use it. Take a look at the appendix now and start your research. You need one of these programs or one similar to manage a portfolio.

CHAPTER EIGHT

SMALL-CAP MUTUAL FUNDS,
BIG REWARDS

When I was in business school, one of my finance professors wanted to start a mutual fund. He hadn't determined exactly what he'd invest in, but he knew what he would call the fund: Up Your Assets. He was sure the name alone would make investors want to buy it.

The name certainly conveyed what every investor wants. Though he didn't develop the fund, there are thousands of others trying to increase investors' wealth. Many of them specialize in small-cap stocks. These funds are perfect for investors who don't have the time, knowledge or money to invest in diversified industry groups by buying individual stocks.

Mutual fund investing in small-cap stocks offers an easy way for investors to participate in this profitable part of the market. Investors with limited capital of less than $1,000 can use mutual funds to diversify their investments. Other investors with large portfolios can buy funds for specialized sectors such as biotechnology or health care, where they have limited knowledge but recognize the profit potential. And investors with little time but great interest in small-cap stocks can let the mutual fund pros manage their money.

Sometime during your investing investigations, you will want to know how to find, analyze and use mutual funds. Similar to stocks, there are many databases and publications waiting your inquiry.

WHAT ARE MUTUAL FUNDS?

Think of a person sitting behind a desk with a sign saying: Give me your money; I will invest it for you. With your money I will buy stocks in companies that are open only on Tuesday. I will charge you fees for doing this.

That's what a mutual fund does. It takes in money from many people and invests it in a specified way. The rules for what or how the fund invests are described in its prospectus. The prospectus is a small booklet with a full description of the fees the management receives, who is managing the fund and what stocks or bonds the fund can buy. By law, every detail about the fund must be contained in the prospectus. That's why you should read it. Then you'll know exactly how your money is being invested.

While the above descriptive paragraph is too simplistic, it adequately describes how a mutual fund works. Investors give money to a fund investing in a way the investors want but don't have the knowledge or sufficient money by which to invest on their own. There aren't any funds dedicated to buying companies open only on Tuesdays, but give the mutual fund industry a few months. However, there are several thousand mutual funds, and at least 300 are dedicated to small-cap investing.

TWO TYPES OF FUNDS:
CLOSED-END AND OPEN-END

Closed-end funds are similar to stocks in that they trade on an exchange, usually the New York Stock Exchange. These funds are also referred to as exchange-traded funds. Closed-end funds have issued shares, like any other company, and the money given the funds is invested in a specific way, described in the fund's prospectus. Once the fund has issued its shares, the shares trade freely on the exchange. Anyone wishing to buy into these funds must purchase them on a stock exchange from investors selling their shares. For the funds' purposes, they are "closed" when the original stock is issued.

Open-end funds don't have stock trading on an exchange. They continue issuing new certificates as long as investors want to give them money. The one exception is when the managers of a fund decide they have enough money for their particular investment philosophy, and they decide to close the fund. This rarely happens, but be aware that the phrase "the fund is closed" does not refer to a closed-end fund. It literally means the fund is closed to new investors.

NET ASSET VALUE, DISCOUNTS AND PREMIUMS

Open-end funds trade at their net asset value (NAV). Every day the fund totals up the value of its investments and divides that by the number of shares it has outstanding. This number is the net asset value of the fund. This amount is what new investors will pay for their shares. There may or may not be a commission, also known as the load, added to the NAV, and there may or may not be a transaction fee. More about that later.

In contrast, closed-end funds can trade at premiums, or discounts, to their net asset value because investors may perceive the funds as great or terrible. The economic law of supply and demand is very evident in this sector. When a fund has performed well, investors bid up the shares beyond their net asset value, happily paying a premium for what they believe will be continued outstanding returns.

If a fund has not done well, investors vent their wrath by selling. Some will sell the fund for less than its net asset value. They want out because they feel the fund's performance will get worse.

At this stage of the book, you should be thinking: When something sells at a discount, like buying dollars for ninety cents, opportunity is pounding on my door. You're thinking correctly.

You can buy many closed-end funds at prices below their net asset value. For some funds at certain times, the discount is small, say 2%. That same fund may later trade at a premium. Or it may trade at a larger discount, say 20%. There are no limits to premiums or discounts because investors can buy or sell shares until a price level is found that stabilizes the price. That may be a very high premium or a very low discount.

Remember, these are funds that invest in stocks or bonds and value their portfolios every day. You can determine how much their investments are worth, or their net asset value, by looking in the *Wall Street Journal* every Monday or in *Barron's*. There is a page devoted to closed-end funds, and each fund's net asset value is published along with its current selling price and the premium or discount that selling price represents to net asset value. Many people make a lot of money buying deeply discounted funds and then selling them when they go to a premium.

OPEN OR CLOSED FUND, WHICH DO YOU BUY?

The one that's right for you. Here's how to determine that:

- First, get in the right sector of funds. Small-cap funds have names with growth or aggressive growth, small-cap and micro-cap in them. The first group, growth funds, invests for long-term growth without undue risk, usually in companies the fund managers believe have long-term growth potential.

  The last three, small-cap, micro-cap and aggressive growth invest in companies the managers believe will have rapid growth in the near term. This group of funds is, as the name implies, the most aggressive, offering the highest risks and rewards of the funds. Many of these funds and their toll-free numbers are listed in Appendix D.

- How much time have you got? If you have less than two years to invest in a growth or aggressive growth fund, don't do it. Some would argue that less than five years is too short a time frame. Like any small-cap stock, give yourself ample time to reap the rewards from your investment.

- Variety is the spice of life, and it doesn't hurt your portfolio, either. Don't commit too much to any one fund, certainly not more than 20% of your available money. You're buying diversity when you invest in the fund. The managers combine your money with other investors' and buy many stocks. No one stock represents too large an investment, usually not more than 3% of a portfolio, so you won't have too much exposure to any one stock.

  You also need to diversify by industry, just as if you were buying individual stocks. You should have at least five small-cap funds, each representing a unique investment: health care, biotechnology, technology, telecommunications, emerging markets, special situations, financial institutions, etc.

- Who manages the fund and how long have they been doing it? This information is available in the prospectus and from your on-line database service. Later in the chapter, we'll go through all the information on mutual funds available from one service, Prodigy.

You're looking for someone with experience. If the manager has had less than five years in a job, he or she probably hasn't experienced a really bad and/or a very good market. You want a real pro at the helm when the markets are crashing, everyone is selling and there seems to be no hope. That's when pros are buying, not joining the herd.

- What's the fund's track record? Look for 10 years of performance, that usually includes most of the volatility of the market. If the fund is newer, look at the experience of the manager.

The performance should be very good in good markets, and good in down markets. One of the problems with certain investment styles is that they outperform the markets in one direction, but are terrible in the other. For example, some funds with returns in the 40% to 50% range in a strong bull market will probably be down 30% to 40% in a bear market. You're better served with a fund that is up with the bull market and only slightly damaged by a bear market.

A good place to compare annual performances at a quick glance is in *Investor's Business Daily*, on the mutual fund page. It compares the last three years with the S&P 500 Index for each year and then gives the performance of the fund year to date. You should also be able to use your on-line service for this information.

Always compare a fund with other funds in the same group, not just to an index. If you like a certain health care fund, check to see how it did against the other health care funds over a three-, five-, or 10-year period. If you only look at the fund against an average, you may not be buying the best fund in the group.

- Has the fund grown too big? Small-cap funds have a limited universe of investments, especially sector funds. A sector fund invests in only one sector of the market, such as medical devices or computer peripherals. If a fund has too much money to throw at relatively few investments, it can hurt the performance of the fund. Any time a small-cap fund has more than $250 million, you want to double-check its invest-ment guidelines. If the fund is narrowly restricted to certain types of investments, it may have to invest in stocks that are overpriced just to get the money out the door.

Remember, if you're buying a fund for its expertise in a certain industry, you have to sell that fund if you think the industry is about to tank. Your fund will keep investing your money in those stocks because that's its job. Don't think fund managers will switch out of one industry into another if they manage a sector fund. They can't. Their charter is to buy those stocks. And keep buying them or hold cash. You have to get out of the fund if you want out of the industry.

- Is the fund charging too much to take your money? There are a number of fees funds can charge: management fees for managing the money as well as a sales charge, or the load, which is a sales commission to pay the broker or financial planner who sold the fund, usually ranging from 2% to 8% of the money invested. Load can be charged at the front end, when you buy the fund, or at the back end, when you sell, or throughout the holding period.

If you buy a front-end load fund with $2,000, and it has a load of 8%, only $1,840 of your money goes into stocks, the remainder goes to the broker. If you pay 12(b)-1 fees, which are deducted annually to pay for marketing the fund, your returns are diminished by the amount of this fee. Other expenses, such as fees charged to cover operating and ad-ministrative costs, are in addition to the management fees.

The amount you want to look for in the fees of a fund is nothing to minimal. You should also have a very powerful reason to buy a fund with a load on it. No study has shown that load funds outperform no-load funds. You're not buying extra performance when you buy load funds; you're buying your broker's lunch.

One more fee you may pay is the transaction fee when you buy an open-end, no-load fund. This fee is charged by the broker, whether it's a discount broker or a full-service broker. However, many brokers have negotiated deals with no-load funds wherein no transaction fee is charged for buying the fund. The broker is paid by the fund from its 12(b)-1 or management fees. When you buy no-transaction-fee funds, all of your money goes to work.

Other fees to look for: back-end loads, charged when you leave a fund; level loads, charged every year you own the fund; and hybrid loads, which charge a little up front, a little along the way, and a little when you leave.

The Vanguard group of mutual funds has some of the lowest fees in the industry. Always check if they have a fund for an industry or type of fund in which you have an interest.

Closed-end funds, because they trade on an exchange, have normal commission charges, like any stock you would buy. If you buy these at a deep enough discount to their NAV, your commissions still won't have you paying a premium for the fund.

- Portfolio turnover, or how much does the manager buy and sell stocks? You know how commissions can hurt your returns. Buying and selling stocks adds costs to your portfolio. Even though mutual funds can buy and sell stocks for pennies per share, if they do it too often, those pennies add up, but not in your favor. Excessive portfolio turnover can sometimes mean the fund manager is trying to trade the market rather than invest in it. Or the manager may be switching among sectors, trying to get on board the hottest group of stocks. Not only is this expensive, it raises the volatility of the fund, creating wide swings in performance.

The prospectus for the fund will tell you how your money will be invested. If it states profits are expected to be made by trading the fund aggressively, it's not investing, it's trading. Also, historical data will tell you the percentage of the portfolio that has been traded. If it's over 200% every year, that's excessive trading. If there's too much portfolio turnover, don't buy.

So Those Are the Questions— Where Are the Answers?

Turn on your computer and follow me. Your on-line service should have the scoop on mutual funds. I'll walk you through Prodigy's data, and you can see if your service has similar information.

If you have Windows, sign on to Prodigy by putting the arrow on the Prodigy icon and clicking your left mouse button twice. Give your membership number and password; once connected, you will be on the Highlights page and can read the news. You can reach the mutual fund information two ways: type the letter "j" and the Jump box will be highlighted. Hit the Return key and then type in "Mutual Fund Reports." You must be a subscriber to the Strategic Investor service to go to this page.

Or when you sign on, you can move the arrow to the Business/Finance box. Double-click with the left mouse button and the screen will change to the news events for the business day.

On the right side of the page, you'll see a box labeled Research. Move the arrow with your mouse and double-click on this box. Another box will appear with a list of options. Choose the one saying Mutual Fund Reports by moving the arrow on the words and double-clicking the left button of the mouse. Once again, you must subscribe to the Strategic Investor option to receive this database.

The screen will change again and two choices are given. Select the one entitled Select Mutual Funds by moving the arrow to the highlighted box and clicking once. This will put you on another screen, which will give you four options: Search by Fund Name or Symbol; Fund Family/Group; Investment Objective; and Performance Period.

Searching by fund name assumes you know the fund you want to analyze. If you do, type in the fund name, and the program takes you to the first of three pages of data on the fund. I've compressed those three screens on the following page and used the Twentieth Century Inv: Giftrust Investors Fund as an example because of its outstanding long-term performance. Let's look at the information on the fund.

The first line gives you the name of the fund: Twentieth Century Inv: Giftrust Investors, and the symbol: TWGTX. This symbol can be added to your Quote Track program on Prodigy, and if you are following or own the fund, the price will be updated daily for you. This symbol is also handy to have when buying a fund because many funds have similar names but each has a unique symbol. The symbol keeps the confusion to a minimum.

The next line tells you the fund's objective: Growth-Aggressive and when the fund started: 11/83. If you want a small-cap fund with

PRODIGY(R) interactive personal service 01/02/95 4:14 PM

MUTUAL FUND REPORTS

Information provided by Investment Company Data Inc.

Twentieth Century Inv:Giftrust Investors Symbol: TWGTX
Objective: Growth - Aggressive Started: 11/83

Period Ending	-Rate of Return (%)-		Difference	-Decile Rank-	
11/30/94	Total	Annualized	from S&P 500	Obj.	All
1 month	-4.24	-40.57	-4.68	7	9
3 months	11.28	53.35	+68.00	1	1
1 year	20.21	20.21	+19.17	1	1
3 years	106.20	27.28	+17.66	1	1
5 years	174.75	22.40	+13.56	1	1
10 years	883.22	25.68	+11.21	1	1
Market Cycle	51.29	15.62	+1.49	2	1

Sales Charge (max)	0.000 %	Expense Ratio	1.00 %
Redemption Charge (max)	0.000 %	12b-1 Fees	0.00 %

Fund Family: TWENTIETH CENTURY GROUP
Fund Manager: Team Managed (since 1983)
Current Prospectus: 04/94 JUMPword: TWENTIETH CEN

ADDRESS TELEPHONE NUMBERS
4500 MAIN STREET Toll-Free 800-345-2021
P. O. BOX 418210 In-State 816-531-5575
KANSAS CITY MO 64111 Facsimile 816-340-4753

MINIMUM PURCHASE REQUIREMENTS FUND FEATURES

	New Account	Existing		
			Phone Switching:	Yes
Regular Acct	$250	$50	Withdrawal Plan:	No
IRA/KEOGH	$250	$50	IRA/KEOGH Accts:	Yes

ASSET COMPOSITION DISTRIBUTIONS PER FUND SHARE

Report Date: 09/30/94		Date	Income	Cap. Gain
Net Assets: $239.4 (mil)		1/1-11/30/94	$0.0000	$0.0000
Cash/Equivalents	5.8%	Last:12/20/93	$0.0000	$1.9107
Common Stock	94.2%		
Preferred Stock	0.0%	KEY VALUES
Convertible Issues	0.0%	Dividend Yield	0.00 %
Warrants	0.0%	Turnover Ratio	143.0 %
Corporate Bonds	0.0%	Average Maturity
Municipal Bonds	0.0%	Beta	1.42
Gov't Securities	0.0%	Alpha	1.08
Other	0.0%	Volatility	6 (med)

aggressive growth with a track record, you know this is one worth considering.

The data presented in the following lines give the performance of the fund for one month, three months, one year, three years, five years, and 10 years. That performance is annualized and compared with the S&P 500 Index. Then it is compared with its peer group and all other funds for the same periods.

Looking at the one-month data, you can see the fund decreased 4.24%, and if it continued to do that every month for a year (annualized), it would have a rate of return of –40.57%. The one-month return was 4.68% below the S&P 500 Index. The final two columns compare the negative 4.24% return for the fund with the other aggressive growth funds, which placed it in the lower 70% (7th decile) of the growth funds, and with all other funds, which placed it in the lower 90% (9th decile) for the one month. As you will see, this was a bad and unusual month for this fund. In the Prodigy database, there were 303 aggressive growth funds at the time of this writing and several thousand for all funds.

Is this performance good or bad? Well, it's pretty bad for one month when compared with all funds, and you know there are better-performing funds because this one only ranked in the lowest 70% of its peer group. But remember, one month's performance does not a fund make. So let's go to the next lines.

For three months, one, three, five and ten years, it scores in the top percentile for its peer group and all funds. It has done very well compared with all funds for a long time period and stayed on top for aggressive growth funds.

The use of deciles to rank the fund refers to a system using 1 through 10, where 1 is the top 10%, 2 is the top 20%, etc.

Should you buy this fund? Based on only these numbers, you know it looks promising. What you don't know, and can't unless you call for the prospectus, is the focus of the fund. What is the niche in which it invests? When you read about the fund, you'll know if it has a specialization which fits into your portfolio and fills a need.

Now we get to the expenses of buying the fund. There is no fee or load to buy the fund. A note of caution, however, is needed. This doesn't mean a broker won't charge you a transaction fee for buying the fund. That fee goes to the brokerage firm for processing the trade.

If there had been a load or sales charge, there would not be a transaction fee in addition to that because the broker would be paid from the sales load. In this case, there is no sales charge, but remember there will probably be a transaction fee if you buy it through a broker.

The next fee to consider is the expense ratio: 1.00%. Is that high or low? It's in the middle to low end of fees charged by aggressive funds. You should know that aggressive growth funds require more trading and more new ideas. Their fees will usually run higher than a more traditional growth or balanced fund.

The next line states there is no redemption charge. That's a fee you'll be charged by some funds when you sell them. Most of the time, this fee diminishes with time until it reaches zero, usually over a three- to five-year period. The objective is to keep you in the fund to let the manager have the time to achieve a good return. If the market turns bad a month after you buy in, and you want your money back, the manager has to sell stocks to give it to you. By charging a high redemption fee, you are penalized for not staying with the fund.

Is it fair? That's not the right question. The right question is: Do you want to pay someone a fee for getting your money back? In this fund, you don't.

Also on this line is the 12(b)-1 fee, or the marketing and administrative fees: 0%. Some funds will charge this fee in addition to the management fee, claiming they need it to market the fund. Watch out for funds charging management fees, 12(b)-1 fees and redemption fees. All of these fees come out of your pocket and affect your return. Compare fees as well as performance data when looking to buy a fund. All of these data are conveniently available on the Prodigy system. America Online uses the Morningstar database and has very similar information. It also doesn't charge for the service.

WHO AND WHERE ARE THESE GUYS?

The next page gives you details on who the fund manager is, in this case, it's a team, not one individual. It also shows how long it has been managed: since 1983. Ideally, a manager has been with the fund for more than five years, and the fund has done well. When making the trade-off between the length of time of the manager and the performance, take the performance every time. In other words, if a manager has been there for 20 years and the performance is mediocre, there is no consolation or better returns in knowing the manager is an old hand.

For this fund, because a team manages it, you can assume an investment philosophy has been well researched and used for guiding the managers. In that way, managers can come and go, but the fund will continue to perform well.

The data for these pages are from the fund's most current prospectus. Prospectuses are usually updated at least once a year. You will want this document if you have an interest in investing in the fund. It tells you everything about the fund. Do not buy a fund without reading its prospectus.

Where can you get this information? From the fund, and the address is given as well as the toll-free phone number and the fax number. If you want to contact a fund, you can do so three ways and all the numbers are given on this page.

The next set of numbers tells you how much you need to buy into the fund. Some funds have a minimum dollar amount. This one does for regular and IRA or Keogh accounts—$250.

The fund also allows phone switching, which means that the fund is part of a family of funds available from the Twentieth Century Group. You call the group up, tell it you want out of one and into another of its funds, and it will switch you into it.

If you do buy into this or most other funds, you don't always need a broker to do it. You can send most open-end funds your check directly, after you've read their prospectuses carefully, of course. The fund will buy the shares for you and send a copy of the purchase for your records. You can then follow the price of the fund in the newspaper on a daily basis or on your on-line service. The Prodigy service has Quote Track, which follows any stocks or funds when you input their symbol. America Online has the Quotes and Portfolios program for tracking, and CompuServe also has this feature.

So What Does the Fund Buy?

The last page tells you what kind of investments the fund buys, how much it paid out for this year and last, and several other key measures.

The Asset Composition column tells where the fund is investing on the day the report is made. In this case, it was September 30, 1994. The fund had $239.4 million to invest and had 5.8% in cash and

94.2% in common stocks. Because the fund is in the aggressive-growth fund category, you know most of those stocks are small-cap.

A comment on the cash position: usually, funds have low cash positions, say 1% to 3%, when the managers feel very bullish on the market. When they're bearish, cash can go as high as 100%, although this rarely happens. A more defensive posture can be assumed once the cash position goes above 10%.

The distributions for the fund look like they come at the end of the year because they are capital gains, and the fund pays no dividend. That is in keeping with small-cap stocks. They rarely pay dividends. You can see the capital gains were $1.9107 in 1993. You won't know what they are for this year until they are paid.

The payment of capital gains is usually made in November or December. As a fund buyer, you do not want to receive capital gains distributions within a short time of owning the fund because you are taxed on those gains as if you had held the fund for the whole year. What is really happening is that the price you pay for the fund includes the capital gains waiting to be distributed. In essence, you will be taxed on the money distributed to you, money which you have just given the fund. If you are investing late in the year, call the fund to find out when the distribution will occur and wait until it has happened, then put in your funds.

The Key Values are the last data entries. The Dividend Yield tells you how much the fund pays out, in this case, as expected, zero. Again, small-cap stocks need their funds for growth and don't have the luxury of paying dividends.

The Turnover Ratio tells you how much trading activity is in the fund. For small-cap funds, turnover ratios of 100% or more are not unusual. In this case, it is 143%. This means that the fund bought and sold the dollar value of the fund about one and one-half times in one year. This reflects an active manager who takes advantage of profits when possible. Again, for a small-cap fund, this isn't unusual. However, when a fund starts getting above 200% turnover, you should read the prospectus very carefully and be comfortable with the philosophy of the fund. When turnover gets too high, volatility increases and investors see wide fluctuations in the value of the fund.

The Average Maturity line refers to bond funds and is not applicable to stock funds.

The Beta number refers to the price performance of a fund compared with the performance of the Standard & Poor's 500 Index of stocks. In other words, with a Beta of 1.42, this fund will move up 142% for every 100% the S&P Index moves. Conversely, if the index moves down, this fund will go down 42% more than the index. High betas are part of owning small-cap funds. When you are bullish on the market and you're right, high beta funds (or stocks) will give you better performance than the market. If you are bearish on the market, you want to find funds or stocks with betas below 1 because they should go down less than the market.

The Alpha number is a measure of selection risk for the stocks in the fund. An investor should seek a positive alpha. In this case, it is 1.08. What this means is that you are being well paid for the risk you are taking in this fund as opposed to investing in the Standard & Poor's 500 stocks. A negative alpha means you're not being rewarded enough for the risks. A positive alpha is sometimes considered the value-added a manager brings to the fund. In other words, investors would see an alpha of zero if the fund is rewarding them equal to the risks taken. A positive alpha says the manager is getting more performance from the stocks selected than the risk inherent in them. This measure is a quick way to tell if the fund is making a high enough return based on its risk characteristics. This fund certainly is.

The final measure is Volatility. This tells you the total risk of a fund, based on a scale of 1 to 10. Ten indicates funds that are most risky. On the other end of the risk spectrum is the money market fund, rated at zero. This fund is rated six or in the middle of the risk pattern. In other words, you're not taking undue risk by being in this fund. Ratings are based on the standard deviation (variation) in fund performance over the latest 36 months.

How to Find Funds

You can look at the funds listed in Appendix D, but that list doesn't include every fund. There are new ones coming out continuously. The funds featured in the appendix are only small-cap-oriented. If you want to check each of these and discover new ones, go to the Prodigy screen for the Mutual Fund Reports, where we started the analysis of the Twentieth Century Fund. On AOL, go to the Morningstar Fund Reports, and on CompuServe, the Mutual Fund Center.

You can get there as described earlier in the chapter, and the screen will change to a page giving you the option to select a fund or find out about the Analyst program. For now, put your arrow on the box highlighted by Select Mutual Funds. Click the mouse button once. Now you're on a screen with four boxes: Search by Fund Name or Symbol; Fund Family/Group; Investment Objective; and Performance Period. Using these last three choices, you can screen mutual funds by your own criteria.

You use the Fund Name or Symbol selection when you know the fund you want to analyze. Let's assume you don't, but do want to know which funds are the best performing for small-cap stocks for the last one month, one year, three years or five years.

That's where the next three boxes will help. Highlight the box next to the Fund Family/Group by putting your arrow on it and clicking the mouse button once. This option will give you the names of groups of funds such as Vanguard, Fidelity or Franklin. If you have a preference for a family of funds or want to know all the funds these companies offer, the information is here.

A good reason to be in a fund that is part of a group of funds is the advantage of telephone switching. Most funds will allow investors to move from one fund to another in their family of funds by simply calling the fund and requesting the switch. Many will not charge for the switch. For example, you may be very bullish on the market and invest in a small-cap stock fund and one year later decide the market may go south. If you are in a family of funds with a money market fund option, you can call the fund on its toll-free line and ask it to move your investment from the small-cap fund to the money market fund. Then when you've decided your next best investment, you can switch again. Remember, this is only available within a family of funds managed by the same company.

KNOW YOUR INVESTMENT OBJECTIVE

The next option on the Mutual Fund Reports screen is the Investment Objective. By placing your screen arrow on this and clicking your mouse button twice, you can see a choice of 24 types of funds, from balanced or bond funds to growth or sector funds.

The choice in which we have an interest is entitled Growth-Aggressive. The majority of these funds will specialize in small-cap issues. You can highlight Growth-Aggressive by putting your screen arrow on the words and clicking your mouse button once. Then you can exit the screen by clicking the arrow on the Escape box twice. That puts you back on the menu screen.

You'll notice next to the words Investment Objective will be Growth-Aggressive. That's the first group of funds you're asking the computer to find. But let's add one more search criterion and ask the computer to find aggressive funds and rank them by performance.

RANKING FUNDS BY PERFORMANCE

There are four options on the Performance Period screen. By putting the arrow on the Performance box and clicking the mouse button twice, you go to a screen with performance options for four time periods: one month, one year, three years and five years.

What you want to determine is the best-performing funds for each of these time periods and see which ones are repeated. Remember, many funds have not been around for five years, so if they don't appear in the five-year performance screen, they started sooner than that. The same is true for the three-year screen. This means a close reading of the prospectus, as always, is needed before you simply buy the fund.

NOW SHOWING ON A SCREEN NEAR YOU

Let's see what the top five performing funds have been over the abovementioned time periods, and see if any of them repeat. The first screen I'll choose is the Five Year Performance. I put the arrow on the box in front of the words 5 Year Comparison and click the mouse button twice.

The screen changes automatically to the menu screen for the Mutual Fund Reports and after the Performance Period it says 5 year performance.

Now you have two screens for the computer to filter: the type of fund, Growth-Aggressive, and Performance Period, five years.

On the last line on the screen, there is a box in front of the words List Matching Funds. When you put your arrow on the box and click the mouse button twice, the computer goes to work. It is searching for all the aggressive growth funds and then ranking them in order of their performance for the last five years.

When it has found them, the screen changes and a list appears. On this search, 136 funds were listed. The returns ranged from up 171.75% to down 11.76% for five years. The top five funds were:

AIM Funds: Aggressive Growth
MFS Emerging Growth Fund/B
Twentieth Century Inv: Giftrust Investors
PBHG Growth Fund
Thomson Fund Group: Opportunity Fund/B

After looking at this ranking, I returned to the Menu page by putting the arrow on the Menu box and clicking the mouse button twice. I went back to the Performance Period and changed the choice to three years. Then I asked the computer to list matching funds by highlighting that box and clicking the mouse button. When it screened for three-year performance, these funds came out best:

PBHG Growth Fund
Twentieth Century Inv: Giftrust Investors
AIM Funds: Aggressive Growth
Thomson Fund Group: Opportunity Fund/A
Heartland Group: Value Fund

Using the same technique for one-year performance, the computer found these:

GT America Growth Fund/A
GT America Growth Fund/B
Robertson Stephens Inv. Tr.: Value Plus Fund
Janus Mercury Fund
Mutual Series Fund: Discovery Fund

Finally, I looked at the one-month winners:

Hartwell Emerging Growth Fund/A
Hartwell Emerging Growth Fund/C
Hartwell Emerging Growth Fund/B
Parkstone Group Fund
TCW/DW Small-Cap Growth Fun

Now What Do You Do?

None of the funds appears in each time period, but three of them show up twice: AIM, PBHG and Twentieth Century. You already know about Twentieth Century. You can investigate AIM and PBHG by using the same techniques. These may or may not be the right funds for you. You won't know for sure until you've read the data from your on-line service, in this case Prodigy, and the prospectus.

The fact that these funds have been in the top five listing in two different time periods is very promising. Remember, they are competing against hundreds of other funds for this honor.

To look at these funds, simply place the arrow on the fund name, and click the mouse button twice. The computer will get the data on the fund and change the screen to the first of three pages of information. If you like what you see there, call the fund, and you will receive a prospectus on how the fund invests. Read it carefully. Then you'll have enough information to make an investment decision.

You should buy more than one fund. Putting all your small-cap dollars into one way of investing may work well one year but not the next. In fact, some of the best funds, with returns over 30% in one year, have had negative returns the next.

Knowing this, you can look at a fund's five-year record, then compare it with its one-year record. If the fund has had poor performance for the last year but shows very good returns the other four, it may be the best time to buy the fund. Conversely, if the returns have been excellent for the past year and poor for the other four, you should be careful about buying into it.

OTHER MUTUAL FUND INFORMATION SOURCES

No discussion of mutual fund information can exclude the Morningstar Service, which offers *Morningstar Closed-End Funds* and *Morningstar Mutual Funds.* (Morningstar, Inc., 225 West Wacker Drive, Chicago, Illinois 60606; 800-876-5005.) One of the pioneers in analyzing open-end and closed-end mutual funds, Morningstar gives the interested reader valuable information on thousands of funds. This is the resource AOL uses for its Mutual Funds Reports.

It divides the world into the two fund groups, and you can subscribe to the open-end fund analysis and/or the closed-end information. Your subscription brings you data and comments on funds every two weeks if you have it delivered on paper. If you only want the data, that is available on a floppy disk. A select number of funds has been chosen and each fund is updated every quarter for closed-end funds and every five months for open-end funds. Each mailing contains a different group of funds.

The information on the funds includes data and an analysis of the funds' investment philosophy, the managers' style, and the success or lack thereof or both. I'll use the description of the Morgan Grenfell Smallcap Fund to give an example of a closed-end fund analysis (pages 188–190). The open-end fund descriptions are very similar, except the issue of discounts and premiums is not a factor.

CHECKING THE FUND OUT

At top left is a description of the fund. In this fund, the focus is on stocks with market capitalizations in the lowest 15%. Market capitalization is the price of the stock times the number of shares outstanding. This fund is in the small-cap universe because all of its stock holdings are chosen from the small-cap stock universe.

In the graph (page 189), the first lines give the name of the fund, Morgan Grenfell Smallcap; the symbol, MGC; its objective, domestic equities; the premium or discount the fund is selling to its net asset value (NAV), 13.1%; the yield, 0%; the market price, $8.88; the NAV, $10.21; and the date of the NAV, 12/30/94.

In the box to the left of the graph is Morningstar's objective rating of the fund's performance: the Return has been average; the Risk is average; and it has a three-star or neutral rating. Five stars is outstanding in the Morningstar universe, and a one-star fund may still be in your portfolio but would require a very good reason such as portfolio diversification.

At the top of the graph is a set of numbers for each year the fund has existed, back to 1983, in this case, since 1987. These numbers are very helpful in timing the purchase of the fund if you decide it's the right one. The widest discount to the NAV for this fund occurred in 1987, at 23.9%. Remember, however, in October 1987, the Dow Jones Industrial Average lost more than 1,000 points in one week. You should keep that in mind when looking at any statistics for funds or stocks for the year 1987. So take that one away.

The next year, in 1988, the discount was as low as 21.5%, but again, because the crash occurred in October, I'm sure the discount was just beginning to close. In future years, the discount was as low as 18.4% and the premium went as high as 11.7%.

The graph gives you the value of $10,000 over the life of the fund in terms of market price and NAV. At the extreme right of the page

MORGAN GRENFELL SMALLCAP

Morgan Grenfell Smallcap Fund seeks long-term capital appreciation. Current income is a secondary objective.

The fund mainly invests in securities of U.S. companies with market caps in the lowest 15% of all equities.

The fund had an outstanding loan payable to Morgan Grenfell Capital Management due in May 1993. It was prepaid on Feb. 14, 1992.

Board members serve staggered terms to discourage takeover attempts; additionally, supermajority voting is required for open-ending, merging, or liquidating the fund.

As of Feb. 21, 1992, Yale University owned 448,900, or 8.2%, of the outstanding shares.

On April 22, 1994, shareholders rejected a proposal to open-end the fund.

Portfolio Manager

Robert E. Kern et al. Since 5–87. BSME Purdue U. Kern is a managing director at Morgan Grenfell. He was previously a managing director at Chase Investor's Management, which he joined in 1965. Chase Investor's Management merged into Morgan Grenfell in September 1986.

NAV Total Return %

	1st Qtr	2nd Qtr	3rd Qtr	4th Qtr	Total
1990	0.65	8.65	−27.86	9.81	−13.37
1991	29.31	−4.62	11.56	10.35	51.83
1992	0.49	−12.22	1.57	15.70	3.66
1993	1.00	−1.91	11.06	−0.13	9.90
1994	−2.53	−7.62	8.62	0.27	−1.93

Performance/Risk

	NAV Total Return %	+/− S&P 500	+/− Wil Sm Grow	% Rank All	% Rank Obj	Mkt Total Return %
3 Mo	0.27	0.29	−0.56	17	22	6.90
6 Mo	8.91	4.05	−4.01	5	10	9.79
1 Yr	−1.93	−3.25	−2.47	20	56	−6.61
3 Yr Avg	3.76	−2.50	−6.56	79	59	−2.29
5 Yr Avg	8.00*	−0.69	−3.26	48	51	7.58*
Incept Avg	7.66	—	—	—	—	4.74

Rating	Risk % All	Rank Obj	Return 1.00 = Equity Avg	Risk Avg	Morningstar Risk-Adj Rating
3 Yr	88	81	0.05	1.01	★★
5 Yr	90	82	0.65	1.18	★★★
10 Yr	—	—	—	—	—

Average Historical Rating: 2.7 ★'s over 56 months

Risk % Rank: 1=Low, 100=High

Investment Style

	Stock Portfolio Avg	Relative S&P 500
Price/Earnings Ratio	28.1	1.52
Price/Cash Flow Ratio	20.3	1.76
Price/Book Ratio	4.3	1.27
5 Yr Earnings Gr %	16.5 #	2.97
Return on Assets %	7.3	0.97
Debt % Total Cap	24.0	0.85
Med Mkt Cap ($mil)	749	0.06

figure is based on less than 50% of stocks

Style: Value, Blend, Growth / Size: Large, Medium, Small

Portfolio 06-30-94   Total Securities: 78

Share Chg (12-93)	Amount	Security	Value $000	% Total Invest
−2000	73000	Xilinx	2491	3.96
0	53000	Leggett & Platt	1988	3.16
−16500	78500	Ceridian	1933	3.07
5000	75000	Outback Steakhouse	1809	2.88
14000	77000	Tidewater	1790	2.85
−6000	47500	Sports & Recreation	1758	2.79
44000	44000	Gymboree	1738	2.76
0	55500	Bed Bath & Beyond	1589	2.53
−2500	56000	Sunglass Hut International	1526	2.43
13000	53000	Altera	1497	2.38
7000	41000	Boston Chicken	1466	2.33
13500	59250	TNT Freightways	1363	2.17
0	50000	Diamond Shamrock	1269	2.02
23500	46004	Legent	1242	1.97
40000	80000	American City Business Jrnls	1240	1.97
−4500	90500	Noven Pharmaceuticals	1222	1.94
45000	90000	Taco Cabana Cl A	1215	1.93
21000	42750	Paging Network	1176	1.87
4000	54000	Crown Crafts	1019	1.62
0	45000	BJ Services	928	1.48

Morgan Grenfell Smallcap (MGC)

Ticker	Objective	Prem/Disc %	Yield %	Mkt Price	NAV	Date
MGC	Domestic Eq	-13.1	0.0	8.88	10.21	12-30-94

3.3	-9.2	-2.2	2.7	9.0	11.7	3.9	-2.7	Highest Prem/Disc
-23.9	-21.5	-16.2	-13.1	-12.6	-7.5	-13.5	-18.4	Lowest Prem/Disc

Historical Profile
Return Average
Risk Average
Rating ★★★
Neutral

Growth of $10,000
— at NAV ($000)
— at Market Price ($000)

Alpha	-2.22
Beta	1.23
R^2	42
Std Dev	15.05
Mean	4.83
Sharpe Ratio	0.09

Premium
Discount %

1983	1984	1985	1986	1987	1988	1989	1990	1991	1992	1993	12-94	History
---	---	---	---	7.45	8.87	10.80	8.70	12.30	11.95	11.85	10.21	NAV
---	---	---	---	-19.72*	19.06	25.05	-13.37	51.83	3.66	9.90	-1.93	NAV Total Return %
---	---	---	---	-5.49*	2.45	-6.63	-10.26	21.35	-3.95	-0.16	-3.25	+/- S&P 500
---	---	---	---	---	-0.24	6.14	5.64	-4.97	-9.53	-8.08	-2.47	+/- Wil Small Growth
---	---	---	---	0.00*	0.00	0.00	0.00	0.00	0.00	0.00	0.00	Income Return %
---	---	---	---	-19.72*	19.06	25.05	-13.37	51.83	3.66	9.90	-1.93	Capital Return %
---	---	---	---	---	18	20	82	7	77	84	20	Total Rtn % Rank All
---	---	---	---	---	26	44	72	12	59	50	56	Total Rtn % Rank Obj
---	---	---	---	-40.00*	22.92	34.04	-2.24	58.02	1.52	-1.62	-6.61	Market Total Rtn %
---	---	---	---	-9.2	-14.2	-11.8	-5.5	-1.1	-1.2	-7.8	-13.9	Avg Prem/Disc %
---	---	---	---	0.00	0.00	0.00	0.00	0.00	0.00	0.00	0.00	Income $
---	---	---	---	0.00	0.00	0.25	0.65	0.97	0.82	1.14	1.23	Capital Gains $
---	---	---	---	4.32	2.56	2.13	2.01	1.79	1.44	1.39	1.46	Expense Ratio %
---	---	---	---	-1.80	-1.30	-1.10	-1.05	-0.85	-0.83	-0.74	-0.61	Income Ratio %
---	---	---	---	98	83	80	75	70	89	89	---	Turnover Rate %
---	---	---	---	37.3	41.4	54.2	45.6	64.5	68.0	67.3	59.1	Net Assets ($mil)

Composition % 12-31-94

Cash	8.0	Preferreds	0.0
Stocks	92.0	Convertibles	0.0
Bonds	0.0	Other	0.0

Index Allocation
% of Stocks

Dow 30	0.0
S&P 500	5.0
S&P Mid-Cap 400	36.6
US Small-Cap	58.5
Foreign	0.0

Sector Weightings

	% of Stocks	Relative S&P 500
Utilities	0.0	0.00
Energy	9.9	0.97
Financials	2.7	0.25
Industrial Cyclicals	9.1	0.56
Consumer Durables	9.0	1.45
Consumer Staples	1.0	0.08
Services	21.9	2.69
Retail	14.2	2.43
Health	6.0	0.69
Technology	26.3	2.87

Most Similar Fund in MCEF

Inefficient Market	Weak Fit
Jundt Growth	Weak Fit

Tax Analysis

% of cumulative NAV total rtn

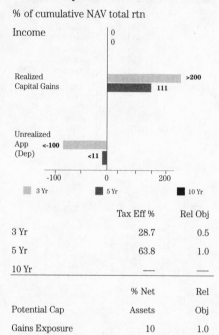

Income
0
0

Realized
Capital Gains   >200   111

Unrealized
App   <-100
(Dep)   <11

-100   0   200

3 Yr   5 Yr   10 Yr

	Tax Eff %	Rel Obj
3 Yr	28.7	0.5
5 Yr	63.8	1.0
10 Yr	—	—

	% Net Assets	Rel Obj
Potential Cap Gains Exposure	10	1.0

Analysis by Carolyn Whitfield 01-27-95

Morgan Grenfell Smallcap Fund's dramatic strategy shift in 1994's second half hasn't dramatically improved its performance.

MGC had a rough time last year. Going into 1994, the fund had 40% of assets in consumer stocks, focusing mainly on restaurants and specialty retailers. Manager Robert Kern expected these stocks to benefit from the recovering economy. Many retailers, though, were hurt in the first part of the year by fierce competition and stagnant prices. At the same time, many of MGC's restaurant stocks were also weak. The fund thus suffered significant losses in both the first and second quarters: At June's end, its –10% year-to-date return landed in the bottom quintile of the domestic-equity objective.

In response to these losses, Kern slashed MGC's consumer-stock position in the second part of 1994. By year-end, consumer stocks took up only 17% of assets. MGC took losses on many of these positions, but it was able to avoid further losses as these stocks continued to weaken throughout 1994. Kern used some of the proceeds to increase the fund's technology stake, which rose to 28% of assets in December from 20% in June. This shift proved well timed because technology stocks came back strongly in the third and fourth quarters. Thus, MGC's –1.9% annual return almost made it into the top half of its peer group.

But while MGC's performance has improved recently, it's still lagging the Wilshire Small-Cap Growth Index. That's because some of MGC's sector picks haven't been so successful. In 1994's second half, the fund's stake in paper stocks grew to 10% from 2%. But while the paper sector in general has done well in 1994, most of MGC's paper stocks show losses for the year.

Indeed, over the long run, MGC has lagged both the value index and the S&P 500, making it difficult to recommend this fund.

Address	885 Third Avenue, 32nd Floor New York, NY 10022	Telephone	212-230-2600 / 800-888-8060
Advisor	Morgan Grenfell Group PLC	Reinvestment Plan	Yes
Subadvisor	N/A	Shares Outstanding	5,785,510
Administrator	N/A	Exchange	NYSE
Management Fee	1.00%	*Date of Inception	05-14-87
Income Dist Sched	Paid Irregularly	Shareholder Report Grade	A-

Volume 14, Issue 2, February 10, 1995. Reprinted with permission.

are statistical data on the fund: the Alpha is negative 2.22 (This is same alpha discussed earlier.) This means the fund has underperformed, given its expected risk-adjusted performance established by its Beta.

The Beta is 1.23, meaning the fund is 23% more volatile than the S&P 500 Index. The R-squared number (42) gives an indication of how much influence the S&P 500 stocks have on the performance of the fund. The closer this number is to 100, the more it resembles the S&P Index. For small-cap stocks, the R-squared number should always be low because investors are buying these funds specifically not to own the large-cap stocks in the S&P 500 Index, and the correlation between movements in small-cap stocks and large-cap stocks can be low.

MORE STATISTICAL INFO. AND THAT'S DEVIATION, STANDARD DEVIATION.

The next box down shows three numbers: standard deviation, mean, and the Sharpe Ratio. The standard deviation is an annualized statistic based on monthly returns from the past 36 months. The higher the standard deviation, the more volatility in the fund. This fund has a standard deviation of 15.05. That's high. That means you need a seat belt to own this fund.

The mean number represents the average monthly total return from which the standard deviation is calculated. This is an annualized number. In this case it's 4.83.

The Sharpe Ratio is a risk-adjusted measure to determine reward per unit of risk. The higher this number, the better the fund's historical risk-adjusted performance. This fund has a ratio of 0.09. It's not high.

THE PERFORMANCE GRAPHS

The graph on page 189 gives you a price history of the NAV and the market price. By seeing where the widest spread is between these two figures, you can buy funds at their historically low relative prices, in other words, when the discount to the NAV is the largest.

Below the price graph is the discount/premium in bar graph form. This is another quick way to see if you're buying the fund at its cheapest relative price.

HISTORICAL DATA

Below the graphs are 12 years of data on a fund, if it has had that long a history. There are 16 fields of data, and without going into each one, here are few highlights:

The NAV Total Return % on the second line gives you the performance for the year recorded. For this fund, the best year was a return of 51.83% in 1991, and its worst year was at the beginning, a negative 19.72%. You can see that this is a volatile holding.

The next two lines compare the fund's performance against two indexes: the S&P 500 and the Wilshire Small Growth. A positive number in the first line tells you in percentages how much the fund outperformed the index. If the number is negative, the fund underperformed by that percentage. The fund then is compared to an index similar to its investments. If the fund is doing well, it will beat its index. This fund has done that in two years, 1989 and 1990.

The returns for income and capital give you the percentage due to dividends for income and capital gains. As expected, the income is zero, while the capital gains have varied widely.

Total Return % Rank All is a figure derived from comparing this fund with all funds in the Morningstar closed-end fund universe. The lower the number, the better the performance with 1 being the best and 100, the worst. This fund's best year was 1991, with a rank of 7. The worst year was 1993, with a rank of 84.

The next line ranks the fund against its peers, or as it says, Total Return % Rank Objective. Again, the fund hit its apex in 1991 with a rank of 12, but its low point came in 1990 with a rank of 72.

What you're looking for in these rankings is a fund that is doing well and that is ranked below 20 against its peers. You shouldn't be overly concerned how it's doing against the universe of all funds or the performance compared with the S&P 500 Index. You're buying the fund for a specific niche in your portfolio: small-cap stocks. Participating in large-cap or mid-cap stocks should be done with other funds or your own stock picks.

The following line gives you the Market Total Return % based on market prices as opposed to the NAV. These numbers tell you how investors have treated the fund. In some years, this return is greater than the NAV return, and some years less. It is greater in years when investors take the market price to a premium of the NAV. In those years, an investor would have received the return from the fund plus the bonus of other investors bidding the price of the fund above the NAV. In 1991, that was an incredible 58.02%.

The Average Premium/Discount % is simply the average for the year, calculated by adding together the month-end premium, or discount for each month, and then dividing by the number of months used.

The next line gives you the income for the fund for each year, in this case zero. The following line gives you the actual dollars paid out for capital gains in each year.

Next comes the expense ratio for the fund. In this case, it has gone down from a large 4.32% to a more reasonable 1.46%. Then you have the Income Ratio %, which is calculated by dividing the fund's net investment income by its average NAV. The net investment income is the total income of the fund, less the operating expenses. Because this fund has no income, this number will always be negative. It also means that these expenses are being taken from the capital gains, if any, and the capital of the fund.

The last two lines give you the Turnover Ratio and Total Assets in millions of dollars. The Turnover Ratio for this fund is not excessive when compared with many other small-cap funds. Again, this ratio is determined by a formula reflecting the buying and selling of stocks by the fund.

The final row of numbers is the total dollars the fund has. If this number is too small, below $10 million, you need to be sure the fund will stay open. If it's too high, above $250 million, you need to be sure the manager's universe of investment options is large enough to prudently employ the money. In other words, too much money in a fund with very specific and tight guidelines, as explained to you in the prospectus, will have difficulty finding undervalued stocks.

WHAT DOES THE FUND OWN?

On the right side of page 188, you see the holdings of the fund, starting with its largest dollar amount. However, these data do not tell you when the stock was bought or for what price. Furthermore, it is usually at least three months old, and many of the positions may have been sold.

There are still two very good uses for this information. The first is that you know what the fund owns and can make a judgment as to your comfort level with these stocks. Second, this is a good place to find stocks for your portfolio. If you have the inclination, you can take each stock, use the method of analysis in Chapter 6 and you might find some real winners.

THE FUND'S ALLOCATION

Where the fund is putting your money is of interest. A table (page 189) tells you the composition of the fund. In this case, 8% is in cash, 92% in stocks. This is what you'd expect and want because you're paying the managers to invest your money in stocks.

Another table provides an explanation of which industries the fund holds. In the Morgan Grenfell Smallcap fund, services, retail, and technology account for more than 62% of the stocks. Are these the areas in which you want your money?

In the right-hand column is Index Allocation information. This tells you what percentage of stocks the fund owns that are in the following indexes: Dow Jones Industrials, S&P 500, S&P Mid-cap 400, U S Small-cap, and Foreign. As expected, most of the stocks appear in the small-cap area.

Also on the right are names of funds from the Morningstar Closed-End fund universe that are most similar to this one. For this fund, there are none that are very close.

OVER TO THE LEFT SIDE OF THE PAGE

Under the name of the fund is a synopsis of the fund's objective: capital appreciation with income as a secondary goal. When you read this portion of the page, you'll know if the fund meets your basic requirements. Because we're looking for appreciation, this one is worth considering. If you're looking for a monthly check, you're in the wrong place.

Below the description and other details of the fund, is the NAV Total Return box. This gives you a quick look at how the fund has performed each quarter for the last five years. Notice in 1990 in the third quarter, the fund lost 27.86% of its value. Then in the first quarter of 1991, it grew 29.31%. As mentioned before, you need to put on your seat belt when you buy small-cap funds or stocks.

The Performance/Risk data show how the fund performed over six time horizons, in absolute percentages and in comparison with the S&P 500, the Wilshire Growth Index, all other funds, and funds in the same category. Finally, it gives the Market Total Return %, which tells how the market value of the stock has performed.

The final set of numbers gives the risk-adjusted ratings for the fund. Under the Return column, look for numbers above 1. In this case, it is 0.65. This means the fund has underperformed when compared with funds in its category. If the number had been above 1, the fund would be outperforming its group.

Similarly, the Risk numbers give you a measurement for the fund's underperformance as measured against a three-month Treasury bill. Like all of us, you want to avoid losing money. If a fund scores greater than 1 in this column, and this fund scored 1.01 for a three-year average, it means that the fund had a greater underperformance measurement than others in its class. For the five-year period, it scored 1.18.

The last category is the Morningstar Risk-adjusted rating. It's the star scale of 1 to 5 with five stars being the best.

THE FUND'S STYLE

To quickly categorize each fund for the reader, Morningstar puts a fund in a box with nine squares. Based on a quantitative measure, the square on the top left represents an investment style called Value Investing in large stocks, theoretically the safest investment. In the bottom right square, there is the small-cap growth investors, the most risky of the funds. Morningstar shades the box that is most appropriate for each fund.

If you are looking for small-cap funds, you want the shading in the lower three boxes. Each represents small-cap enterprises but with three different approaches: value, blend and growth. The growth square in the lower right corner is the most volatile and potentially most rewarding sector of the market.

If you want a less-jolting investment and still want small-cap performance, take a fund with the shading in the middle or left square on the bottom row.

Obviously, you can't pick a winning fund by simply looking at a square and picking one of the boxes or counting the number of stars.

However, these quick references will tell you if you should spend more time with a particular fund. You may want to establish a minimum of four stars and only value investing as your minimum criteria. If these requirements give you investing comfort, you can eliminate all of the funds not leaping these hurdles.

RATIOS AND MORE RATIOS

Under the Investment Style category are seven bits of data you'll find helpful. The first is the average Price-to-Earnings (P/E) Ratio for the fund's portfolio and how that compares with the S&P 500 Index stocks. Remember, this particular fund is a small-cap fund and you would expect higher P/E multiples because investors will pay up for growth stocks. However, if the P/E comparative ratio for the fund is above 2, you should have a very good reason to own the fund. In this fund, the average P/E is 28.1 which is 1.52 times the S&P 500 Index average P/E. Is it too high? It's not bad, but I would look for a strong performance to justify the higher multiple.

The next ratio is Price to Cash Flow (PCF), which is the fiscal year-end market price divided by the cash earnings per share. Cash flow is a measure of a company's ability to generate cash from its business or its liquidity and solvency. Cash flow measurement is a good gauge for the company's financial health. For our example, the ratio is 20.3 of 1.76 times the S&P 500 Index stocks. You want this number to be reasonably in line with the P/E ratio. In this case, it's not (28.1 versus 20.3). That may mean the companies in the portfolio are short on cash because they are growing quickly or that they're financially in trouble. P/E and PCF ratios should follow the same trend.

PRICE-TO-BOOK RATIO

This ratio is the weighted average of the price/book (P/B) ratios of all the stocks in the fund. The P/B ratio of a company is calculated by dividing the market price of its stock by the company's per share book value. The per share book value is the historical accounting value of the company's assets. This figure does not include intangible assets such as patents and trademarks.

If a fund has a high P/B value ratio, it can signal danger. Some investors will only buy stocks or funds with book values of 1 or less.

These are the value investors. However, these investors would never buy service or software companies, which have very few tangible assets but can make good money for their investors. In our example fund, the P/B is 4.3, a bit on the high side but not too bad. It's 1.27 times the P/B for the S&P 500 Index stocks. For growth stocks, this isn't out of line.

GROWTH: GIMME ALL YOU GOT

You want a growing stock. The faster the better. The next line tells you how fast the stocks in the fund, on average, have been growing for the last five years. In this fund, it's 16.5% per year. That's very good. In fact, it's 2.97 times the rate of the S&P 500 Index. That's a big plus. However, you have to determine if you're paying too much for that growth. One quick way is to compare the P/E ratio with the growth ratio.

In our example, the P/E is 28.1 versus a growth rate of 16.5. If these numbers were reversed, you could get very excited. Ideally, you would like to see the growth rate higher than the P/E ratio. Some investors make a rule of only buying stocks with P/E ratios less than half their growth rates.

RETURN ON THE ASSETS OF THE COMPANY

This measures the after-tax and after-debt-service profitability of a company. It shows how profitable a company is after it pays its taxes and all the interest on its bonds. You want a high number here because it tells you how well the management exploits the assets it has, such as plants and equipment. In our example fund, the average return on assets (ROA) for the stocks in the fund is 7.3% while it is much less for the comparable index stocks (0.97).

DEBT AS A PERCENT OF TOTAL CAPITAL

This number is important because it tells you how much a company has borrowed relative to its total capital, which is debt plus equity. In this fund, the percentage the stocks have borrowed is 24. This is a good conservative number. Any time the ratio gets above 50% you should be concerned. That would mean half the capital for the stocks in the fund has been borrowed. As you can see, the comparison with the index stocks tells you these stocks are more conservatively capitalized than their larger counterparts in the S&P 500 because the relative ratio is less than 1 (0.85). That's a plus for the fund.

MEDIAN MARKET CAPITALIZATION OR HOW BIG ARE THESE STOCKS?

This gives you the halfway point for the size of the companies in the fund's portfolio. Half of the stocks are less in market capitalization and half are greater. In this fund, the median market capitalization (stock price times the number of shares outstanding) is 749 or $749 million. You can see how small these stocks are relative to the S&P 500 because the median is only 0.06 the size of the median for the index. In this fund, you know you have small-cap stocks.

WRITTEN ANALYSIS OF THE FUND

This is one of the best value-added sections of the Morningstar service. Because Morningstar doesn't accept payment or advertising from investment companies, the analysis is honest and straightforward. Morningstar doesn't care if you buy the fund or not. In fact, part of its service is to help you avoid bad funds.

The analysis section (page 190) gives you one professional's opinion on the management and philosophy of the fund. It explains moves the fund has made in the last quarter. It also points out the environment in which the fund is working, in particular how it's doing against relevant indexes such as the Russell 2000 and the Wilshire Small-Cap Growth Indexes.

It's wise to remember that this is one analyst's opinion. You may have knowledge of an industry in which the fund is investing and feel comfortable with owning the fund even if the analyst is dropping bombs on it. That's why looking at the fund's holdings is most important when analyzing a fund. By using the methods in Chapter 6, you can make your own judgment as to your comfort level with the fund's investments.

THE FUND'S DETAILS

The last section of information gives the address, phone numbers, and other pertinent data. From these, you can tell who runs the fund and for how long; what the management fee is; how many shares are outstanding; if you can use a reinvestment plan, which is a plan that allows you to reinvest any proceeds from the fund back into the fund without paying a commission; on what exchange the fund is traded; when the fund started; and what Morningstar thinks of the information sent to the shareholders.

MORNINGSTAR SHINES BRIGHTLY BUT OTHER STARS ARE APPEARING

If there is anything you want to know about a fund, whether it's closed-end or open-end, Morningstar has the longest history of providing information for funds. Its closed-end fund work stands alone for its thoroughness. Its User's Guide for either group of funds is very understandable and highly recommended reading. Also, every two weeks, there is an update for the covered funds, which includes a ranking of the best- and the worst-performing funds for each sector.

However, there are other sources which do a fine job as well: *Value Line Mutual Fund Survey* (800-284-7607, ext. 6672) has recently joined the group and covers the open-end fund arena. It charges less than Morningstar ($295 versus $395) and has a few more features such as more funds (2,250 versus 1,300) and a comparison of a fund's performance in bull and bear markets. This statistic is a very helpful addition, especially when you're feeling defensive.

There are many newsletters dedicated to ranking mutual fund performance. None of them covers all funds and many are specialized for certain sectors such as emerging markets or international. Some of the newsletters are:

> *Mutual Fund Forecaster* – (800-327-6720) or (800-442-9000)
> *Mutual Fund Investing* – (800-722-9000)
> *The Mutual Fund Strategist* – (802-425-2211)
> NoLOAD Fund, DAL Investment Co. – (415-986-7979)
> Investment Information Services – (312-649-6940) has several
>   publications: *The Mutual Fund Letter, Investment Horizons* and *Mutual Fund Newsletter*.
> *Handbook for No-Load Fund Investors* – (914-693-7420)
> *The Telephone Switch Newsletter* – (714-536-1931)

Wiesenberger's Investment Co. Service – (800-232-2285) has three publications: *Wiesenberger's Investment Co. Service; Current Performance and Dividend Records*; and *Management Results*

There is a trade association for mutual funds called Investment Company Institute (202-326-5800), which represents about 90% of the outstanding mutual funds. They have several books and publications on mutual funds and investing. Some titles are: *Guide to Mutual Funds; Mutual Fund Fact Book; Money Market Mutual Funds; Free List of More Than 1,200 Mutual Funds; Investment Strategy for Busy People*; and *Monthly Statistics*.

There is also the No-Load Mutual Fund Association (914-693-7420), which represents about 400 no-load funds. It publishes *Investor's Directory: Your Guide to Mutual Funds* and *Bibliography*, a one-page guide to books, magazines, newsletters and financial advisory services for the beginning investor.

CHAPTER NINE

A SESSION ON
AMERICA ONLINE

In the on-line jungle there is one dominant lion: America Online (AOL). With more than six million subscribers as of this writing, it is the most popular way of going on-line, finding data, buying and selling stocks, checking the weather, airline schedules or whatever interests you. The odds are most readers of this book are on America Online, have tried it or will. Let's look at some of the financial features on the service, and then I'll describe how to buy and sell stocks on-line.

PERSONAL FINANCE

When you sign on to AOL, you first see the Welcome page. There are several icons to choose from, each with a different interest: the news, a magazine, a special site on AOL, etc. If you go to the top right of that page, you'll see a small box. By clicking on that box, you'll close the page and see the one immediately behind it, the Main page.

The Main page is always being updated, but as of this writing there are about twenty-five icons, each with its own subject. The one we're interested in is the Personal Finance section. Put your arrow on the box labeled Personal Finance and click on it. Your screen changes and a new one appears. There is a scroll box and several icons on the page. Since this page is revised from time to time, I will only describe it generally.

There is a scroll box with many choices in it, ranging from brokerage firm information to mutual fund sites, from independent information providers to the famous Motley Fool. Also on the page are several icons. Among them are: Company Research, Quotes and Portfolios, and the Banking Center. There are usually four more icons which are changed frequently to highlight certain financial sites. Let's look at a few of these areas.

No Added Fees for AOL Sites

An important financial point: none of these sites costs extra. On AOL, there are no premium services. Everything is included in your monthly fee. Currently the pricing program is for subscribers to receive ten hours of usage for $9.95 per month and then a charge of $2.95 for additional hours. Another option is for heavy users: the fee is $19.95 for twenty hours of use. You can gather a great deal of information for little cost at these rates.

The Personal Finance Icons

COMPANY RESEARCH

This is a great site, loaded with data and graphs on thousands of stocks. For on-line investors, this is where you'll spend most of your time.

When you click on this icon, your screen changes and there are five icons on the right side of the page. On the left is the scroll box containing several site links; one of them is to the Online Investor.

This site, devoted to on-line investors, is written by my partner, James C. Hale, and me. You can reach it by using the keyword search function and using the keyword OI or OLI or Online Investor or you can click on the words "Online Investor" in the scroll box.

Once at the Online Investor site, you'll find a guide for using the Company Research database on AOL, featured companies in the news, a guest columnist from major newsletters or investment advisors, an explanation of the economic news releases and what's expected to be announced during the week, a guide to mutual funds, as well as a message board for questions, a daily column on the markets, and other helpful hints on how to exploit what's on AOL for stocks and mutual funds for better investing. Our purpose is to inform and direct investors so they can make better investment decisions. It's really an extension of this book but dedicated to understanding the databases and information on America Online.

This site is only one of the many possibilities on the Company Research page. Starting at the top: the first icon is for Stock Reports. You'll definitely use this. By clicking on the box, your screen changes to a page with three choices: Search the Database; Special Screens; and About Morningstar. The first two are the most used.

As the name implies, you can search through the database of stocks by clicking on this box. A new menu appears and asks for the symbol or name of the company you wish to investigate. Type in either choice and the screen shows another box with the name of the company highlighted, if it's in the database. Some companies are too small and won't be shown. But there aren't too many you won't find.

When you double click on the highlighted bar, the screen changes and a page appears full of financial goodies: the full name of the company, the ticker symbol, its industry, the address, a description of what the company does, the phone number, the stock's performance statistics, its market capitalization and six key ratios: P/E, PSR, Price to Book, Debt to Equity, yield, and ROE. Then there are five years of revenues and earnings, EPS, and net profit margin. The next section gives the growth rates for Revenues, Earnings, EPS and Dividends for the last four years with a Compounded Annual Growth Rate for each category for the previous three years. Following that are abbreviated quarterly reports for the last eight quarters, and then a synopsis of the balance sheet for the previous five years, and finally a cash flow figure.

As mentioned earlier, this is a great place to start your investigation of a stock. A number of the important ratios (which were described in Chapters 5 and 6) are given here, and you'll need to check them before considering a stock for your portfolio. This is a quick way to find these numbers.

After you've checked out some stocks, go back to the Stock Reports page by clicking the box at the top right of the page. The screen changes to the Stock Reports page and the next box to look at is called Special Stocks. Click on the box entitled AAII Special Screens.

THE AAII SPECIAL SCREENS

This area gives you stocks with special characteristics, ones from certain models chosen by the AAII (American Association of

Individual Investors). One of the constant models used is the Peter Lynch program. It picks stocks from a large database that mathematically fit the mold Peter Lynch has defined.

The three other screens enter the database and find stocks with Earnings Surprises, stocks with low P/E ratios and stocks with good dividend income. This is a great place to find an idea, not to pick an investment. Just because a stock has made it into the screen doesn't mean it's right for your portfolio. Do the same analysis described in Chapter 6 on these stocks.

After you've checked out several of these screens, go back to the Stock Reports page by clicking on the top right box of the page.

THE MORNINGSTAR DATABASE

At the bottom of the Stock Reports page is the icon for the Morningstar database. When you click on it, you go to a page with two options: the stock database or the mutual fund database.

By clicking on the Stock Reports box, you return to the Stock Reports page. Earlier in the chapter, I described this area.

MORNINGSTAR MUTUAL FUNDS ON-LINE

By clicking on the Mutual Fund box, you go to a main page with several icon choices. The one on the top left is the one to get into. It's the one entitled Top Performing Funds. It's got lots of good information.

Click on the icon and the screen changes to a page of choices. You can have the computer go in and find the best 25 funds from any of twenty categories, including: all funds, aggressive funds, balanced funds, income funds, Europe funds, global funds, mortgage funds, etc. This is one of the fastest and best ways to find a fund worth investigating.

One caveat: these funds are drawn from Morningstar's database, which has over 7,000 funds, but it does not include all funds. There may be funds you want to analyze that aren't in this database. Morningstar can't possibly cover every fund. But it does an excellent job of giving a great deal of information about each fund included.

Among the data you'll find on any one fund: how to contact it; its performance over the last month, three years, and five years; who's running the fund and for how long; the major holdings of the fund;

the risk of the fund; the fees the fund charges; and much more. If you're on AOL and want to find some good funds, this is definitely a site for you.

That's a quick summary of some of the many sites on AOL dedicated to providing good financial data and ideas. Now let's look at how to buy and sell stocks.

BUYING AND SELLING STOCKS ON-LINE

Let's assume you've found a stock worthy of your investment dollars. Now you want to buy it, and since you've done all the research, you don't want to pay additional charges to a broker for taking an order. You want execution only. You want to trade on-line.

There are many on-line brokers, ranging from discount brokers to deep discount brokers. Some of them have software for setting up an account directly with the brokerage house, others have Internet sites where you open your account, still others are on AOL, Prodigy or CompuServe and you can open an account on the on-line service.

The commissions vary, some as low as $12 for a transaction regardless of the number of shares traded (eBroker offers this rate, found on the Internet at www.ebroker.com), and some go above $30 per transaction. There is a difference in service and information capabilities.

BROKERAGE BASICS

When you open an account with an on-line brokerage firm, whether it's a deep discount or discount broker, you should look for these qualities:

- Insured accounts: SIPC (Securities Insurance Protection Corporation) is standard with every account and covers up to $500,000 of your investments (limit of $100,000 in cash). Every broker who is a member of NASD (National Association of Securities Dealers) has this insurance, and every broker must be a member of NASD. Most brokers have purchased additional, private insurance, and most accounts are now protected up to a minimum of $2,500,000 or more.
- Access to a person for help if and when the broker's computer isn't working. During the market meltdown of 1987, the

biggest complaint about discount brokers was that clients couldn't get through to place orders. Make sure you ask your brokerage firm what it has done since then to help you place orders when the market is moving quickly and with heavy volume. At the very least, get a phone number and ask for the name of a person you can contact when everything hits the fan.

- Real-time quotes when you're placing an order. Many firms will have delayed quotes you can access to keep track of your stocks, but when you place an order, you want to know what's going on now. Stocks can move a great deal in fifteen or twenty minutes, the usual delay time for quotes. If you don't know where the stock is, you certainly don't want to put in a market order (an order that tells the broker to buy a stock at the current offer price or sell a stock at the current bid price).

- Timely reports on your trades. Many trades are done electronically, but if your broker doesn't have the ability to send your trade back to you, it will take a while to know whether you bought or sold a stock. Some firms use a telephone call to confirm a trade. I was told by one investor that the broker wouldn't leave the confirmation of the trade on an answering service so the investor never knew if the order had been executed unless he called the broker or saw the confirmation in the mail. You want a broker who will confirm your trade on the wire while you're waiting or if you've put in a limit order, will E-mail the confirmation to you upon execution. (A limit order is when you put a limit on the price of a stock, either to buy or sell it at a specific price. Sometimes limit orders don't get executed because the investor's price is never reached.)

- No minimums on order sizes. Some brokers require you to do a minimum size trade to get their price advantage. Work with the ones that don't have a minimum.

- No fees for IRAs or other accounts. Paying fees for most accounts isn't necessary, especially an IRA. Many brokers still charge an annual fee. Avoid them.

- Account access. You need to see your account. Make sure you can pull it up on your computer whenever you want. You will always get an account statement in the month you have activity in an account, but this is not timely enough for most investors.

THE SAFETY ISSUE

Most investors have an understandable concern about the safety of trading stocks over the telephone lines, which is what you do when you buy and sell on-line. And there is also the anxiety of some hacker getting into your brokerage account and transferring out money or securities. Here's what the brokerage community has done:

- When you open an account with a firm, you are given an account number and a Personal Identification Number (PIN), just like the bank account PIN that lets you access your account at ATM machines. No one knows your PIN except you. That's the first level of protection.
- When you enter an order, your instructions are encrypted from the time they leave your computer until they reach the computer at your brokerage firm. Encryption, in its most easily understood form, is simply scrambling information. So your PIN and account number and your transaction request is just a jumble of gibberish until they are reconstituted at the other end by the host computer. Anyone picking up your message wouldn't be able to read any of it.
- No money or securities can be removed by an on-line request. In other words, you can't have money wired to a bank or have securities sent to you via the computer. These requests need to be made in writing and sent to the broker. In this way, if a hacker ever did break into your account, the only activity would be buying and selling stocks. Since there is no economic incentive for anyone to do this, you can feel comfortable that your account is secure.

OPENING AN ACCOUNT ON-LINE

Since the Online Investor has a site on AOL, we have several brokers who advertise on our program. By clicking on one of their ads, you can find out more about each of them. One of them, PCFN, however, has established its own site on AOL and you can go directly to that site and open an account. Here's the process:

Either click on the ad banner or use the Keyword search function and enter the letters PCFN. The screen changes to the main page for PCFN. You have five choices: access your account (hard to do when you haven't opened one yet); a commission comparison box; an account opening option; a trade demonstration box; and a special offer. By clicking on any of the options, you can go to the site and see what's there.

The Compare Commissions site does just that. When you go to this page, it asks you to enter the number of shares you want to buy and the price of the stock. Then it calculates the cost of doing that trade with PCFN. It also shows what the same trade would cost at several other firms, most of them well-known discount brokers or a full-service broker. After you've checked that, go back to the main page by clicking on the box in the upper right corner of that page.

Back on PCFN's main page, you can click on the box entitled Try Our Online Demo. This takes you to a screen with a hypothetical trade that has already been entered. It shows the order that was entered: the amount of shares, the price requested, if it's a limit order, or no price if it's a market order, and if the shares were bought. It also shows other hypothetical trades that are outstanding and the prices for the open orders; the prices for the trades previously done, and the dates the trades were executed.

You can look at the order page by clicking on the box on the bottom of the screen entitled Change Order. On this site, you'll see the boxes you need to fill in. Here's what they ask for (these are the same questions you need to answer when you enter a real order):

QUANTITY

There's an open box where you enter the number of shares you want to buy. Put in the total number of shares, such as 100 or 200 or however many you're looking to buy or sell on this order.

ORDER TYPE

Market—this is when you want a fast execution and are willing to buy stock at the last price it is offered (the offer or ask side of the market) or sell stock at the last price it is bid (the bid side of the market). Be aware that this is not the last price at which the stock traded. A stock can trade between the bid and the offer price, but when you enter a Market order, you are telling the broker making a market in the stock or the specialist on the floor of the exchange that you want to buy stock at the offer price or sell it on the bid side, and you will accept whatever price exists when your order is entered.

LIMIT ORDER

This order puts a limit on the price at which you will sell or buy stock. The limit is a dollar price that you specify. It tells the specialist (if a stock trades on an exchange like the New York or American) or the market maker (if a stock trades on the NASDAQ) that you will buy stock only if it is offered at the price at which you wish to buy, or you will sell only if a stock is bid where you wish to sell.

Major caveat: When you're working with NASDAQ stocks, the ones with four letters in their symbols, these are all traded by market makers. When you enter a limit order, a market maker must actually bid for your stock at the price you entered to sell or offer stock at the price at which you wish to buy. In other words, the stock may trade all day at a price you entered, but you may not buy or sell any stock because no market maker bid or offered stock at any time during the trading day at the price you want to transact stock. It is very frustrating to watch stock trade and not get limit orders filled. Be aware this can happen to you. Also be aware that many brokers will not accept limit orders for NASDAQ stocks because the broker has to work the order with each market maker. There is no central exchange where you can leave your order, so the broker fills that function for you. Not all of them do. (Update: The NASDAQ is currently changing its rules to accommodate limit orders better.)

On the two exchanges, the New York and American, your limit order will become the bid or offer when a stock moves to your level. In other words, the specialist trading the stock cannot go ahead of your bid to buy stock once the stock gets to your level. Your bid then becomes the bid on the exchange, and you will buy stock if someone comes in to meet your bid. The same is true when you use limit orders to sell stocks on an exchange. When a stock reaches the level you want to sell at, your stock price (the limit order price) is the next offering price level on the exchange. The specialist cannot step in front of you and sell stock first.

You can see that if you're working with exchange stocks and a stock is moving quickly one way or the other, your limit orders have a good chance of being executed. Many times on the NASDAQ, because of the wide spreads (the difference between the bid and ask prices of a stock), limit orders have a difficult time being executed. Knowing this before you place an order can help you think about the realistic levels you want to place on any limit order.

STOP ORDER

This is an order that is placed above or below the market price and is only used on the exchanges. The NASDAQ stocks, because there is no central marketplace with one specialist but rather many different brokers making a market in the stock, don't facilitate stop orders. The Stop Order is used when you want to buy or sell a stock, but only after it has reached a certain level.

If the Stop Order is entered above the market price, it means you want to buy the stock and the price you are entering is the trigger price. Once that price is hit, you want to buy the stock, and your order becomes a Market Order (see page 208). You will buy the stock wherever the next offering is. Sometimes that is above the last price, sometimes at the same price, sometimes below the last price. Stop orders for buying stocks are usually used by investors who have sold a stock short and want to limit the pain when the stock starts going up, or they are used by technical traders who are looking for a certain price that pushes the stock above its trend line or other technical indicator, making the stock an attractive buy to them.

If investors use a Stop Order on the sell side, they usually are getting out of a stock because they're concerned it will go much lower. Like the Buy Order, your Stop Order to sell a security is triggered when your stock trades at the price you have given. Then your Stop Order becomes a Market Order (see page 208) and the next bid is the price you will receive for your stock.

ALL OR NONE ORDER

This order is used two ways: when you have a position in a stock and want to get out of all of it or you won't sell your stock, or when you want to buy a block of stock and want the whole block or nothing at all.

Sometimes when a stock trades only a few hundred shares in a day, these orders can help. If you don't use this order for a large sale of stock, sometimes you can sell only a hundred shares and then the bid (what a specialist or market maker is willing to pay for a stock) will go lower. By using the All or None Order, you are saying to the specialist or market maker that if they want your stock, they have to take all of it or they don't get any of it. Sometimes they'll take all of it, but sometimes, if they see a large enough block of stock, they won't buy it, and you'll see the bid move lower without any stock trading. That's because the market maker or specialist knows there is stock for sale, and since they have a legalized monopoly, they know you won't sell it anywhere else.

However, lowering their bids doesn't always work in their favor. If a buyer comes into the market while you're trying to sell your stock, they may need your block of stock and pay your price without hesitation. And if the market maker who lowers the bid also lowers the offering (this is not required and often is not the case), a buyer may come in and buy stock at the lower offering price. Now the market maker needs your stock, but you may not have left the order with your broker and your block is gone. The market maker then must raise the bid price to attract more sellers so the stock sold to the buyer at the lower price can be replaced. Sometimes the bid price moves above the level where the stock was sold and the market maker actually loses money. The reverse of the whole process, buying a block of stock, works the same way.

Use an All or None Order only when you have a large trade.

FILL OR KILL ORDER

Think of this as a flash order: do it now or don't do it. In other words, fill the order I have placed (buy or sell), or kill the order. When you enter an order with a limit price and make it a Fill or Kill Order as well, it gives the market maker or the specialist the opportunity to respond to your order. You're saying, in effect, here's my price and I want it now or I don't want to do business. The specialist can do it your way or not. But the order does not stay with the broker. If the order isn't filled, it's killed. You haven't bought or sold any stock.

PRICE

This is an empty box that can stay empty if you want the order to be a Market Order (see page 208). If you want to buy or sell a stock at a certain price, this is your opportunity to enter that price.

When you enter the order, use the decimal system. In other words, if a stock is trading at $32 ¼ and that's the price you want to buy it at, enter $32.25.

DURATION

This tells the broker how long you want the order you have entered to be in effect. The choices are: Day or Good Till Canceled (GTC). The Day Order means you only want your order to be active for the day you enter it. If it is not executed, the order is canceled. If you want to try again the following trading day, you must reenter the order.

The Good Till Canceled Order means just about that. These orders stay in effect until you cancel them or until ninety days have elapsed, at which time they are automatically canceled. I would caution against using this order unless the stock you are buying or selling is relatively quiet. With highly volatile issues, your order can be executed after news has been released, pushing your stock in one direction quickly. If the news is bad, you may not want to own the stock. But because you have an order waiting to be executed, it will automatically get filled once your price level is reached. This can be particularly devastating if you wake up one morning and see a poor earnings report or other bad news on a stock you're looking to buy, and your stock takes a tumble. If you had a GTC Order in to buy the stock, you now own it. With this latest news, you may wish you didn't.

ACCOUNT

You have three choices: Cash, Margin or Short.

Think of the *Cash account* as you would a checkbook. You can't write checks without money in the bank. In the Cash account, you can't buy stock unless you have money in the account or you have the money to pay for the stock within three business days of the trade date. In other words, all stocks purchased settle (the settlement date) for cash in three business days after you execute a trade (the trade date). You either have the cash in your account to pay for the trade or you put cash in the account by settlement date (three business days after trade date). Conversely, if you sell stock in the Cash account, you will receive cash for your sale three business days after you sell.

The *Margin account* gives you greater flexibility. Think of the Margin account as an account that gives you the right but not the obligation of borrowing money against securities you own. You can use it like a Cash account if you wish, buying and selling securities that are fully paid for on the settlement date. But you can also use it to leverage your investing. You want to be very careful if you use this facility. Much like credit cards for certain individuals, Margin accounts can bury you if you don't use them wisely.

This is the way a Margin account works: You buy stock, and instead of paying for all of it, you put in only 50% of the money due. The other 50% comes from the brokerage firm where you bought the stock. When you buy the stock, the seller on the other side wants 100% of the proceeds of the sale. If you put in only 50%, the other 50% has to come from somewhere. Where does the broker get its 50%? It pledges your stock to a bank and borrows from the bank on your behalf.

The broker will use your stock as collateral for a loan. The bank will then lend the money to the broker. The broker, in turn, will take those proceeds and pay off the seller of the stock. The seller is happy. The bank has a fully collateralized loan that pays a good rate of interest. The bank is happy. The broker is charging you the rate of interest the bank is charging plus adding on a certain amount for its troubles. The broker is happy. You have more stock than you would if you had to use a cash account since you've only paid for 50% of the position. You may or may not be happy.

What could be wrong with this picture? Let's look at what might happen after you've bought your stock. Keep in mind that the money you've borrowed is costing you every day the loan is outstanding. Much like a small hole in the bottom of a boat, a little water comes in at a time, but eventually, unless you correct the problem, you will sink. Similarly, if the stock you've bought on margin doesn't move up after a while, even if it stays at the same price, you lose money because you have to pay interest on the money you've borrowed to buy the stock. If the stock has a dividend, that will help defray this cost, but it's a rare stock that pays a dividend anywhere near the margin cost of funds.

Another problem comes when the stock goes down. If the price goes down to a level where your equity is only worth 25% of the value of your original purchase, you will get a margin call requiring you to deposit money or securities to bring the value of your equity to a 50% level. Let's look at an example:

You buy 100 shares of stock X at $10 per share for a total cost of $1,000 plus commissions (you're using a deep discount broker and you've kept this number very small). For our purposes let's just round it off to $1,000. You deposit $500, and use margin to pay for the remainder of the purchase. You now own $1,000 worth of stock, for which you've paid $500. You are now leveraged. If the stock goes to $20 per share, you own $2,000 worth of stock that cost you $500 and you've made a 200% return on your investment. You are now ecstatic. (Here's the math: sell the stock at $20 for proceeds of $2,000. Pay off the $500 borrowed in the purchase. You go home with $1,500 from an investment of $500. That's a 200% return. I have ignored the commissions and interest charges as well as the capital gains tax in the example, something you can't do in the real world.)

Now let's see what happens if the stock goes to $6 a share. Your total investment is worth $600. You still owe $500. Your original equity of $500 has diminished to $100. Notice the bank loan remains the same size and is growing every day because of added interest. The bank is not comfortable. Your collateral of stock is not valued highly enough for the bank's loan. Much like a teenager, it wants more money, and it will not be denied. If you don't come up with the money, the broker has the right to sell you out of your position, pay off the banker and send you whatever is left.

Before the brokerage takes any action, it sends you a notice called a margin call. In this example the call would ask for $200 because you have to bring the value of the account to a 50% level of the value of the securities. (Remember your equity is only worth $100.) You can put in cash, if you have it, or you can put in securities worth twice the value of the margin call, if you have them. The reason for twice as much value in securities is because you can only borrow 50% against them. If you don't have the cash or the securities, the broker will sell you out.

And when do you suppose investors get the most margin calls? Not when the market is moving up. The banks are happy then, the broker is happy then, and investors are very happy then. The margin calls start shooting out when the market heads south. And if you don't have the ability to meet them, you will lose your securities. What is also true is that you will lose control of your investments. Just when you least want to sell your securities, you may be forced to because of too much borrowing.

Don't lose control of your investments. Don't put yourself in a position of weakness by borrowing more than you can comfortably maintain. I would go so far as to urge you to use margin only on a temporary basis, not as a permanent part of your investment strategy.

One other comment about margin: not all securities can be put on margin. The general rule is that the stock must be selling at $5 or more. But that general rule isn't always applicable. Every security is scrutinized by each broker, and even if a stock costs more than $5, if it is not liquid or has other factors that make it unsuitable, it will not be eligible for margin. Don't buy a stock assuming you can buy it on margin. Ask your broker before you enter a trade if the stock is eligible for margin accounts. If it isn't, you'll have to pay the full amount due on settlement. The broker makes the decision whether a stock can be put on margin, keeping in mind the rules prescribed by the Securities and Exchange Commission on which stocks can be margined.

To sum up: margin, like all borrowing, can be used wisely and well if it isn't done excessively. Use your margin ability sparingly. Sometimes it can be very profitable. But if it's a constant investment tactic, you will eventually be caught in a down market, forced to sell out securities you want to hold, and suffer considerable loss. Keep margin use to a minimum and keep control of your investments.

The *Short account* is a special account used for shorting stock. You must use this account if you are going to sell a stock short. When you think a stock will go down in value, you can sell the stock short and buy it back later at a lower price. By entering your order in a Short account, you are notifying the broker you don't own the stock but want to sell it. The broker will then check if you can sell a stock short because the broker must borrow the stock from another account or from another broker.

When you sell a stock short, you are selling the stock to another buyer. Since you don't own the stock, you won't be able to deliver it to the buyer. Your broker, however, may be able to borrow the stock on your behalf and deliver it to the buyer. If the broker doesn't have the stock in another account and can't find another broker from whom to borrow the stock to deliver to the buyer, you can't short the stock. There isn't any available to satisfy the other side of your trade. Therefore, your broker will come back to you and tell you, no, you can't short the stock. Most of the time, you can short a stock, but many times you cannot.

One more warning about shorting stocks: short squeeze. This is when a stock is heavily shorted and then starts to go up in price. When it goes up, the owners of the stock want to sell it. When they want to sell, they must have their stock. If you have borrowed their stock for your short, you will lose your short position. Your broker will buy you stock at this higher price to deliver back to the original owner. Your short will be squeezed. This is not pretty, fun, or profitable. Shorting stocks is a very sophisticated strategy and is best left to professionals who understand all the ramifications of what it means to be short a stock.

THE MOST COMMON ACCOUNTS AND TRADES

The vast majority of investors don't need all these options. You are best served if you open a Cash account and place Market Orders. As you get more experienced and knowledgeable, you can experiment with margin, limit orders, short selling, etc. Initially you don't need to know about these options. Just get started with the basics and build on those.

It's really that easy. You open an account by filling in the forms right on your computer. Depending on your answers, you may be able to trade a small amount of stock before you have to put in any money. The forms are self-explanatory and ask for your name, social security number, address, income and other relevant data. If you have sufficient income or experience, you may be approved within seconds and enter your trade. If you are not immediately accepted, you will need to mail in a check to the broker and have the deposit in the account before you do your first trade. All of this is fully explained on-line as you are opening the account.

Opening your account and buying and selling stocks on-line can be somewhat confusing initially because there seem to be so many options. Not only can you use the above descriptions to help you answer your questions, but all on-line brokers will be happy to walk you through the choices and explain which account is best suited for you. If you make the effort, you will save money. After the first few trades, you'll feel very comfortable with the process.

The following are a sample of on-line brokers who have Internet sites, direct on-line access through proprietary software or through on-line services such as AOL:

Accutrade	800-228-3011
Brown & Co.	800-822-2021
Ceres	800-669-3900
Charles Schwab & Co.	800-e-Schwab
eBroker	E-mail address only: www.ebroker.com
E*Trade	800-786-2575
Fidelity	800-544-7272
Jack White	800-753-1700
K. Aufhauser	800-368-3668
Lombard Securities	800-LOMBARD
National Discount Brokers	800-4-1-PRICE ext. 700
Olde Discount Brokers	401-841-5600
PC Financial Network	800-825-5723
Quick & Reilly	800-837-7220

More About AOL Financial Sites

Here's a sampling of more financial resources on AOL:

Company News: a site that compiles news articles from four sources such as Reuters and PR Newswire. Brings you up to date quickly on any news affecting a stock. Keyword: Company News.

Company Research: a site that includes financial statements on more than 6,000 stocks; Earnings Estimates supplied by First Call, helps you know what analysts expect for the next quarter and year's earnings; a link to EDGAR (Electronic Data Gathering and Retrieval), the SEC site on the Internet for all 10-K and 10-Q reports from publicly held companies; historical stock quotes, a graphing service that gives you a price history for one month, one year or three years. This is where on-line investors will spend the most time. Keyword: Company Research.

Current Quotes: a site that gives you a quote on most traded stocks. Just put in the symbol of the stock, or if you don't know it, the name of the company and it will find the symbol for you. You'll get the following information from your inquiry: last price on the stock;

the change for the day from the previous day; the high price for the day; the low price for the day; the opening price; the previous day's close; the volume for the day; the average volume per day for the last 30 days; total shares outstanding; the 52-week high and low for the stock; the beta of the stock (an historical measure of how volatile the stock is compared to the market in general; if a stock has a beta of 1, it means the stock has gone up and down as much as the market; if the beta is less than 1, the price has moved up and gone down less than the market; if the beta is over 1, the stock has moved up and gone down more than the market); the yield of the stock; the P/E of the stock; and finally the earnings per share. Keyword: QUOTES.

Portfolios: This feature lets you enter the stocks you want to follow or own. You enter the symbol and the price you've paid for the stock, and the program tells you how much you are making or losing with every change in price, as well as how the total portfolio is performing. You can put as many portfolios on the system as you like. Keyword: PORTFOLIO.

AND THE BEAT GOES ON

AOL, like Prodigy and CompuServe, is continually evolving. By the time you read this summary, there will have been changes, additions and deletions. The exact site or bit of information is not as important as your desire to get on-line and start digging. If you are using AOL, start with our site, The Online Investor. It will help you find the data sources needed to make better decisions, and it explains how to use the information after you've found it.

Eventually, all the information an investor needs will be on-line. It may reside in a combination of places, some of it on an on-line service such as AOL, some on the Internet. Some of it will be free, and some will cost. The on-line evolution continues, and the beneficiary is the individual investor. The sooner you start your investing program on-line, the more information you'll have.

CHAPTER TEN

NOW GO DO IT!

The biggest obstacle to investment success is yourself. This book gives you the tools needed for making better investment decisions. Now it's up to you to take those tools and make them work for you.

Like walking, the first steps to building your computer system and portfolio will be the hardest. You'll make mistakes. Frustration with your new computer will make you say bad words, loudly and often. You'll pick losing stocks and feel like a failure. At times, you'll hate the stock market, the computer, and life in general. Get over it, and get on with investing.

At other times, you'll feel like a genius when a stock you bought gains several points in one day or is bought out by another company for a hefty premium over your purchase price. I hope that doesn't happen on your first trade. You'll think investing is easy, and that you've found a sure-fire way to make money. As soon as you make quick profits, enjoy them and then become more cautious. The market will not often give you easy money. As with a loss, get over it and get back to investing. And *never* confuse a bull market with genius.

ONCE AGAIN, THE BASICS

You need a decent computer and a good on-line service. All three of the main services, AOL, CompuServe and Prodigy, are very good. I have a strong affinity for AOL because of my site on it, The Online Investor, and the fact that it charges a flat rate without add-on charges for certain features. You can find almost every data point in this book on AOL, you just have to look a little more to find it. You don't have to pay extra for it, however. For about $120 per year, you can access financial information on stocks and mutual funds as well as the Internet for many other resources. If you want a more professional package, you can move up to Bloomberg's financial service, which goes for about $20,000 per year. It, too, represents value, but you need a large portfolio and full-time attention to it to justify that kind of money.

With your computer and on-line service, you're on the hunt for stocks which historically have given the best returns. Those are small-cap, growth companies that ideally have the following characteristics:

- Decent P/E Ratio. Be suspect of P/Es that are too low or too high. Too high or too low are relative to the current average P/E on the S&P 500 Index or the Russell 2000 Index.
- Low Price-to-Sales Ratio (PSR). You want this below 1 and if it's over 3, you should have very good reasons for owning the stock, and contact with a fairy godmother.
- Low Price-to-Book Ratio. The closer this number is to 1, the closer you are to buying the company's stock for its book value.
- High Relative Strength. This measures the stock's price performance relative to the market. A higher number, above 80, is good.
- A Relatively Decent Beta. Beta measures the volatility of a stock versus the market. The higher the Beta, the more ups and downs you'll have. Betas above 1 mean you'll move up and down faster than the market in general. If you're bullish, you want a high Beta.
- A High Profit Margin. The closer you get to 100%, which is impossible, the better your stock will perform. Realistically, you want above 15% for a small-cap growth stock.
- A High Return on Equity (ROE). Make 15% your minimum interest level.
- A High Return on Assets. This is a number that varies depending on the industry group. Always check the industry average and make sure you're buying a stock with above-average returns.
- Low Debt-to-Equity Ratio. Look for less than 1.00. That means all debt is less than 100% of the equity. Too much debt is like too much of anything.

- Low Long-Term Debt-to-Equity Ratio (LTD/Equity). This should be a small number, less than 0.50. It gives you the amount of long-term debt divided by the equity.
- High Quick Ratio. This measures the amount of cash available for paying bills. More cash is better than less. Many small-cap stocks have a ratio less than 1. Above 1 is better. It means that the company has enough cash to pay its bills for the next year if the bills are the same as they were the previous year.
- High Current Ratio. This puts inventories, marketable securities and receivables in with cash. This should be above 2 for comfort. Higher is better.
- High Growth Rates for Sales and Earnings. Look for earnings growing faster than sales. It means that your company is getting more efficient.
- Don't Worry About Dividends. Small-cap stocks don't pay too many dividends because they need the cash for growth. If you want dividends, buy utilities.
- Mid to High Capital Expenditures. This number is related to depreciation. If the company is replacing old machines and adding new ones, it's growing.
- Strong Free Cash Flow (FCF). This is earnings plus depreciation. Look for 10% or better by dividing the FCF per share by the price of the stock.
- Small to Medium Percentage of Outstanding Stock Held by Institutions. This should be at least 5%, but not more than 30%. Too much institutional ownership leaves no one else to buy the stock. Too little means no one cares about it.
- High Management Ownership of Stock. The more management owns, the better it'll manage your company. It's in its best interest.

GETTING INTO THE RHYTHM OF
CHECKING OUT STOCKS

The above list is a shortened version of Chapter 6 and can be used to quickly check a stock. Those attributes are the hot buttons for good investing. They're not the only ones, but they represent major influences on a stock's success. And with a computer and an on-line service, you can quickly determine each of them within a matter of minutes. Yes, it's that easy after you've done it several times.

Once you've set up your computer, you can spend just a few minutes a day looking for new stocks, reading news stories on ones you own, or checking out the latest tip from a taxi driver. You'll find each stock has its strengths and weaknesses. And you'll develop your own sense of the ones you want to investigate further, subjecting them to the rigors of analysis described in Chapter 6 and Appendix B. As with everything, the more you practice, the easier the routine gets.

That's really the purpose of this book, to let you know you can do it. There are new easy-to-use tools such as computers and on-line services that make digging for investments easy. You don't need to be brilliant to do it. You do need to be persistent and diligent.

OTHER IMPORTANT INGREDIENTS

There's more to investment success than finding stocks with the right numbers. The most important ingredients are:

- Patience. Give your stock time to perform. If the market goes down, most likely your stock will also. It may generate strong earnings and still lose ground because investors perceive the industry as having already peaked with a bleak future. Reexamine your reasons for owning the stock. If you're comfortable and the earnings keep going up, eventually, the stock will also.

- Buy on down days, sell on up days. This is difficult to do initially because everything seems so hopeless on down days and so limitless on up days. If you can be the only buyer when everyone else is selling, you may not buy at the bottom, but you will definitely get better performance from your portfolio. Conversely, when the market is roaring, put in a day order to sell above the stock's current price. Similar to a rainbow trout going for a caddis fly, if someone pays your price and you've made your profit target, take home your profits and come back another day. Unlike the trout, you can always keep the money.

- Take losses. Don't have a percentage where you cut and run. Have a good reason for selling, such as lack of earnings growth and no foreseeable change in the future. Watching a stock slowly erode and then drop like a slippery jar of jam is most unpleasant. A loss can happen for any reason, such as a promising drug not performing as planned in clinical trials. If you own the stock because you were banking on that drug, take your loss.

Taking a loss is probably the best demarcation line separating pros from amateurs. There are unexpected events that change the nature of a stock or the perception of it, such as an earnings estimate being revised downward shortly after you buy the stock. If you've done your homework, read all the available reports, and made a decision based on those, there's no way you can possibly know an earnings estimate will be revised. Or that three top executives will mysteriously leave the company in one day, which is what happened to Micron Technology. When these news bombs explode, you need to take in those facts, determine their significance and be brutally honest with yourself. If you feel the company has changed because of the news, get out.

- Enjoy the adventure. Investing can be like a photo safari without the mosquitoes. It's very exciting to come across a stock with most of the right numbers, read the company's reports, and track the ticker symbol across the tape. When the stock gets to your buying level, you take monetary aim and capture your prize. How the investment develops will depend on many factors, but part of your enjoyment should come from the hunt and discovery. Some investments, unfortunately, don't turn out. Some are works of beauty, giving you the thrill of victory and a good story to tell your friends.

THE EVENING RITUAL

Your ultimate goal should be to spend less than 30 minutes per day on your portfolio once you have purchased stocks. That's easily done with the computer.

Set aside a designated time for your investment work. Have your computer in a relatively quiet place, if possible. Sit down every night, turn on the computer, check your holdings and any stocks you're following by using the Portfolios feature on America Online or other on-line service, and read news on your stocks by using the Company News feature of America Online.

The Portfolios page on AOL has the News by Ticker icon. When you click once on this icon, a box appears asking for the symbol of the stock. After it is entered, a scrolling box of headlines appears; they have been collected from the last month of news. By double clicking on the headline of your choice, you can see the full story.

If you have 10 stocks, each one won't be in the news every day. Sometimes none will be mentioned for several days or weeks. Other times, especially at the beginning of each quarter, there will be earnings announcements or new developments reported. That's when you need to make a decision on a stock: leave it alone, buy more of it or sell it.

With new earnings, you can plug in the numbers in the stock evaluation form (Appendix B). Have the latest data made the stock more or less attractive? Besides the numbers, were there any new products or management changes announced? Consider every piece of information. Review why you own the stock. Make it a daily habit.

On the weekends, you can use the AAII screening program on AOL or the Stock Hunter Feature on Prodigy to find new stocks. The Stock Hunter is part of the Strategic Investor option, which you must buy as an extra to the basic service. On Saturday morning, all of the data on more than 6,000 stocks is updated.

By using the various investment screens from CANSLIM to Wall-flowers in the Stock Hunter program, you can pick out new stocks to investigate. Do not buy a stock because you like all the numbers in this program. Those numbers are not adjusted, and you must get the annual and quarterly reports from the company or the Company Reports section of Prodigy or read an updated research report in *Value Line* or from a brokerage firm to determine what really happened during the quarter.

Also, these are only numbers. They do not give the news on the company. You'll need to check the Company News feature on Prodigy or AOL to see what has happened over the last few weeks at the company you're considering.

If you're thinking that this is a lot of work, you're still in the past. With the computer, all of these tasks can be done in minutes, from screening for stocks, looking at the appropriate ratios and then reading the news articles. And each step is easily done by moving the screen arrow to the right box, double-clicking and then letting the computer do the work.

YOU CAN DO THIS!

There has never been a better time to be an investor. We are very fortunate to live in a time when the computer does much of the work for us, especially searching databases and computing ratios. And the cost is very affordable, especially if you choose your on-line service carefully. I have found each service has its strong points and would recommend you try each to find the one that fits your style. Certainly, the most cost effective one is AOL.

The computer is also getting easier to use. If you tried several years ago and gave up in frustration, no one can blame you, especially if you tried a DOS-based computer. Those were sadistic machines, released to an unsuspecting public with great promise and tremendous complications.

Those days are gone. Computers are getting closer and closer to their objective: easy use for everyone. As an investor, you can't go another day without one. They're not as easy as they're going to be, but they are way ahead of where they were only two years ago. Buy one and with one good investment, you'll pay for it. In a few years, you can upgrade to a faster, better model.

Even with a computer, investing is a challenge. In one sense, it is easier than ever to invest because you can get information in seconds. But remember, that means so can everyone else. That makes the public more informed and better investors. That means that stock prices will reflect news more quickly. If you don't have a computer, you are at an investing disadvantage.

However, if you have a computer and use the methods described in this book for buying stocks, you will make better, more informed decisions. You will feel more confident about investing, have good reasons for buying a stock or mutual fund, and by investing in small-cap stocks or funds, know you have as much or more knowledge than other investors.

Good luck and *now go do it*!

SMALL-CAP NEWSLETTERS

The following is a sample of newsletters that specialize in small-cap stocks or have small-cap stock features as part of their publication. This is not an endorsement of any of them. I highly recommend you call or write the ones of interest and ask for a free sample. If you like it, subscribe for a trial period of three months or if there is a money-back guarantee, subscribe for a year and cancel if you become dissatisfied. If they won't send a free sample, perhaps you shouldn't subscribe.

A good review of most of these newsletters is published annually in *The Hulbert Guide to Financial Newsletters*.

> *The Addison Report*: P.O. Box 402, Franklin, MA 02038
>   Phone: 508-528-8678
> *Bi Research*: P.O. Box 133, Redding, CT 06875   No phone given
> *Better Investing*: National Association of Investors, 1515 E. Eleven Mile
>   Rd., Royal Oak, MI 48067   Phone: 313-543-0612, 810-583-6242
> *The Cabot Market Letter*: P.O. Box 3067, Salem, MA 01970
>   Phone: 508-745-5532
> *California Technology Stock Letter*: P.O. Box 308, Half Moon Bay, CA
>   94019   Phone: 415-726-8495
> *The Clean Yield*: P.O. Box 1880, Greensboro Bend, VT 05842
>   Phone: 802-533-7178
> *Common Stocks, Common Sense*: P.O. Box 224, Concord, MA
>   01742-0224   Phone: 508-371-1677
> *Dow Theory Forecasts*: 7412 Calumet Ave., Hammond, IN 46324-2692
>   Phone: 219-931-6480
> *Emerging & Special Situations*: Standard & Poor's Corp., 25 Broad-
>   way, New York, NY 10004   Phone: 212-208-8152
> *Financial World*: P.O. Box 7098, Red Oak, IA 51591
>   Phone: 212-594-5030

Growth Stock Outlook: P.O. Box 15381, Chevy Chase, MD 20825
    Phone: 301-654-5205
Investment Horizons: 680 N. Lakeshore Drive, Tower Suite 2038,
    Chicago, IL 60611   Phone: 312-649-6940
Kinsman's Low-Risk Growth Letter: 584 1st St. East, Sonoma, CA
    95476   Phone: 707-935-6504
Laloggia's Special Situation Report: P.O. Box 167, Rochester, NY
    14601   Phone: 716-232-1240
MPT Review: P.O. Box 5695, Incline Village, NV 89450
    Phone: 702-831-7800
Market Mania: P.O. Box 1234, Pacifica, Ca. 94044
    Phone: 415-952-8853
Medical Technology Stock Letter: P.O. Box 40460, Berkeley, CA
    94704   Phone: 510-843-1857
New Issues: The Institute for Econometric Research,
    3471 N. Federal Hwy., Fort Lauderdale, FL 33306
    Phone: 800-327-6720
OTC Insight: Insight Capital Management, P.O. Box 127, Moraga, CA
    94556   Phone: 800-955-9566
OTC Review Special Situations: 37 E. 28th St., New York, NY 10016
    Phone: 800-237-8400, Ext. 61
The Oberweist Report: Hamilton Investments, 841 N. Lake, Aurora, IL
    60506   Phone: 800-323-6166
The Outlook: Standard & Poor's, 25 Broadway, New York, NY 10004
    Phone: 800-221-5277 or 212-208-8812
Personal Finance: P.O. Box 1467, Alexandria, VA 22313-9819
    Phone: 800-832-2330 or 703-548-2400
The Princeton Portfolios: 301 N. Harrison, Suite 229, Princeton, NJ
    08540   Phone: 212-717-5125
The Prudent Speculator: P.O. Box 1767, Santa Monica, CA
    90406-1767   Phone: 310-587-2410
The Red Chip Review: 50 S.W. Second Avenue, Suite 320, Portland,
    OR 97204   Phone: 503-241-1265
The Turnaround Letter: New Generations, Inc., 225 Friend St.,
    Suite 801, Boston, MA 02114   Phone: 617-573-9550
United & Babson Investment Report: Babson-United Building,
    101 Prescott St., Wellesley Hills, MA 02181
    Phone: 617-235-0900
Value Line Investment Survey: 220 East 42nd St., New York, NY
    10017   Phone: 800-634-3583
Value Line OTC Special Situations Service: 220 East 42nd St.,
    New York, NY 10017   Phone: 800-634-3583
The Zweig Forecast: P.O. Box 360, Bellmore, NY 11710
    Phone: 516-223-3800
Zweig Performance Ratings Report: P.O. Box 360, Bellmore, NY
    11710   Phone: 516-223-3800

EVALUATION SHEET MATH ◄----┘

By using a mathematical approach for ranking investments, you can compare stocks and invest only in the strongest ones. However, just because a stock comes out well based on the numbers does not mean you have a winning stock.

For example, consider the stock of Russ Berrie & Co. This is a fine company with a good balance sheet that during 1992 and 1993 had banner years. The numbers generated from my evaluation sheet put this stock well ahead of any others at the time. When I looked at the price of the stock, it was selling very cheaply by almost any measure. But that was just by using the numbers.

After receiving the annual report, I called the company. The president, who was most gracious, returned my inquiry. I learned the strong earnings had come from one source: Troll dolls. Even the president didn't think it was possible to duplicate the company's success or exceed it until there was a new product. Troll dolls, as you can imagine, were very hot and then not.

You will find companies like Berrie with very exciting numbers. However, if the stock is very cheap, there is probably a reason. That's why, at the very least, you need the reports from the companies or a call to the investor relations department or a senior officer. You can't buy companies by the numbers. If it were that easy, the largest, fastest computers would screen all stocks every day, pick the winners and make money. Some firms do screen stocks every day, but the successful ones use that as a starting place, not an investment decision point.

AN EVALUATION SHEET FOR RANKING STOCKS

The following is one way to rank stocks. Most of the numbers can be found on most on-line services, *Value Line Investment Survey, Investor's Business Daily*, or be calculated by hand.

I recommend you put this program on a spreadsheet, such as Excel or Lotus 1-2-3, and let the computer do your work for you. Refer back to Chapter 6 for explanations of terms.

THE BIG PICTURE OR WHAT YOU'RE TRYING TO DO

The basic concept for this procedure is to assign a value for each ratio or number generated by a stock, add up those valuations, divide by the P/E of a stock, and compare that number with all others. Then you can rank the stocks from the highest value to the lowest.

I use a scale from 1 to 10 for the relative value of a ratio. For example, I give PSR (Price-to-Sales Ratio) a value of 8, Profit Margin a value of 10, and Five-Year Earnings Per Share Growth a 5. You may want to change the valuations according to your preference. However, this formula will provide you with a good starting point for valuing stocks.

THE GRID

Across the top of a page, put the following abbreviations: PSR, P/Book, PFT MGN, ROE, ROA, D/E, QCK RTO, CUR RTO, 1 YR EPS, 3 YR EPS, 5 YR EPS, QTR EPS, FCF, MGT %, INST %, REL STR, REL EPS, P/E. Let's look at each of these:

PSR is Price-to-Sales Ratio. Ideally, a stock will have a PSR below 1. Beneath the heading of PSR, allow for five spaces. The first space should be labeled "Actual PSR." In the second, put "Below 1." In the third, put "Between 1 and 2"; and in the fourth, put "Greater than 2." Label the last one "Total Value." It looks like this:

PSR

Actual PSR
Below 1
Between 1 and 2
Greater than 2
Total Value

Now I find the PSR for the stock on Prodigy, and write it in the first space. Let's say it's 0.5. Then I give the line "Below 1" a value of 10. The next line has a value of 5, and the last one has a value of 1. Since our mythical stock has a PSR of 0.5, that number goes on the first line.

In this program, I have given the PSR a relative value of 8. I will now add that to the heading and use that number as a multiplier. The filled-in headings and lines look like this:

PSR (Value: 8)

Actual PSR:	0.5
Below 1:	10 points
Between 1 and 2:	5 points
Greater than 2:	1 point
Total Value:	80 points

Here's how the math works: Since the PSR is under 1, I multiply the value of the "Below 1" column times the Relative Value of the category. In this case, it's 8. Therefore, Total Value is 8 times 10 = 80. If the PSR had been 1.3, then Total Value would be the product of 8 times 5, or 40.

Now we're going to do this for all headings, using relative values and points for each category. The next is Price to Book or P/Book. Using the same mythical stock with which we started, I found the P/Book in Prodigy and America Online with a value of 1.7.

P/BOOK (Value: 7)

Actual P/Book	1.7	
Below 1:	10	points
Between 1 and 2.5:	5	points
Greater than 2.5:	1	point
Total Value:	35	points

Remember, I'm multiplying the relative value of the category times the number of points, not the P/Book ratio. Since this stock had a ratio which put it in the second category, the formula was 7 times 5 = 35.

The next category is PFT MGN or profit margin. This one has a relative value of 10, and the stock I'm creating has a profit margin of 17%, a number I found on the Prodigy service and AOL.

PROFIT MARGIN (Value: 10)

Actual Profit Margin:	17%	
Greater than 25%:	10	points
Between 15% and 25%:	8	points
Between 10% and 15%:	5	points
Below 10%:	1	point
Total Value:	80	points

I've used four categories here for a little more fine-tuning. I multiplied the relative value of the category (10) times the points in the category. In this case: 10 times 8 = 80.

Next, look at ROE or Return on Equity. My stock has an ROE of 22%, a number I found on Prodigy and AOL.

RETURN ON EQUITY (Value: 8)

Actual ROE:	22%	
Greater than 30%:	10	points
Between 20% and 30%:	8	points
Between 10% and 20%:	5	points
Below 10%:	1	point
Total Value:	64	points

You probably understand the formula by now. I'm going to continue to fill in each category with relative values and points. When I've entered all of them, I'll sum the total values and divide that by the P/E of the stock. That will give me a ranking number which I assign to the stock, but I'll explain more about that later. For now, here are the remaining categories:

RETURN ON ASSETS (Value: 6)

Actual ROA:	6%		Source: Prodigy
Greater than 20%:	10	points	
Between 10% and 20%	5	points	

Between 5% and 10%:   3 points
Below 5%:   1 point
Total Value: 18 points

This category is a little tricky because a banking stock is doing great if its ROA is greater than 2%. That's why it's important to compare stocks within their industry groups and not against all other stocks. You'll discover each industry has some peculiarities. Again, that's why you can't use numbers as the sole measure for investing.

DEBT-TO-EQUITY RATIO (Value: 5)

Actual D/E:	0.05	Source: Prodigy
Below 0.10:	10 points	and America Online
Between 0.10 and 0.25:	8 points	
Between 0.25 and 0.50:	5 points	
Greater than 0.50:	1 point	
Total Value:	50 points	

QUICK RATIO (Value: 7)

Actual Quick Ratio:	2.35	Source: Prodigy
Greater than 2:	10 points	
Between 1.5 and 2:	8 points	
Between 1 and 1.5:	6 points	
Below 1:	1 point	
Total Value:	70 points	

CURRENT RATIO (Value: 5)

Actual Current Ratio:	3.5	Source: Prodigy
Greater than 3:	10 points	
Between 2 and 3:	8 points	
Between 1 and 2:	5 points	
Below 1:	1 point	
Total Value:	50 points	

ONE YEAR EARNINGS PER SHARE (Value: 9)

Actual 1 Year EPS Growth:	40%	Source: Prodigy
Greater than 50%:	10 points	and America Online
Between 40% and 50%:	8 points	
Between 30% and 40%:	6 points	
Between 20% and 30%:	5 points	
Between 10% and 20%:	3 points	
Below 10%:	1 point	
Total Value:	72 points	

THREE YEAR EARNINGS PER SHARE (Value: 7)

Actual 3 Year EPS Growth:	25%	Source: Prodigy
Same as above in one year EPS		and America Online
Total Value:	35 points	

FIVE YEAR EARNINGS PER SHARE
(Value: 5)

Actual 5 Year EPS Growth:	15%	Source: Prodigy
Same as above in one year EPS		
Total Value:	15 points	

QUARTER EARNINGS PER SHARE (Value: 10)

Actual Quarterly EPS:	57%	Source: Prodigy
Same as above in one year EPS		and America Online
Total Value:	100 points	

FREE CASH FLOW PER SHARE
(Value: 8)

Actual Free Cash Flow Per Share:	$1.00	Source: Prodigy
		and America Online
Free Cash Flow (FCF) divided by price of stock:	12%	
Actual FCF/Stock price:	12%	
Greater than 15%:	10 points	
Between 10% and 15%:	8 points	
Between 5% and 10%:	6 points	
Below 5%:	1 point	
Total Value:	64 points	

MANAGEMENT OWNERSHIP (Value: 8)

Actual Management Ownership:	24%	Source: Prodigy
Greater than 40%:	10 points	
Between 30% and 40%:	8 points	
Between 20% and 30%:	6 points	
Between 10% and 20%:	5 points	
Between 5% and 10%:	3 points	
Below 5%:	1 point	
Total Value:	48 points	

INSTITUTIONAL OWNERSHIP (Value: 7)

Actual Institutional Ownership:	10%	Source: Prodigy
Greater than 50%:	1 point	
Between 30% and 50%:	3 points	
Between 20% and 30%:	5 points	
Between 10% and 20%:	8 points	
Between 3% and 10%:	10 points	
Below 3%:	1 point	
Total Value:	70 points	

RELATIVE STRENGTH (Value: 8)

Actual Relative Strength:	85	Source: *Investor's Business Daily*
Greater than 90:	10 points	
Between 80 and 90:	8 points	

Between 70 and 80:	6	points
Between 60 and 70:	4	points
Between 50 and 60:	2	points
Below 50:	1	point
Total Value:	64	points

RELATIVE EARNINGS PER SHARE (Value: 10)

Actual Relative EPS:	74	Source: *Investor's Business Daily*
Same as above		
Total Value:	60	points

PRICE-TO-EARNINGS RATIO

Actual P/E:	25	Source: Prodigy, America Online, *Investor's Business Daily, Wall Street Journal*

Now add up all Total Values for the stock and divide that number by the P/E. The sum of the Total Values is 975 for this hypothetical stock. Now divide the P/E ratio of 25 into that number (975 divided by 25 = 39). The number 39 is assigned to our stock.

The reason we divide the total by the P/E is this: the P/E is an equalizer in the marketplace. If a stock is very strong in several categories, such as earnings and cash flow, the P/E should reflect that. If you find a great stock, don't be surprised if other investors agree with you and push the stock's P/E up to reflect their enthusiasm. Your efforts become much more worthwhile when you find a low P/E stock with strong earnings, cash flow, ROE, ROA and several other categories. By using this formula, those stocks will have the highest rank.

You should know several things about this formula: It is a starting point for studying stocks. It can be adapted to your particular biases. For example, you may think Institutional Ownership is more important than Relative EPS. In that case, give each category a different weighting than the one I have. You may also want to fine-tune the points, giving narrower ranges or assigning more points to outstanding performances such as greater than 50% quarterly EPS growth.

You can also add items, such as number of insiders buying their own stock or number of insiders selling. Or some people feel accumulation and distribution of a stock is important. Whatever you want to add is fine. You should take this set of numbers and make it reflect your thinking and comfort levels.

Please remember, no matter how exciting a stock looks after you've ranked it, don't buy it. Get the reports from the company, talk to the officers, read research reports from analysts following the stock—watch the stock trade for a few days or weeks and get to know it before you become an owner in the company.

If you would like a copy of the Excel file which I have developed for this program, please send $35 plus $3.00 for shipping and handling, to:

> Allrich Investment Management
> 761 Arlington Road
> Redwood City, CA 94062-1856.

APPENDIX C

PORTFOLIO SOFTWARE ◄----'

Software is one area in which free or the lowest price should not be the driving force behind using a program. The most important consideration is your need. You may be able to use free software, or you may have to pay dearly for a special program. In either case, you will get value for your money, and I advise you to carefully consider every possibility before starting with new software.

The biggest concern is growing out of the capability of a program. Your record-keeping increases as you invest in various stocks, receive dividends, interest and stock splits. If you have mutual funds reinvest in the fund instead of sending you money, each of those entries must be made in your portfolio software. Over the years, hundreds of entries are made.

If your software can't handle your portfolio's changes over time, you will have to reenter each of those items on any new program you purchase. This is not a pleasant task, and furthermore, it virtually assures you of making errors in the data. Avoid the problem by buying the best program now and growing into it.

The following are a sample of portfolio management programs. New ones will be out next week, and some of the ones described here will be bought or have a name change or stop doing business. I've tried to include the larger, more established names and what their programs do.

SCHWAB'S STREETSMART

This is first because it's free and very good. The only catch is: You must open a Schwab One Account to get it. A minimum deposit may be required; contact the company for information. Because Schwab offers discounts on transaction fees for buying and selling stocks and has discounts or no fees for mutual funds, you may already intend to use the firm. This software is an added incentive.

StreetSmart performs most of the basic functions: tracking portfolio values, recordkeeping for purchase date and price, gains and losses, and daily valuations of the portfolio. As a bonus, this program can be used with Schwab's own database of your account. In other words, you can go on-line with Schwab to check your portfolio.

Furthermore, you can buy and sell stocks through your computer. When you go on-line through the Trading icon, you can place orders electronically and receive an additional 10% discount on Schwab's discount commissions. Whether you enter a limit or market order, or place other conditions on the trade, you have choices and control over your trading. You don't have to speak to anyone, and no one will call you. It's your computer working with Schwab's.

StreetSmart allows you to view all your transactions, positions, get quotes for stocks, print information, access various news and research reports for an additional cost and graphically display the performance of your portfolio as well as its asset allocation.

The program also downloads your new purchases and sales, relieving you of the manual task. In fact, if you open your account with money, the program will take care of everything for you relating to recordkeeping and performance details as well as transactions. In addition, the program has great flexibility.

If you are transferring in securities from another firm, you will need to manually input the data such as purchase date, quantity, symbol, etc. That's no problem. The program lets you customize your information, and, if necessary, change data from Schwab.

One more notable feature is the price history for securities. When you request a price for a stock you own, the Schwab main computer will download the last price, and, if requested, the high and low for the day. By doing this every day, you can have the price ranges for a stock over whatever period of time you own it. Furthermore, StreetSmart will take that data and draw a price graph with them. It's a neat bonus.

This is certainly an exceptional program. I like the ability to check your portfolio against Schwab's database, which gives you your monthly statement. By using StreetSmart, you can keep daily tabs on your portfolio, transact on-line and generate important tax information. Check this one out.

MANY, MANY MORE!

According to the 1995 Individual Investor's *Guide to Computerized Investing*, there are 141 portfolio management software programs. I'm going to list the ones with the most features suitable for individual investors, the last price given as well as where to buy the software. For a complete listing of portfolio software, see the above book. If you are a member of the American Association of Individual Investors, you can purchase most of these programs at a discount, ranging from 10% to 40%.

Advanced Total Investor, $129, Hughes Financial Services, 2 West
    Hanover, Suite 212, Randolph, NJ 07869   Phone: 201-895-5665
    Comment: Good import/export capability with spreadsheets.
Andrew Tobias' Managing Your Money, $80, MECA Software, Inc.,
    55 Walls Drive, Fairfield, CT 06430-5139   Phone: 203-255-1441
Captool, $149, Techserve, Inc., P.O. Box 9, Issaquah, WA 98027
    Phone: 800-826-8082   Comment: Has every feature you want.
Fidelity On-Line Xpress, $50, Fidelity Investments, 82 Devonshire St.,
    R20A, Boston, MA 02190   Phone: 800-544-0246
    Comment: Similar to StreetSmart.

Folioman, $89, E-Sential Software, P.O. Box 41705, Los Angeles, CA
 90041   Phone: 213-257-2524
Investor's Accountant, $395, Hamilton Software, Inc., 6432 E. Mineral
 Place, Englewood, CO 80112   Phone: 800-733-9607
Money Maker for Windows, $59.95, Q-West Associates, 13233 Black
 Mountain Road, #1-410, San Diego, CA 92129
 Phone: 800-618-6618
PFROI, $79, Techserve, Inc., P.O. Box 9, Issaquah, WA 98027
 Phone: 800-826-8082   Comment: Good value.
Portfolio Watcher, $150, Micro Trading Software, Inc., Box 175,
 Wilton, CT 06897   Phone: 203-762-7820   Comment: For Mac
 users only.
Pulse Portfolio Management System, $195, Equis International,
 3950 South 700 E., Suite 100, Salt Lake City, UT 84107
 Phone: 800-882-3040
Quicken, $60, Intuit, P.O. Box 3014, Menlo Park, CA 94025
 Phone: 800-624-8742   Comment: Data is fully integrated so
 user only has to input it once for all functions.
Viking, $495, Delphi Economics, Inc., 8 Bonn Place, Weahawken, NJ
 07087   Phone: 201-867-4303   Comment: Has good technical
 and fundamental research characteristics.
Wealthbuilder, $70, Reality Technologies, Inc., 2200 Renaissance
 Blvd., King of Prussia, PA 19406   Phone: 800-346-2024

MUTUAL FUND ←---┘
INFORMATION

The following lists are samples of mutual funds and newsletters dedicated to mutual funds. New funds and newsletters spring forth daily. These mutual fund selections were based on performance: the first group of aggressive-growth funds has been in the top 25 performing funds in the one-year, three-year and five-year categories, an extremely difficult feat; the remaining groups are the best-performing aggressive-growth funds over the last 10 years, then the best for the five-year period, and lastly, for the three-year period. As always, these are names for you to investigate further by using your on-line service and then receiving information from the companies.

MUTUAL FUNDS SPECIALIZING IN SMALL-CAP STOCKS

There are more than 100 mutual funds listed under the heading of Aggressive Growth Funds (all focusing on small-cap stocks) in the Morningstar Funds Reports on America Online. It lists them alphabetically and gives the following information on each:

> The Morningstar Star Rating of one to five stars, with five being the
> highest
> The maximum load charged
> The return for the previous three months
> The return for the previous year
> The annualized return for the last three years

By looking at these columns, you can quickly pick funds with no loads and good returns. Then you can click on the ones of interest and get much more detailed information.

By using the screening program for performance for one, three and five years, available on AOL on the Morningstar site, I was only able to find one fund that appeared in the top five funds for each category: The Stein Roe Capital Opportunities Fund. That shows how difficult it is to stay on top.

THE BEST FIVE AGGRESSIVE GROWTH FUNDS FOR THE LAST FIVE YEARS

As of July 15, 1996, these were the best funds. The annualized rate of return, the load and phone numbers are given. Keep in mind that the last five years represent one of the great bull market periods of our time. Do not expect these kinds of returns over the next five years.

Name	Phone	Ann. ROR	Load
AIM Aggressive Growth Fund	800-347-4246	32.66%	5.50%
Putnam New Opportunities: A	800-225-1581	31.44	5.75
PIMCo. Advisors Opportunity: A	800-426-0107	29.29	5.50
PIMCo. Advisors Opportunity: C	800-426-0107	28.35	1.00
Stein Roe Capital Opportunities	800-338-2550	26.50	None

THE BEST FIVE AGGRESSIVE GROWTH FUNDS FOR THE LAST THREE YEARS

AIM Aggressive Growth Fund	See above	37.55	See above
Stein Roe Capital Opportunities	See above	33.84	See above
Putnam New Opportunities: A	See above	30.76	See above
Putnam New Opportunities: B	800-225-1581	29.76	5.75
USAA Aggressive Growth	800-382-8722	29.39	None

THE BEST FIVE AGGRESSIVE GROWTH FUNDS FOR THE PAST ONE YEAR

Stein Roe Capital Opportunities	See above	84.88	See above
USAA Aggressive Growth	See above	83.10	See above
Alliance Quasar: A	800-227-4618	76.40	4.25
Alger Capital Appreciation	800-992-3863	75.59	5.00
Alliance Quasar: B	800-227-4618	75.17	4.00 deferred charge

MUTUAL FUND NEWSLETTERS

These newsletters specialize in tracking mutual funds, offering advice on the best-performing ones and recommending types of funds for current market conditions. Call them and ask for a sample newsletter. If they won't give you one, ask for a short subscription period, say two or three months. If they don't offer that, ask if they have a money back guarantee on a subscription. If they do, subscribe, read several issues and then make a decision.

Cabot's Mutual Fund Navigator – 508-745-5532

Fidelity Insight – 617-235-4432   Comment: Covers only Fidelity funds, but is not affiliated with Fidelity.

Fidelity Monitor – 916-624-0191   Comment: Covers only Fidelity funds, but is not affiliated with Fidelity.

Fund Exchange – 800-423-4893

Fundline – 818-346-5637

Graphic Fund Forecaster – 508-470-3511

Growth Fund Guide – 605-341-1971

Investech Mutual Fund Advisor – 800-955-8500

Investor's Guide to Closed-End Funds – 305-271-1900

MPT Fund Review – 415-527-5116

The Marketarian Letter – 800-658-4325

Morningstar Closed-End Funds – 800-876-5005
Morningstar Mutual Funds – 800-876-5005
Mutual Fund Forecaster – 800-327-6720
Mutual Fund Investing – 800-722-9000
Mutual Fund Letter – 312-649-6940
Mutual Fund Strategist – 802-658-3513
No-Load Fund Investor – 914-693-7420
Noload Fund*X – 415-986-7979
Personal Finance – 703-548-2400
Peter Dag Investment Letter – 216-644-2782   Comment: Focuses on
        funds from Vanguard, but is not affiliated with Vanguard.
Sector Funds Newsletters – 619-748-0805
Stockmarket Cycles – 213-465-5543
Switch Fund Timing – 716-385-3122
Telephone Switch Newsletter – 714-536-2201
United Mutual Fund Selector – 617-235-0900
Value Line Mutual Fund Survey – 800-634-3583
Weber's Fund Advisor – 516-466-1252

BIBLIOGRAPHY

Computers: The Plain English Guide, Phillip A. Covington. Jackson, Michigan: QNS Publishing, 1991.

How to Make Money in Stocks, William J. O'Neil. New York: McGraw-Hill, Inc., 1991.

The Hulbert Guide to Financial Newsletters, Mark Hulbert. New York: New York Institute of Finance, Simon and Schuster, 1991.

The Individual Investor's Guide to Computerized Investing, The American Association of Individual Investors. Chicago: American Association of Individual Investors, 1994 and 1995.

The Intelligent Investor, Benjamin Graham. New York: Harper & Row, 1973.

The Investor's Information Sourcebook, Matthew Lesko. New York: Harper & Row, 1988.

Keys to Reading an Annual Report, George Thomas Fiedlob, PhD and Ralph E. Welton, PhD New York: Barron's Educational Series, Inc., 1989.

One Up on Wall Street, Peter Lynch. New York: Penguin Books, 1989.

Quality of Earnings, Thornton O'Glove. New York: The Free Press, 1987.

The Stocks, Bonds, Bills, and Inflation 1995 Yearbook, Ibbotson Associates. Chicago: Ibbotson Associates, 1995.

Super Stocks, Kenneth L. Fisher. Homewood, Illinois: Business One Irwin, 1984.

The Warren Buffet Way, Robert G. Hagstrom, Jr. New York: John Wiley & Sons, Inc., 1994.

ALLRICH INVESTMENT
MANAGEMENT

The author is the founder of Allrich Investment Management, an investment advisory firm. If you have a minimum
of $250,000 in securities or funds and would like to discuss
with the author how the firm would develop and manage an
individual portfolio reflecting your objectives, please contact:

Allrich Investment Management
761 Arlington Road
Redwood City, CA 94062-1856
415-363-8587